Luggage By Kroger

Luggage By Kroger

A True Crime Memoir

Gary Taylor

iUniverse, Inc.
New York   Bloomington

Luggage By Kroger

A True Crime Memoir

Copyright © 2008 by Gary Taylor

iUniverse books may be ordered through booksellers or by contacting:

iUniverse
1663 Liberty Drive
Bloomington, IN 47403
www.iuniverse.com
1-800-Authors (1-800-288-4677)

ISBN: 978-0-595-53030-4 (pbk)
ISBN: 978-0-595-63084-4 (ebk)

Library of Congress Control Number: 2008942284

Printed in the United States of America

iUniverse rev. date 11/24/08

Dedication

This memoir is first for my descendants, because they should have an accurate record of these events.

It is second for all those folks over the years who kept me out too late in bars demanding I tell it again with more details.

And third, it is also for anyone else who just enjoys a good yarn.

"I'd rather laugh with the sinners than cry with the saints."
—Billy Joel

"I don't care how beautiful she is. Somebody, somewhere is sick of her shit."

—Anonymous graffiti on the men's restroom wall of Rudyard's Pub in Houston

Author's Pledge

This is a work of non-fiction. I solemnly affirm that the events in this memoir are all true to the best of my recollection and verified by numerous legal documents. Much of the dialogue comes from trial transcripts and depositions. Other conversations have been reconstructed from memory. But this was not difficult. The reader will quickly realize that most of these conversations should have been unforgettable.

In addition, I want to emphasize my good faith and honest effort to protect the personal privacy of everyone mentioned in this book. To accomplish that goal, I have referred to many acquaintances by first names or nicknames only and have created first name pseudonyms for others in at least four instances. Only one of those involves a character central to my story. Wherever I considered acquaintances to be public figures I have identified them by their complete names. In my own case I have held nothing back. To successfully tell my story, however, I have had to include many instances where it intersected with the lives of others. I have worked diligently to include only information necessary to explain their influence upon me. If I caused anyone pain, I would apologize in advance to those who deserve their privacy. To public figures who feel they have been maligned, however, I will just invite them to set the record straight when they produce memoirs of their own.

Prologue: Once upon a time in Houston…

"OK, Gary, let's hear this famous Texas fatal attraction story."

It was February of 2001, and I was sitting around the bar in the Singapore Cricket Club, sharing drinks with some British and Australian expatriates during a work assignment in the Far East. One of my colleagues had heard about my "Texas fatal attraction story" from someone in the states and now wanted to know more. Although the life-changing events of my Texas story had occurred twenty years earlier and more than eight thousand miles away, my audience appeared as eager to hear about them as if they had happened the day before in their backyard.

And why not? It was a yarn I had recounted many times since 1980 with drinking buddies all over the world. It was a true tale about murder and adultery. It was a story dramatic enough to have been twice optioned by Hollywood and aired three times on TV in documentaries. It was a story that had made me a guest on a dozen talk shows from Oprah Winfrey to Regis Philbin, where I discussed the dangers of obsessive relationships and showed my wounds as the poster boy for true-life fatal attractions. It was a story engaging enough to have been reported in magazines and newspapers on several occasions since it occurred, most recently the year before. It was a story driven by an unpredictable and classically manipulative femme fatale who could have been dispatched straight from central casting for a Bogart flick. It was a story with universal appeal that touched a wide range of issues central to the human condition: survival and redemption; love and lust; second chances ignored and embraced; trust and betrayal; weakness and strength; the futility of violence as a solution in life; the limits of ambition; the boundaries of trust; fatherhood; and, the dilemma of moral ambiguity.

It was a story I never minded telling. It was a story that happened to me. And I began the way I always had in the past.

"I am basically just an ordinary guy," I said. "But once upon a time, I had a truly extraordinary year. So, if you want to hear about that, let's order another round and keep 'em coming. It may take a little while."

Part One:

The Widow Wore Red

ONE

January 15, 1979

When Houston homicide detectives arrived at the southwest Houston townhome of anesthesiologist George Tedesco, they found patrolmen guarding a gruesome scene in the garage. The Argentine doctor's nursing staff at St. Joseph Hospital had asked police to check Tedesco's home because he failed to show up for a surgery the week before. Arriving there, the police found blood seeping from under the garage door and drag marks leading to his body in the back. A metal pipe wrapped in a rag lay beside him on the concrete floor, and police surmised it had been used to bash his skull. Repeated blows had splintered the bone, crushed his right eye, broken his nose, and knocked out several teeth. They started trying to solve the crime.

At first, theft of the thirty-year-old doctor's missing silver Corvette appeared a possible motive for the mayhem. But the sheer viciousness of the attack made that seem like overkill. Instead, police already knew that Tedesco had spent the last year embroiled in a messy and unusual common law divorce case that seemed bizarre for those days in the late 1970s. In fact, trial of that divorce had been scheduled for that very day—January 15, 1979. They decided to focus on it as a potential cause. But they never realized things could get even more strange. The circus was just opening its doors.

Dictionaries define a "femme fatale" as a "calculating woman of dubious ethics," and Tedesco's adversary in the divorce action was an attractive, blonde thirty-two-year-old criminal defense attorney already building such an image around the Harris County Courthouse. Her name was Catherine Mehaffey, and she had launched the divorce action after living with Tedesco for just three months. Long before words like "palimony" and "stalking" joined our legal vocabularies, Catherine appeared to be pioneering those concepts by deeds in Houston. Asserting herself as Tedesco's common-law wife under Texas laws of the time, she had sued him for half of his assets, claiming all sorts of abuse. Tedesco chose to resist, hiring a lawyer to challenge Catherine's claims and stubbornly refusing her invitation for a quick payoff that might spare them the embarrassment of court.

So she had spent the year before his death making him miserable. Oh, the cops were well aware of the Tedesco divorce. He had sought their help on several occasions, claiming she had followed and spied on him. He even accused her of orchestrating a burglary at his townhouse late in 1978. His attorney had instructed him to tape all phone conversations with her in an effort to document her threatening activities. In those days, however, even a pint-sized five-foot-six-inch, 166-pound guy like Tedesco generated little sympathy when he came sniveling around the police substations seeking protection from a woman. They couldn't arrest her for making him nervous. She had committed no crime. Maybe he should just grow a pair of balls and handle it himself. After all, what's that little lady going to do? Kill him?

After finding him in that pool of blood, however, they began to question those initial reactions to his pleas. They wondered if maybe they hadn't been too hasty with their macho dismissal of Tedesco's complaints. Catherine Mehaffey instantly took an express elevator ride straight to the top of their "interesting persons" list within minutes after the homicide investigation began. And discovery of a taped conversation between them from just a couple of days before—possibly on the day of his death—only made detectives more anxious to question her.

"Hello," he answered as that tape began.

Her voice replied: "George? We need to talk."

He continued: "Yes, Catherine, we certainly do. We need more than that. You need to bring back my stuff. Those artifacts are priceless and your people stole it all."

Suddenly, the tape depicted a change of tone for her, a snarl and an admission of her stalking: "I saw you with that whore, that slut. Who was she?"

Obviously familiar with her tactics and, of course, aware he was creating a tape that might some day surface in a courtroom, Tedesco remained emotionless and focused, refusing to even acknowledge her question about a recent date where she had followed him. Instead, he quietly asked: "Are you returning the art?"

Then her voice shifted to an overdramatic whine with dialogue straight from a soap opera: "Why do you do these things? You've ripped the heart right out of my chest and stomped on it. Why can't we end this like adults?"

He stood his ground and candidly asked: "Why did you have to steal everything?"

Just as quickly her voice regained composure. She sounded every bit the lawyer in a cross-examination: "I don't know what you mean. But we can talk, can't we? I can come over…"

He interrupted with an angry retort, shouting, "You can come over and bring my shit home. Then I'll tell the police to stop the investigation. If I don't get my shit you'll be sorry."

Catherine's voice dissolved into that of a frightened girl, showing that she, too, was playing for the tape recorder, preserving the record on her allegations of abuse. Almost sobbing, she said: "You will promise not to hurt me again?"

He ignored the trap and avoided a debate on whether or not he had been guilty of violence. Instead, he simply replied: "I'll be here."

The tone on the tape was chilling and the implication clear. Recently, it appeared, Tedesco and Catherine had arranged a meeting at Tedesco's home where he had been found murdered. That tape was destined to become a classic in the police department's archives, a conversation piece for the next year or more as top cops and prosecutors analyzed the range of emotion, the danger it betrayed, and the sound of a dead man talking to someone who might have become his killer just hours after it was made.

Homicide detectives spoke briefly with her after they left the scene. Questioned at the police station, Catherine dazzled with her verbal footwork and intellectual agility. Later, for a magazine interview in 1980, she would recall the interrogation and laugh about the end of it. As she started to leave, she would say, one detective leaned over and asked, "Just one more question. Did you love him?"

Cackling with laughter, Catherine would describe her response: "I guess he was expecting me to break down and cry out, 'Yes, yes, and I killed him!' But I just said, 'No' and walked out."

Detectives believed they had the right track with her. But the murder was horrific and raised many questions about Catherine. Could a woman actually have beaten someone like this? Did she have an accomplice? And what purpose did Tedesco's murder serve? Didn't she need the divorce to get her share of their alleged community property?

They had an answer to that last question soon enough. Within days of the murder, Catherine Mehaffey marched into the Harris County Clerk's office and filed a new cause of action. No longer just the estranged wife of

George Tedesco, she sought new status as the doctor's widow. She wanted the whole estate and planned a probate action to grab it.

The cops realized they needed additional brainpower and legal savvy on this case. So they recruited assistance from the Special Crimes Bureau of the Harris County District Attorney's office, a unit created to unravel criminal activities too complex for the regular cops.

And I'm sure that Catherine was tickled giddy by the attention. For her it would have been like the county just raised the bounty on her reward poster.

At least, that's what she told me later.

TWO

Summer 1979

I wouldn't formally meet Catherine until about nine months after Tedesco's murder. Before I did meet her, however, I had become well-acquainted with her reputation throughout that year after his death. You might call it part of my job description. As the criminal courthouse reporter for *The Houston Post*, I made my living through knowledge of newsworthy crimes. Although the Tedesco murder remained unsolved with no one charged and nowhere near a trial, it certainly looked like a case eventually headed my way.

And she was just getting started. Twenty years later, award-winning journalist Howard Swindle eventually would summarize her career for a *Dallas Morning News* article noting that in the "high drama" of Catherine's life "the characters around her are stalked, threatened, wounded, or killed while the diminutive star eludes an ever-changing cast of investigators. Hers is a real-life road show of cat-and-mouse that has played in five Texas counties over three decades. The script is byzantine, the scenes often brutal. Many of those who have been cast as victims share a story line: They had close associations with the fifty-something blonde that, at the time of their misfortune, had turned bitter."

Today, I couldn't have said it better. But back then I didn't realize I was about to audition for a crucial role in her opening act.

Surprisingly by the summer of 1979 the Tedesco murder had not generated much news interest, even though it boasted all the elements for a prime time splash in the two newspapers and local television. The victim was a doctor brutally murdered, and a possible suspect was an attractive female lawyer back in the days when female lawyers were pretty rare, particularly among those slugging it out in the sewer of the criminal courts. In fact, Catherine was probably one of about five females even practicing in my courthouse back then, and it was among the largest in the country.

Then came the unique twist of her decision to start a probate court battle for Tedesco's estate. It wasn't supposed to be an exceptionally large estate, maybe two hundred thousand dollars in a region known for multimillion dollar probate wars. But Tedesco's parents in Argentina decided to fight for it, something Catherine might not have anticipated. Instead of snatching Tedesco's estate quickly by filing as his widow, she immediately found herself backed against the wall. Challenging her claim as their son's widow, the family hoped to use the discovery afforded them as litigants to implicate her in his murder. They hired attorneys and a private investigator to work toward two related goals: destroy her claim on the estate and find enough evidence to charge her with murder.

In response, she hadn't flinched. Catherine had managed to persuade a couple of lawyer pals to represent her as the estate case moved toward a September jury trial in Harris County Probate Court. She seemed to enjoy this high stakes game that included a private eye on one hand dogging her tail and the police continuing to hit dead ends on their leads. She would laugh later telling me how one of her lawyer drinking buddies had called the Tedesco family's reward hotline masquerading as a Greek sea captain who knew the identity of the killers. Indeed, the probate and investigative files for the Tedesco estate case read like black comedy, introducing a colorful cast of characters with Catherine leading the pack.

Tedesco's next door neighbor told investigators she saw Catherine and her law office partner hopping the fence at Tedesco's townhome the evening of January 15, 1979, just after police had left the scene. Catherine would later explain the episode as one of her attempts to secure her "community property." According to the neighbor, however, Catherine did not even feign the role of a weeping widow.

"You'll be sorry if you don't forget everything you've seen and heard," the neighbor recalled Catherine's threat when interrupted while using a crow bar to open Tedesco's back door. The neighbor said Catherine continued: "If you do talk to anyone about what you've seen and heard, you'll be sorry, I promise you, you'll regret it."

Later on Catherine would cackle with glee telling me how lawyers from all over town pillaged Tedesco's place for weeks after his death, helping her reclaim her share of their estate so the parents couldn't haul it away.

Police and Tedesco's investigator thought they had a good lead when they discovered Tedesco's stolen Corvette parked at a shopping mall. They staked it out for three days until they spotted a man sneaking around only to discover he wanted to steal the thing himself. So they gave up and just listed the car as abandoned.

Their investigation of Catherine's client base and previous life did turn up a connection to another possible suspect named Tommy Bell. He was destined to become a defendant with Catherine in an unsuccessful, last gasp, $10 million wrongful death civil lawsuit filed by the family one year after the murder alleging the two of them had conspired to kill Tedesco.

Investigators uncovered other sordid tales of repeated confrontations with the men in her past. A former court bailiff said an extramarital affair with Catherine had ended with her blackmailing him for money so she could abort his child. Then she told his wife anyway, destroying his life and leaving him penniless.

Farther back in her mid-1970s law school days at the University of Houston, they found a former law student who had dated her. After their break-up, he suspected her in several acts of violence that included the beating of a new girlfriend, the burning of his apartment, and the ramming of his car in a fit of rage. After graduating, he said, he took his law degree, joined the US Marine Corps, and quietly relocated to another state, glad to be out of her life.

Prior to that, they learned Catherine had been married to a classmate from the University of Texas who had joined the Navy and taken her to Tokyo with him. The product of a private Catholic girls' high school in Houston, she had returned home after that split determined to become a lawyer. She earned her undergraduate degree in 1974 from the University of Houston and stayed on to collect a law degree there in 1977. But the first husband, like most everyone else in her past, remained out of sight as foggy rumors filtered into the investigation. They heard tales of a military probe that followed complaints she had tried to shoot him while they lived in Japan. But no firm evidence emerged to do more than just color her reputation.

Although frustrated by their failure to tie her to Tedesco's murder, the family's investigators still felt confident they could destroy her claim to ever have been Tedesco's common law wife. And the lawyers waited with great anticipation for what they believed would be the highlight of their pretrial campaign: the July deposition of Catherine herself and a chance to question her under oath in a setting where invocation of the Fifth Amendment against self-incrimination would blow a big hole in her desire to convince any jury she deserved George Tedesco's estate.

THREE

July 17, 1979

To win Tedesco's estate under Texas' common-law marriage rules, Catherine would have to convince a jury that the three months they had lived together in late 1977 constituted a state of informal matrimony. She could argue that length of cohabitation is not an element in proving a marriage, and Texas laws would bolster that contention. Texas allowed couples to declare themselves married without the trappings of a ceremony if they chose. But she knew jurors likely would want some strong evidence to counter any disgust with the short duration of their actual cohabitation. So she hammered that philosophy repeatedly during a marathon, ten-hour pre-trial deposition most remarkable for its moments of X-rated anecdotes and angry exchanges with a pair of lawyers representing the parents of the murdered anesthesiologist.

Unencumbered by the need to clear all questions, answers, or voluntary responses with a judge, that session deteriorated immediately into a legal free-for-all with Catherine using the forum to torment her adversaries. Just like police detectives investigating Tedesco's murder, the Tedesco family's team of estate lawyers would leave the session with nothing in the way of confession about the crime. But they would compile a written record confirming suspicions that Catherine boasted special skills for frustrating anyone who stood in her way.

The session was scheduled to start promptly at eleven in the morning with Catherine, her attorney, the two Tedesco lawyers, and a certified stenographer to make an official record. But Catherine managed to delay until after noon with an unusual demand that a third party attend and watch the entire proceeding. That third party was an attorney named Robert who had known Catherine since their days a few years before as law students at the University of Houston. He also had represented Tedesco in some business matters, and Catherine came determined to embarrass him with wild allegations about everything from sexual antics of his former wife to his relationship with Tedesco. She capped off the day insisting that Robert answer some questions himself under oath in a night-cap session that didn't begin until forty minutes after ten.

During all of this, neither lawyer ever asked her directly if she had killed Tedesco or knew who had. But it became apparent early in the day that she had come prepared to deny any involvement and hint her own theory that Tedesco might have been killed by a gay lover, disgruntled drug smuggling associates, or...Robert. While slipping those theories into the record, she managed to avoid answering a number of specific questions about her background by forcefully ordering the Tedesco team to "move along" whenever they asked something she didn't like—such as the date of her birth.

"George made known his feelings that he wanted to be married, and that he felt that you could be married without a piece of paper, and that he felt he was married to me," she said recounting a discussion she said occurred in October 1977. She believed that sealed their love when she moved into his townhouse about then. She conceded, however, that their common-law marriage had lasted only until January of 1978 when she vacated the place. But she couldn't be too specific about the date.

"There was much moving in and out between the 21st of December and the 31st," she said. "You don't just move out in one day when you are moving out. You move out some things, and you come back and get some more, and then you move out some more things."

She had met the anesthesiologist a few months before when introduced by a female acquaintance who worked for another doctor.

Catherine told the lawyers: "He started calling me but I didn't remember him...I usually don't go out with people that have accents. I mean, I have never except for him."

Asked if she had ever admitted targeting Tedesco for his money, Catherine denied it, then added: "Undoubtedly one of George's endearing qualities was that, I suppose, he did have some money. But nobody really understands. I think I am probably one of the only people in the world who ever really cared about George, and I would have liked him if he had acted a little better even if he didn't have any money."

She said: "If I was going to get somebody's money, I wouldn't go around telling everybody about it first. I can get money for myself through my honest labors."

According to Catherine, she and Tedesco announced their common-law marriage to her parents about that time in 1977 at a dinner. Her parents ran a day care center in southwest Houston, but her father died of natural causes just after Catherine filed for divorce from Tedesco in 1978.

Questioned about her use of Tedesco's name, she noted she had helped him change his first name from Jorge to George so he could present a more Americanized image. As far as her using Tedesco for her last name, Catherine told his family's lawyers with a hearty laugh that Tedesco had been thinking about changing his last name to Mehaffey.

Volunteering extended answers to questions about their relationship, however, she managed to portray him as the jealous tyrant of the house. She said he established rules limiting her phone conversations to one minute and prohibiting her from drinking in the house. And, she said, they clashed immediately over her lack of culinary skills: "I think I fixed dinner maybe once or twice, and he threw it down the sink, and said that it was shit, and he always did the cooking."

She tried to bolster her claim that George agreed to a marriage by relating an incident at a party when a black man invited her to dance. She said by this time their relationship "had reached a crescendo of jealousy and insanity with George, and he told them that I was his wife."

On January 2, 1978, she claimed she sought help from a friend because George had beaten her with a belt for "several days on and off." She said they started fighting because she took an old boyfriend to the airport after a party. Then she added an offhand slap at the man she considered her dead husband: "We fought about a trip George was going to take, and, again, he was taking this young boy with him."

Continuing that homosexual theme, she volunteered at another point in the deposition: "A couple of times I asked him who a couple of guys were that came there, and one worked at the hospital. I think he was one of the orderlies, and he was a faggot, and I didn't care for him. I don't recall his name. He didn't like me because he was George's boyfriend, and one time I came home and found out George had gone some place with him, and I got mad, and left."

Catherine used a question about bills from a hospital to mention that George had taken her there to have her stomach pumped after a suicide attempt.

Of course, Tedesco wasn't around to refute any of this. Catherine made observers wonder how all that abuse could have occurred in just five months. She decided to draw her old attorney pal Robert into the mix by slandering his ex-wife. She charged that Tedesco had publicly consecrated an affair with the woman by having sex with her on the living room floor of their townhouse while Catherine and Robert watched.

Catherine said she wasn't shocked, however, because she already had watched one time when Robert's ex-wife serviced a soccer player while waiting to welcome the rest of the team. Carried away by the recollection, she said she had secured an affidavit from the soccer player. She described the scene for everyone at the deposition, including Robert.

"It was wonderful," she said. "You have got to hear this one affidavit, it is the best. The guy was quite a rider. The noises were unmistakable, and I turned around. She forced this guy. I mean, you know."

Robert needed a recess to compose himself as a member of her audience, so they took a break. Then she tried to soothe everyone's nerves with a disclaimer: "Oh, come on. We are just having a little fun."

Asked how the tryst with a soccer player could relate to the Tedesco estate case, Catherine mumbled something about "legal strategy." Then she said she couldn't quite remember. One of the Tedesco family lawyers asked her to notify him if she ever recalled, and she responded with sarcasm: "You will be the first one to know. I will call you."

Obviously frustrated, he replied, "Will you, as soon as you have that? All right. Will you make me the first to know? Please don't call me. Call your attorney, and I will talk to him."

Unable to resist a jibe, his associate jumped in and instructed Catherine to "call him at home."

"Don't hold your breath," she replied. "Just wait until trial time."

Of course, none of this would ever surface in a courtroom without some relation to the Tedesco case, and Catherine kept trying to tie it in. She said she suspected Robert of killing Tedesco because the anesthesiologist had seduced his wife in front of him. She said Robert aimed to take advantage of the doctor, and had grown to hate him because of the affair.

"It wasn't a general feeling," she said of her charge he wanted to take advantage of Tedesco. "When you stand in a room, and you watch a man have anal intercourse with your wife while she kneels on the floor on all fours laughing and screaming, I would say that is advantage."

She added with dramatic flare: "I begged Robert to stop them. I begged him to stop them, and he said it is just good, clean fun. He had this really silly look on his face."

I wish I'd have been a fly on the wall for that deposition. While reading it years later, I wondered what kind of silly look Robert had on his face while Catherine was recounting the alleged scene. And they were only just warming up. Next they moved forward with more serious questions about the burglary of Tedesco's townhouse, the reason for their split, and the events surrounding his brutal demise.

FOUR

July 17, 1979

Surprise pregnancies seemed to occur frequently in Catherine's relationships. At least, that's what investigators would tell me later, warning me to beware if she started warning how she'd missed a period. They would charge she had used the threat of pregnancies in the past to extort money or other concessions from discarded lovers. And the Tedesco estate case files included not just one, but two examples of the pregnancy wedge. Not only was an alleged pregnancy central to her break-up with Tedesco, but Tedesco lawyers located another old boyfriend who received similar news.

That old boyfriend was a six-year veteran of the sheriff's department who admitted to a recent extramarital affair with Catherine. He became material to the estate case in 1979 when attorneys learned he had fenced an antique sword removed from Tedesco's collection at Catherine's request, netting $175. Besides locating a missing item for their probate inventory, Tedesco's attorneys received an added bonus from the deputy's pre-trial deposition. He had testified she later demanded three hundred dollars to finance an abortion with the threat: "Remember George? Remember what happened to him? Remember your son and wife."

He rejected her pregnancy claim and denied her the money. But Catherine told me later she had the last laugh by snitching him out to his wife, who responded with divorce papers. Catherine cackled as she told his story, adding the moral: "He saved three hundred dollars, but it cost him everything else."

Then she would turn sullen and add, "If I saw him and his precious kids in a desert needing a drink, I'd pour their water on the ground."

With Tedesco, she levered the surprise pregnancy theme differently. Instead of using it as blackmail with a threat to tell the wife, in this instance she *was* the wife. So she raised the issue of an unborn child in the waning days of their life together, apparently hoping to stampede Tedesco into a quick settlement in exchange for an abortion. So the Tedesco family lawyers naturally asked her about the baby that never came. And Catherine used her explanation to launch another assault of the dead doctor's character, charging he had forced her into an abortion.

"He had stopped beating me because he was ready to do anything to procure this abortion," she said. "He was willing to eat much dirt and be real nice to me, 'Oh, come back, it's so wonderful and so sweet. Just do what I say.' So I went back, and this was after the beating, and I already knew what I was going to do. I was going to liquidate the community assets at that time fairly and equitably."

She claimed he told her he had performed between three hundred and four hundred abortions in South America and in New York. She said she believed her pregnancy test had registered a false positive.

Catherine admitted warning Tedesco at one point that the child might be illegitimate. But she softened that blow by reminding him that a lot of great people were illegitimate. In the deposition, she listed Alexander Hamilton, and Napoleon Bonaparte. Then she looked around the table and added Robert.

"I was dealing with a mad man, and I would have said anything necessary that George wanted to hear that would keep him from going completely wild," she testified.

She admitted taking items from their home, including parts of Tedesco's collection of pre-Columbian art from South America. She argued that he had acquired it during their marriage so she considered it community property. She said she needed the money because he wouldn't give her any.

Catherine listened patiently while one lawyer presented his list of items he felt were stolen from the house: three tuxedos, three suits, two African headdresses, a Persian sword, a Chinese matchlock rifle, a Jivaro blowgun, a Hoover vacuum cleaner, a designer lamp, a machete in a holster, and 120 record albums.

"George was strange, but I never saw him in headdresses," she fired back. Then she added: "I took one other thing that is probably not on this list that I returned to him because I was fascinated with it, and I knew it meant a great deal to him. It was a human fetus that he kept in a jar. That was his only child, and I gave it back."

Adding that the lawyer's list looked like "padding for the insurance company," she admitted getting $950 for some of the art, but refused to identify the buyer.

She admitted knowing that Tedesco was taping their telephone conversations in the months prior to his death as they continued to squabble about her divorce case.

"You have obviously gone over all the tapes and prepared questions from them," she told the lawyers during her deposition. "We both know. Let's not insult each other's intelligence."

Jumping to her challenge, one of the lawyers asked: "Did you ever tell Dr. Tedesco in a telephone conversation back in January 1978, 'I came there tonight to kill you. Can I kill George Tedesco?'"

She replied: "I don't recall but I could have. I think anybody who ever knew George probably at one time or another—*including Robert*—wanted to kill George, but George just was not worth it."

The lawyer continued: "Did you ever tell him in January of 1978 that 'You are going to be very, very sorry as far as threatening me. I am a lawyer, and I know the tricks of the trade.' Do you know the tricks of the trade?"

That question brought an answer that twenty years later would hover as a *Dallas Morning News* headline above a lengthy article the paper called "Tricks of the Trade."

"Me?" she asked rhetorically. "Tricks?"

Asked if she ever bragged about getting into his house through the mail slot, she replied: "Yes. I had a little bottle and on it, it would say, 'Drink me.' And I would drink it, and then I would shrink to an incredibly small size, and I would literally walk through whatever it was that Alice walked through."

But her sarcasm turned dark at one point when the lawyer elaborated, and accused her of sticking her "skinny" little arm through the mail slot to open the door. She shot back: "Wait a minute. I don't have a skinny arm. I look just fine. You ought to re-examine yourself a little bit physiologically."

Tedesco's family had charged that her removal of items occurred in 1978 and again after the doctor's death in January 1979. Dancing like a prize fighter along the ropes, however, Catherine bobbed and weaved around questions that tried to trace the trail of Tedesco's property. Investigators apparently had tied some of the loot to Catherine's acquaintance, Tommy Bell—a character destined to play a significant role in the violence of my confrontation with her.

While evading questions that would link the missing art to anyone, however, she admitted her role with a comment that sounded like a boast: "And I sold it. How about that?"

Not even Tedesco's murder in January 1979 stopped Catherine's removal of their "community property." If anything, it added more urgency as she told lawyers she suddenly feared that Robert would race inside the townhouse and grab some for himself.

She told the lawyers she had not learned of Tedesco's death until mid-afternoon on that day when she went to the Family Law Center for the divorce hearing. The police had contacted her divorce attorney, and he told her they wanted to talk.

"I couldn't tell them much," she recounted in her July deposition. "I was stunned. I didn't really believe he was dead until I saw this little purse he carried sitting on the desk."

She said she went to the townhouse that night "because I wanted to know what had happened. I wanted to know how he had been killed, where he had been killed. I found it incredible."

Catherine said she saw the report on the detective's desk while he was out of the room. She said she only talked to the detective for twenty minutes. But, before going to the townhouse, she said, all that she knew had come from him. She said the detective approved her trip that night to the townhouse.

"It looked like there had been a ferocious battle in the garage," she testified in her deposition. "I saw a lot of blood. It was all over the right side of the garage. There were pieces of more than blood out there, and I never saw anything like that in my life."

She admitted she took documents that night but nothing else.

"When we got there somebody had poured glue in the lock, and they had pasted a sign on the front door written in paper that said, 'Sealed by order of the court.' We did not know what court—the kangaroo court?" she testified. "We didn't know, so we went around to the back."

She said they entered through the garage because she suspected Robert would be "in there plundering heavily, so I decided to take that which was mine out of the house."

Catherine began to ramble in her testimony. She told the lawyers: "I think the next day somebody told me the homicide detectives figured that it was either a homosexual who killed him or a drug-related deal because they had found some boxes there, crates, packing crates, and I started to receive a large input of information at this time from many people who began telling me things that they had heard, and I could not tell you what one told me and what the other didn't."

She said: "I also heard that they thought that if I had done it, I would have used a gun."

Catherine said she couldn't recall the names of the locksmiths or a friend who loaned her a van to transport property from the home. She said: "It passed like a dream."

No one expected Catherine to present the image of a grieving widow when she took center stage at the deposition in July, barely six months after the brutal murder of the man she claimed had been her husband. But none of the lawyers either could have predicted the dark mix of sarcasm that spouted from her mouth. They knew she had flaunted her role in interviews with police investigators. And the way she handled questions in the civil deposition just enhanced her image as someone who felt untouchable in Tedesco's death.

I never had a chance to read her deposition until ten years later. By then, I was able to smile about her cocky comments, shake my head with a laugh, and whisper softly to myself: *Yes, that's my gal.*

FIVE

September 28, 1979

"That's her. She's here. That's the bitch everybody is talking about."

It would not have mattered if I'd been at that deposition two months earlier, or if I had known in September about the other things I learned later on. It would not have changed what happened between Catherine and me. This was a special, peculiar time for me—a period that left me vulnerable for a dance down the dark side of the street with Catherine Mehaffey as my escort. Freshly separated from my second wife, I was looking for adventure. Although Tedesco had complained about the way she cooked food, I thought she might make the perfect chef for serving plates of action.

Responding to my friend's whispered alert—"That's her"—I turned to look out in the yard where he was pointing his finger not so discreetly at Catherine as she strolled toward the house looking for the bar. We had come after work on a Friday afternoon to some lawyer's cocktail party organized to celebrate nothing more than the end of the week and his purchase of this upscale townhouse near Houston's bustling downtown. The lawyer's name was James, and he had offered his verbal invitation a few days earlier during a personal visit to our office in the criminal courthouse press room.

"There'll be lots of nasty crack," James had said, announcing his party.

"Nasty crack, huh?" I had said. "How can I refuse?"

So it was that I came to be standing in James's living room, staring through his French doors, and watching the nastiest crack in the courthouse as she headed my way. This widow, of course, wore red. But at least it wasn't a flaming firehouse red that might have offended old-schoolers who prefer their widows shrouded in black. Her dress had splotches of yellow to complement the golden curls parked just above the shoulders. At five-feet-three-inches and about a hundred pounds, she really didn't look the menace that most would have us believe. She was considered attractive but not necessarily a knockout. In later years I would recall her as resembling the adult actress Reese Witherspoon, who was only three years old at that time. But she also had the hard look of a bad girl, and that played to my weakness. A menace? She just looked like fun to me.

"So this is the notorious Catherine Mehaffey," I teased, approaching from behind as she ordered a scotch from the bartender. I figured this might be the only time in my life I'd be able to use that opening line.

She turned and squinted from the corner of one eye. I could tell she was not immediately impressed with my attire. I stood out from the legal crowd in their pinstripe suits. My khakis and herringbone jacket betrayed my station. But after all, I did represent the working press, and I had a reputation to maintain. I also offered a display of red and yellow with my tie: a field of red decorated with yellow images of the three monkeys warning observers to see, hear, or speak no evil. It was a tradition at the courthouse for me to wear the thing when juries deliberated big cases, and now it seemed fitting as I began to flirt with Catherine Mehaffey. I asked for a scotch and saw her watching.

"And you would be…?" she asked, waiting for me to fill the blank.

I offered my right hand in a professional greeting, took the drink with my left, and said, "Gary Taylor. I cover courts for *The Houston Post*."

Immediately she jerked back with a sneer, as if someone had thrown a dead skunk on the floor. She sipped her drink and peeked over the edge of the glass. I stared her down until she spoke.

"I used to like that paper. It used to be the start of every day for me. Now it just makes me sad. I still read it, but not my mother. She can't stand it anymore just because of Fred King."

"So Fred wrote a story you didn't like? Those police stories can be gruesome," I said, realizing that, as our police beat reporter, Fred had written the story about Tedesco getting his head caved in. I recalled how Fred had managed to work Mehaffey into that story, noting police had questioned her about the common-law marriage lawsuit and suggesting to even a casual reader: "gold digger" or, worse, "femme fatale."

"If this ends with Faye Dunaway playing you in the movie, you'll feel better about Fred," I said.

That made her giggle because, as I would learn later, she was a sucker for old crime movies, particularly those with bushwhacking babes, dangerous darlings or murderous muffs. "I can't apologize for Fred, he's one of our best reporters," I continued in a professional vein. "I only control my own stories, and I don't think you've made any of those yet. But I do remember that Tedesco story was buried on the inside with no pictures. Maybe nobody read it but you and your mother."

"It was read by everyone I know," she said, swishing a mouthful of scotch as she spoke. "Now I have the estate trial starting Monday. We'll see who gets the last laugh on this. Are you covering that?"

"Nope. I'm strictly criminal courts. I don't even know if we're going to cover it. We're in one of those periods where editors see stories like that as detracting from more serious stuff like the mayor's race."

"That would suit me just fine if no one is there to hear me tell about the merciless beatings and abuse I took from that man."

We were starting to click. Two or three times in everyone's life they find another person playing their tune. This was happening then to us. As we talked, I knew both of us were thinking in the back of our minds: I'm going to fuck you, sooner or later. That's where this conversation is headed.

If you say you've never had such a Norman Rockwell moment yourself with a potential sex partner, I'm sorry. But our roadmap to the bedroom was marked in scarlet letters from the moment we met. I can't explain how. But it happens. It's happened to me maybe four times in life. And this was one of them.

"So, where is Mrs. Taylor tonight?" Catherine finally asked, not so subtly digging for a crucial piece of information.

I sipped my scotch and took the bait: "Which one? You might say I'm estranged at the moment from wife number two. So I hope she's home with the girls."

"Ah, Mr. Taylor, that's too bad. Just when we were getting along so well. But I have such bad luck with the estranged. You know, they always take what they want then run back to wife number two or one or whatever. Then I get the broken heart."

"I don't think that's an option on this one. You can trust me on that."

"Trust you, huh? You'd like that, wouldn't you? You'd be panting like a dog and begging for more if you could get some of this. Then you'd go off and run back to that wife number two the minute she says: 'Oh, Gary, I think we've made a terrible mistake. The girls need their father.' And you'd have this big, shit-eating grin on your face like you just scratched the seven-year itch with a steel sheep's comb and got away with it."

She finished off her scotch, then continued: "I've been there. But it is fun to flirt with you a little. Once that divorce is final, you give me a call, and I'll buy you a decent scotch and maybe, uh, a new suit if you think you'd wear it."

"You ever been married?" I asked.

She tilted her head, batted her eyes, and laughed as she replied, "You mean to anyone other than George?"

"Oh, yeah," I said almost apologetically. I was surprised she'd even snapped on the omission. It didn't seem he would count. "Forgot about him."

"I sure can't call you as an expert witness, can I? You might qualify as an expert on marriage, but I can't have that attitude."

"Well, besides George Tedesco. Anybody else?"

She chatted a bit about her first husband and their time in Japan while he served in the Navy. Of course, she omitted the part about taking a shot at him. I guess it might have been confusing to discuss more than one wounded husband at a time. She quickly turned the conversation to my situation.

"What makes you think this is so permanent?"

"She's got a new man in her life. That's why we're estranged."

"So sad. You're the stooge on this one?"

"I came home from a trip and asked my four-year-old daughter about her weekend. When she said, 'It was terrible. Uncle Al was here all weekend,' I figured a separation was in order."

By this time Catherine had ordered another scotch and was drinking it just as I provided the details. My misery caused her to spit a mouthful on the floor as she laughed in my face. I realized the image of the victimized cuckold really wasn't earning the proper respect from her. She obviously had her own code of acceptable conduct. So I shifted to my charming rogue personae.

"I got even. We had a chat, and I went ahead and told her about my eight affairs."

"How long were you married?"

"Four years."

"You had eight affairs in four years of marriage and confessed it? Your lawyer must love that. Why in hell would you confess to eight affairs in four years of marriage?"

I shook my head, sipped some scotch, and mumbled, "That was all I could remember."

Another mouthful of scotch hit the floor.

"You know," I said, "it's kind of a joke to say it, considering I've been married twice, but I'm really not the marrying kind."

Just then, one of my reporter pals walked up and inserted himself into our conversation. Jim Strong was destined to play a crucial role in the saga about to unfold. At the time, we shared adjoining desks in the criminal courthouse press room. While I wrote for a newspaper, Jim reported his stories for a string of local radio stations. We often covered the same trials and events, played bridge together on slow days, and had started trading life stories over beers now and then. He lived alone in a house in north Houston, and I was already thinking about possibly renting a bedroom from him so I could have a cheap place to live during the divorce. For the last couple of weeks, since Uncle Al had arrived, I'd been sleeping for free on the living room couch of a sympathetic editor who had warned his sympathy would vanish by the end of the month.

"I see you've met the belle of the ball," said Strong, hooking a thumb in Catherine's direction. To her, he introduced himself by saying, "Mehaffey, right? I'm Strong."

"Strong?" she asked, obviously a little confused.

"Jim Strong," he continued, adding with a laugh, "It's my name." Introduction complete, Jim turned to a new conversational assault on me, asking her: "Is Taylor making you bored? I came to tell him he's late for the Herpes Help meeting. But don't let that scare you away."

"Let me guess," she said, ignoring his inference that I might have Herpes, and she should find a new date. "You're another one, aren't you?"

"Another reporter?" Jim asked providing clarification. "You have a nose for shit, don't you? Smell us a mile away? But you're right. I do radio reports."

Suddenly Catherine stepped back and looked at both of us. Then she said, "Say, wouldn't you guys like to see James's house? Can I give you a tour?"

"Can't wait," said Strong.

She turned then and led us around the living area, into a side room, and up a flight of stairs. She opened the door at the top, and the three of us entered James's bedroom. We started walking in different directions looking at his stuff. Catherine rifled through one of his dresser drawers and grabbed a pair of underpants. Clenching her fist, she shoved it inside and jammed it against the crotch.

"The host with the most," she giggled, stretching the shorts like they had a massive erection and mimicking a ring master at the circus. "Yes, folks, our James is all man."

"Uninhibited little gal, aren't you?" I said, while I watched Strong pawing through James's closet, pulling out a pair of trousers.

"Must be his cheap scotch," she mumbled, tossing the shorts on his king-sized bed while rooting through more stuff in the dresser. "Now he can tell all his friends I've been in his drawers."

I spied a large Bible on an antique lectern he had placed at the foot of his bed. In the living room it would have been an intriguing conversation piece. Up here, however, it seemed out of place. I imagined him reading the scriptures before hopping into the sack with some prostitute. I turned the pages and found the section where God turns Lott's wife into a block of salt. When I started to read out loud, Catherine and Strong hopped on his bed and lay next to each other listening pensively. Then I could hear her mumbling only half to herself.

"What's the matter with me?" she was asking. "I don't know what I am doing. Where is the payoff on this? These guys have nothing."

I stopped reading and asked, "You were saying?"

Before she could answer, a small, secret side door burst open and James stormed into the room.

"What the fuck is going on in here?" he yelled, as Strong and Catherine just continued to lay on the bed. Catherine started laughing and slowly stood up.

"Ah, James, what's the problem? I'm just doing my job. I thought you wanted all your friends to see your fine new place."

I watched his mutilated shorts slide off the bed and onto the floor as she stood up to look at him. Strong just laid there laughing. James looked at me and I said, "Nice Bible, James. Family heirloom or did you buy this specially for your new townhome?"

James just scowled, looked us over, and then stomped out through the main door to the bedroom. I looked at Catherine and said, "What's the big deal?"

Catherine picked up his underwear and tossed it in a wicker basket by the dresser. Still laughing, she made her way to the door while Strong got to his feet. In the doorway she turned and started to laugh.

"He's just pissed, I guess, because I'm supposed to be his date for this thing. I'd better go back downstairs and pretend to be the hostess. He's also very sentimental about the bed. It's a five-hundred-year-old antique."

I looked at Strong and said, "A five-hundred-year-old bed? Think of the stories that piece of furniture could tell. We probably should leave, huh? Seen enough of his place? Let's find a bar."

Strong nodded and made for the door. Catherine said, "Good idea, I'll show you guys out."

Downstairs Catherine asked for my phone number. I asked for two of her cards. I used one to jot down my office extension and handed it back. The other I dropped in my pocket.

"I'll call you some time," I said, walking across the porch.

Just then we heard a tremendous crash to the side of the building as James slammed a bag of empty liquor bottles into the trash can, breaking all the glass and mumbling something that sounded like, "Motherfuckers."

"Again I ask, What's the big deal?" I said to Catherine. She looked to the side of the building, started laughing, and said, "This is going to be a long weekend. Call me some time."

Then she turned to the trash cans and yelled, "Hey James, quit making so Goddamn much noise over there. We were just having some fun."

I heard her cackling as she walked toward the trash cans all set to make up with James. Then I drove away wondering what the future might hold.

Part Two:

I Led Three Lives

SIX

September, 1979

Catherine was destined to become several important things to me. But most prominently, she would become my problem-solver. Before I met her, I had a bunch of problems. Then, all of sudden, with her in my life I had only one.

I didn't see her again for about two weeks after the party while the Tedesco estate jury trial raged in Harris County Probate Court. I wasn't covering it, and I was busy with cases on my own beat. So I stayed away. I spent the time self-absorbed in my personal dilemma, something I had been doing a lot. And I thought about Herbert A. Philbrick.

For those who don't recall, Philbrick shared his life story in the early Cold War 1950s with a tension-filled book and then a television series entitled *I Led Three Lives*. The stories followed his adventures living three secret, separate lives simultaneously. To most of the world, Philbrick was a private citizen working in a Boston advertising agency. To the Soviets, however, he was a communist sympathizer and spy in his own country. And, for the U. S. government, he was a double agent, placing himself in danger to help his nation fight the Red menace. On one level the program thrilled viewers by dramatizing the dangers of a regular guy acting as international spy. On another level, however, Philbrick offered a message for everyone, even those in more mundane walks of life. To a certain extent, each of us lives several lives that often intersect. Some follow more contradictory simultaneous paths than others. But each of us must learn to balance those lives, adjusting the tempo to make the combination a tool for growth rather than destruction. If those paths cross and conflict, sooner or later you have to choose one and leave the others behind.

So it was that I came to analyze my three lives and now, years later, recognize how they worked to first lead me into the turmoil ahead, and then, in the end, deliver me from disaster. It's been hard for me to appreciate the story of Catherine and me without first understanding my three lives and how she helped to forge them into a single path. They weren't as glamorous as Philbrick's, but each had its moments. First came my life as a dedicated, professional journalist. Second was my life as a responsible husband and father. And, third came my life as a reckless, but charming, rogue. I had no regrets about any one of them while realizing there were times when one interfered with another. Somehow I had managed to maintain them on separate but parallel lines for more than a decade—my entire adult life to that date—until they led me to Catherine, and I had to choose. I enjoyed each life in its own way and would be hard-pressed to pick one over another. Actually, now that I think about it, the charming rogue beats hell out of the other two. But seriously, how long can you effectively juggle that one against anything else—unless you are a congressman or member of the Royal Family?

Of the three lives that comprised my existence, however, "professional journalist" dominated as the strongest thread among three layers of twine twisted into a single rope. That life overlapped the others and drove them along. And my focus on the integrity of that professional life would turn out to be my strongest weapon in the battle of wills about to ensue with Catherine Mehaffey.

SEVEN

The 1950s

The professional emerged first and at a surprisingly early age, spawned by ego and its inspirational sidekick, ambition. Who can explain the roots of a work ethic? Nature versus nurture traditionally frames the debate. Is anyone born with a work ethic? Although I tend to doubt that, I recall things I did as a child that would indicate I had one before I even became aware of the concept of work or watched my old man bury himself alive with it. In trying to understand it over the years, I have transferred the concept to ambition, which might be a more natural explanation of how a disposition toward success could trigger the conclusion you must work hard to get ahead. Whatever the explanation of the work ethic, I had it. And I harnessed it to push forward in a career of journalism that perfectly fit my talents.

Almost as soon as I could write at all, I started turning that skill into story telling. I remember writing Christmas plays in the fourth grade about Rudolph the Red-Nosed Reindeer and then following with a historical epic centered on a Colonial era Yankee peddler hero named Will. We actually performed these scripts in my fourth grade class, and I got a big kick from the attention. So it was an interest in writing that drew me toward journalism in the beginning, but it was the work ethic that helped me achieve it.

Looking at the genes, I now know that my ancestry included hard workers. Poor white trash doesn't leave much of a paper trail, but I still have found records of some. They all trod similar paths toward the future, traveling west into central Missouri in the 1830s from Virginia and Kentucky. My mother's primary line, the Wrights, are traceable back to Scotland. Meanwhile, my Taylors begin as far as I know with a man named Joseph Taylor born in 1811 to unknowns in Madison County, Kentucky. Before Joseph there is simply a void. But I do know he farmed land in Missouri and worked his grandson mercilessly, according to a diary kept by the boy, Cicero Hampton Taylor, who grew up to become my great grandfather. Cicero lived to the age of ninety-six and did not die until I was in my teens. I regret that I never took the trouble to talk with him about his life when I had the opportunity. No one ever starts caring about genealogy until all the good sources are dead. But at least another relative shared Cicero's diary with me as well as some observations on the son that became a grandpa I would never know, Elsus Bower Taylor. He died of natural causes in 1944, three years before my birth.

Folks called Elsus "Nub" because of a dreadful accident he suffered as a child when he burned off a hand after falling into a fireplace. But the handicap didn't stop him from becoming well known in central Missouri for his skills at breaking mules. He also earned a reputation as a hard-drinking scoundrel. My dad used to joke about their practice of moving every year to a new farm space and talked about times when they were so poor he couldn't have shoes. The Great Depression hit them hard, and my father, Dale Kempster Taylor, escaped by lying about his age to join Franklin Roosevelt's Civilian Conservation Corps. He returned to the farm in the late 1930s determined to make something more of himself. He met my mom, who came from more stable farming stock, and they moved to the nearest big city of St. Louis about the time World War II began.

A CCC-related hernia kept my dad out of the service until near the end of the war when he volunteered and accepted an assignment guarding prisoners in Washington State. For some reason only Dale could fathom, he decided to leave the exciting Pacific Northwest after the war and return to grungy old St. Louis to seek his fortune and provide me a place of birth in 1947. Armed only with a grade school education and ambition, he found a job pumping gas and eventually turned that into a prosperous life, first owning a gas station and then launching what would become the city's largest lawnmower sales and service business.

So it would seem that Dale's offspring might be expected to have "worker" stamped on their genes. That predilection received reinforcement when I learned to accept twelve-hour workdays as the norm just from watching him never come home. I was destined to become intricately acquainted with those twelve-hour days in just a few years ahead, but back then, like any other kid, I saw my old man as a hero and concluded that twelve-hour days must be the hero's schedule. Since I, of course, wanted to be a hero, too, I jumped into that lawnmower work alongside him as soon as I could, joining the business as a little gofer the summer after sixth grade at the age of twelve.

Outgoing and witty, my dad was more of a salesman than a mechanic and had earned his living just after the war selling Fuller Brush products door-to-door. My mom used to joke about his first day on that job, when he left to sell brushes and came back with a 1948 set of the *World Book Encyclopedia* sold to him by a prospect. Another family legend claimed he once won a bet by successfully selling a bag of dog poop within his first dozen doors after bragging to a rival that he could sell anything. He told me later the buyer wanted the poop to fertilize a garden. As a lawnmower magnate he took great pride in sometimes loading a new lawnmower into his truck and toting it door-to-door until he could find some homeowner cutting the grass. Then he would carry on like a vacuum cleaner salesman, unloading the mower and cutting a section to demonstrate the wonders of the new machine.

As proof you can't ever take the country out of the boy, Dale one time scored a big burlap sack filled with live chickens from an uncle who still lived on a farm in central Missouri. He carried the chickens home in the trunk of his 1952 DeSoto and proceeded to wring their necks in our driveway while I sat on the steps with my younger sister, watching in absolute humiliation. Thanks to Dale, our neighbors would qualify as experts the next time they accused someone of running around like a chicken with its head cut off. They clamored to their doors and windows to watch his chicken show, mesmerized by the scene of headless birds dancing their death jigs while blood gushed from their open necks. But no one complained.

For me, this silence-of-the-chickens-episode stirred my first emotions of empathy and compassion. I sat horrified watching him clutch each bird around the neck and then spread his legs for support while spinning his right arm clockwise in a windmill motion before snapping his wrist at the bottom of the circle with a jerk that kept the bird's head in his fist and sent the headless body sailing through the air to finally bounce across the concrete and then leap up in one final frenzy of fluttering confusion. I was glad I wasn't a chicken. I also was glad I'd have the freedom to become my own man and leave that part of my heritage behind.

A rural traditionalist on corporal punishment as well, Dale lashed me occasionally with a belt and one time employed a willow switch in the backyard after I had vanished for an entire afternoon walking the three miles home from his shop at the age of seven with my five-year-old sister in tow. At least he acknowledged the ingenuity of my feat before laying on the wood, mumbling: "I can't believe you found the way." When I was a toddler, I'd been told, he once bought a dog harness with a leash to restrain me from running around in a store and then had to remove it after some Good Samaritan intervened with a threat to stomp him stupid.

Despite embarrassments like those, however, I thoroughly enjoyed his eccentricities and fully respected his discipline, which also served as the foundation for our comfortable middle class life in suburban St. Louis with a stay-at-home mom. I never even thought about abuse and actually reveled in that switching as a badge of honor for what had been my greatest personal adventure to that point in my young life. I wallowed in the pride that the switching failed to make me cry. And he seasoned the rod with plenty of love. I just considered those episodes as the dark side of growing up rural in suburban America. On the bright side, he founded our neighborhood's unit of the YMCA's fathers-and-sons Indian Guides program, forming the Osage Tribe for us and several of my friends. As the inaugural chief he took the name Straight Arrow while I became Broken Bow. Through the Indian Guides he taught me to fish and camp. But he never was a hunter.

While my dad emerged as a role model for discipline and responsibility, my mother was a different story. I loved my mom, of course. She gave me life and did other considerate things like reading daily at noon while I sucked my thumb before nap time. But I just didn't like her, and she never had my respect. She seemed helpless, terrified of life, and unable to function outside the home, where she often operated like a bully. She could swing that belt, too, and usually administered her whippings with an order for me or my sister to "Bend over and hold your ankles." She didn't have to wait for our dad to come home. I learned later that she suffered from a clinical depression so severe that a psychiatrist would treat her with shock therapy in the 1970s. In my formative years, she emerged as a reactive role model, providing traits for me to observe as an adult in rejecting women who might otherwise seem attractive.

Despite those potential problems, I still recall our household as a wholesome, comfortable, and nurturing place. Dale worked Monday through Saturday and barbecued on Sunday. I had a sister two years younger and then, later, another sister came along when I was fifteen, allowing Dale to repeatedly boast: "There's still some fire in the furnace." Neither of my parents drank alcohol. They took us to church every Sunday at the Overland Christian Church where Dale served as a deacon, elder or something like that. Although the name sounds a tad cultish, the Disciples of Christ was and is just a simple denominational Christian group differentiated only by its doctrine of accepting new members after they've made what they call the "good confession." In this ceremony, the convert merely confesses belief in Jesus Christ as lord and savior, and then the minister baptizes the convert by immersion. Historically the group began in the early 1800s as a frontier offshoot of Presbyterianism, its members rejecting the rituals of the larger church and adopting democracy as a governmental structure.

I made the good confession at the age of fourteen and joined the congregation before I had matured enough to deeply examine my true beliefs. Once I did a few years later, however, I realized I had no faith in God's existence and decided it would be pointless to pretend I did. After all, I reasoned, wouldn't God see through the hypocrisy of pretending to believe? So what would be the point? And if he couldn't, would he be much of a God? Someday I figured an epiphany might strike. Until then I decided to create a value system from common sense. Of course, my agnostic conversion occurred after my childhood, and I concede that youthful exposure to the Overland Christian Church served me well. I read the Christian Bible and enjoyed its stories, taking lessons from the mythology and admiring the literature.

As a kid I must have seemed a walking contradiction. To some I appeared as a shy introvert. The summer after fifth grade, for example, I read most of that 1948 edition of the *World Book Encyclopedia*, A to Z. I also learned the game of chess from the girl who lived next door. From chess I learned the power of planning. From her I learned the traits I wanted to find in female companions: intelligence, wit, attractive looks, a forceful manner, and a hint of mystery. I nurtured a serious crush, and we became inseparable that summer, playing chess or learning to dance, unless I was out on one of my adventures.

That quest for adventure formed the other side to my childhood. I enjoyed disappearing on my bike to explore the neighborhoods. I played baseball and roamed at will in those days before helmet laws and child molestors. Even reading fed my imagination as I embraced the tales of historical figures like Daniel Boone. I dug rock and roll for the rebellion as much as the rhythm. And from television I learned appreciation for the antihero in literature as a fan of James Garner's Brett *Maverick*, the riverboat gambler who avoided fights but usually did the right thing at the end of each show.

In *Life* magazine I read the exploits of the twentieth century adventurer John Goddard, who had sat down at the age of fifteen and wrote a list of 127 goals he hoped to accomplish in his life. These included everything from climbing Mt. Everest to visiting the moon. By the time I read about him, he had traveled the Nile in an historic expedition by kayak as he continued to work his way down the list.

While other ambitious youngsters focused on goals like getting rich or becoming president, I emerged from childhood hooked on adventure and determined to pick a career that offered action as well as a chance to deploy my language skills. I recognized the opportunities my household could provide.

More than anything else I wanted to become an adult who was independent and self-sufficient. Journalism or the law loomed as my answer.

It was purely coincidental that I managed to attend one of the top three schools of journalism in the United States. As a state resident, I had bargain-rate tuition at the University of Missouri about 120 miles west in Columbia. Since I funded my education myself on earnings from the family lawnmower shop, it also was all I could afford. Fortunately, for aspiring journalists, it also was the best there was. So off I went in the fall of 1965 to Mizzou, hitching a ride with a buddy's big sister. I never looked back.

Mizzou's School of Journalism was very different from its reputed rivals on the highbrow campuses of Columbia and Northwestern. Some academics actually looked down their noses at old Mizzou. While students elsewhere spent their hours listening to lectures and pretending to cover make-believe events, Mizzou employed the trade school formula. Missouri J-school students actually worked for a commercial paper, called the *Columbia Missourian*. It supported itself by covering the governments and culture of central Missouri and selling advertising there. To get a three-hour credit in basic reporting, for example, a student would attend class on the city desk and might work the whole semester covering Columbia City Hall, the local police, or anything else found in a real daily newspaper. Instead of taking tests, the student just received a grade from the editors based on job performance.

And these editors were not your typical college professors. One of the best at Mizzou had never even graduated college himself. Tom Duffy had started working during high school in East St. Louis, Illinois, as a copy boy during the Great Depression. Marshalling his natural nose for news and a fascination for the written word, Duffy made his mark at the paper there, hammering away at local corruption and rising to an editor's job. Upon retirement he accepted a job running the city desk at Mizzou's *Columbia Missourian* with a title as associate professor. He was the kind of guy who would wad your incompetent copy into a ball and throw it at your face, an inspirational old style newsman from the real world.

Students could not enter J-school until their junior year, after consuming the usual diet of coursework required to prepare all of us for life: English, history, math, science, etc. You know the drill. Although I had expressed an early interest in communication with my Rudolph the Red-Nosed Reindeer plays, I wasn't that clear about journalism until forced to submit my course plan for my third year. By then I was considering an eventual shot at law school after graduation and I saw journalism as a means to that end. After I covered my first murder case for the *Missourian*, however, it became something more. I was hooked on the rush of being at the center of the action.

Beyond the action and the fun of writing, however, I also began to develop the concept of a "higher authority" in journalism. It was Duffy who explained the principle of public service and I took it to heart. He warned us we couldn't really ever have friends among the sources we would cover. The time would come when we might have to expose anyone as a fraud or a thief. That was our duty. And it flowed not from the publisher who paid our salary or the politicians we might quote. Our duty was to serve as that independent monitor to provide our true superiors—the readers—with the facts to help them make their daily decisions. It sounded great, I thought. Not only can I have fun and get paid for asking rude questions, but I also would actually be doing something important.

Near the end of my senior year, I received a letter from the school inviting me to report in person to the Dean's secretary. When I arrived, she told me I should plan on attending the 1969 awards assembly scheduled a month away. She said I would be receiving something called the Walter Williams Award.

"Huh?" I said. "Are you sure you have the right guy?"

She laughed but I was serious. She compared my student identification card with the name on her list and confirmed it. Honestly shaken, I visited the library and researched the award. It went annually to the J-school student who ranked as the "outstanding writer" there.

I already had a job offer before I won the Walter Williams Award. So I collected that accolade and then shipped off to Flint, Michigan, for a spot on *The Flint Journal*. It was summer of 1969, and all I had to fear was the Vietnam War. I figured I'd end up in a rice paddy anyway before I could establish myself as a reporter. I wanted to eventually cover a state legislature or the federal government for a newspaper, but I also felt war experiences could be character builders. Newspapers and war—wasn't that how Hemingway got his start?

The Flint Journal was the flagship of Michigan's Booth Newspapers chain. Outside of Detroit, Booth owned the state with a daily paper in every major city and no competition. Flint was a boom town in the early 1970s as home to Fisher Body, Buick, and other General Motors units. And it would serve as the first rung on my ladder of professional development.

EIGHT

Early 1970s

My romanticized notion of the classic American outlaw disintegrated on September 10, 1969, when I entered the real world of crime and punishment as the official observer at the Genesee County Courthouse for *The Flint Journal*. That was the day Judge Donald R. Freeman sentenced the city's two most notorious felons of all time for the murder of a Flint policeman during the January robbery of the El Toro Lounge and the related killing of an innocent bystander who lived in a home where they had sought refuge. A jury had convicted them some weeks before of capital murder. Because Michigan had no death penalty, however, that conviction included an automatic sentence of life in prison without parole rather than execution. So Freeman had no discretion on the fates of Norvel Simmons and John J. Moran as deputies ushered them suddenly into his courtroom a day earlier than their appointed date on a tip that the pair had a dramatic plan in the works to escape from Freeman's court. That rumor only added to the tension in the courtroom as the two killers stood before a judge with a penchant for verbal abuse and no option for leniency in the outcome.

Their saga offered another intriguing twist with the involvement of a woman named Constance Haines. The mother of eleven children, Haines had pleaded guilty to charges of helping them with the robbery and murder. She was scheduled for sentencing the following day, giving me my first look at an authentic bad girl.

Looking back, it's hard to understand my naiveté as I watched Simmons and Moran standing there in shackles and handcuffs. I'm glad they were white like me because that allowed me to experience my epiphany without any hint of racial prejudice. I'm not sure exactly what I had expected before entering that courtroom for my first look at authentic killers. Perhaps, in the back of my mind I had envisioned someone sad and defeated by life, someone who never had a break, forced into violence by circumstances beyond their control. If so, that picture vanished in a heartbeat when I looked into the eyes of Simmons and Moran. Not only did those eyes communicate a lack of concern about their situation, but they also burned with contempt and hatred for everyone in that room. They were shackled, and still I felt threatened. My mind formed only one thought: *I hope I never meet those guys on the street.* Can society rehabilitate a rabid dog? All you can do is destroy it, or, in the case of Simmons and Moran, lock them away in a hole. And that is exactly what Freeman prescribed in his speech sending them to the state's highest security prison in Marquette on the Upper Peninsula.

"A judge can send you to prison but only the Almighty can send you to hell," thundered the judge, introducing me to what would become a weekly dose of Freemanisms delivered to whatever poor slobs appeared before him on his sentencing day. He enjoyed seating his sentencing targets in the jury box in progressing order of the prison times they would receive. On any occasion he might have half-a-dozen convicted felons awaiting their fates with those last in line realizing the sentences were growing harsher as the judge came closer to their seats on the bench. During the next two years, I repeatedly would hear Freeman tell felons things like, "I wish we had the death penalty in Michigan," or, "You are the lowest form of life"—comments that would constitute judicial abuse outlawed in later years. But Freeman drank his fill before higher courts took exception to such behavior. One time a felon cracked during a particularly aggressive lecture, pushed the court stenographer to the floor, and leaped onto the bench hoping to strangle his honor in his black robe. Deputies pulled him off and I had a great story. Of course, I couldn't write it until I stopped laughing.

Professionally, *The Flint Journal* proved the perfect stop for me straight out of school. The city was big and complicated enough to humble me into a rookie more willing to learn than dictate demands like a prima donna. And the veteran journalists working there provided plenty of education on asking the tough questions while developing a skeptical view of the world.

As the courts reporter for *The Journal* between 1969 and 1971, I presided over a colorful cast of characters who provided a thorough education on criminology and our legal system. Besides Freeman, the county bench included five other judges with their own eccentricities. The county prosecutor, Robert

F. Leonard, was a firebrand in his own right with Democratic Party political ambitions well beyond that office at the time. Later on in the 1980s, he would be convicted himself for embezzling federal law enforcement grant funds. In the 1970s, however, he ranked as the ringmaster for action that ran the gamut from administrative battles with county government to his crusade for a special grand jury to investigate corruption in both county and city government—a crusade that bore fruit and made my time in Flint even more exciting with bribery indictments pending against Flint's mayor and the county's top elected officer by the time I left in 1971.

Besides the judges, the prosecutors, and the criminals, Flint's courthouse community also boasted an intriguing array of defense attorneys eager to teach me their points of view. In the process I learned to get along with all kinds of folks, even dangerous characters like Simmons or Moran. But I also learned to maintain a skeptical eye while listening to anyone's version of the truth, just taking notes and saying nothing in a state of absolute detachment. For me, they were a story. For them, I was their soapbox. Life as a reporter became just a never-ending parade of symbiotic relationships.

My typical workday began at the courthouse, where I would make rounds looking for news. I maintained a diary on the dockets and knew in advance about trial dates and such. I became a part of the infrastructure there, visiting the secretaries of each of the judges, chatting with Leonard, sitting through trials, or joking with the defense attorneys. I gathered research on two levels, one for that day's breaking news and another for enterprise or feature stories I might craft when time allowed. About three every afternoon I would gather my notes and walk the four blocks back to *The Journal* offices where I would hunker down at my desk and hammer out the stories of the day on my manual typewriter for the evening deadline. Sometimes, when an important story broke during the day, I would find a phone at the courthouse and call a rewrite reporter in the newsroom so he could combine my news from the scene with necessary background from our files to develop a finished product superior to what I might eventually deliver after waiting all day.

I didn't realize how much of a professional I had become until my father paid a visit the summer of 1971. He had always scoffed at my journalistic ambitions, viewing them as a self-indulgent crapshoot when compared with the hard work of real men who fix lawnmowers. Or, maybe he just felt jealous that I had chosen my own way in a world alien to him rather than accepting my legacy as heir to his lawnmower repair empire. At any rate, I didn't know what to expect when he tagged along on my beat, following me every step of the way as I moved through the back stairwells like an invisible ghost from courtroom to courtroom.

We attended a Donald R. Freeman sentencing session—always a treat for the uninitiated—and for once that judge was at a loss for words. Freeman invited his featured felon-of-the-day to beg for mercy before sentence was passed. We listened intently as the prisoner sought leniency because the night before, in his cell, he recounted: "An angel of the Lord appeared and said, 'Tyrone, straighten yourself up.'" Freeman closed his eyes, shook his head and simply replied: "Sixty years." Before the judge left the bench, I grabbed my dad and escorted him into the hallway, around a corner, and through a side door where we emerged into Freeman's private chambers, employing a maneuver I repeated almost every day without even thinking about it. My dad was even more surprised when Freeman joined us without a word, as if we were part of his furniture.

While we sat and talked with the judge, I watched my dad's expression and actually felt satisfaction beaming as he realized I had become my own man. In later years, as a father myself, I've often thought that must have been a great moment for him to actually live a day in the life of his grown child. It's something I'd like to do with my own daughters. A bring-your-dad-to-work-day might give all dads a chance to start seeing their offspring as people, rather than the kids they only recall.

When I began my tenure in Flint I had expected to be there only a short time while waiting for my draft date. But a funny thing happened on the way to Vietnam. Richard Nixon instituted a draft lottery, and just days after passing a pre-induction physical exam in Detroit my birth date came up roses at number 343. Essentially that meant I would not be drafted unless the Viet Cong managed to mount an invasion of California. Suddenly, the whole world opened wide. I no longer had to plan my life around a two-year hitch in the Army. So I reviewed my options. Although I loved my job, I focused on a reality of my existence. Michigan's winters are cold, dark, and long. And my professional ambitions went beyond *The Flint Journal*. So I sent letters to the editors of every newspaper in the Sun Belt. *The Houston Post* was the first to call.

NINE

Early 1970s

Before I left Flint, an assistant prosecutor there had warned me I'd find guys in Houston who could chew up Simmons and Moran before breakfast then spit them out for lunch because they just weren't mean enough to make a good meal. I didn't realize then that list of Houston's toughest "guys" eventually would include a five-foot-three-inch, green-eyed blonde. But I was still nearly a decade away from hooking up with Catherine when I arrived in December of 1971 in Houston for the next level of post-graduate education in journalism and crime reporting. While *any* murder in Flint rated a story for *The Journal*, the two Houston papers had to prioritize. They did not have enough room to cover all, so each murder story needed its own "man-bites-dog" element to justify the space.

I had my first taste of the fast lane when I reported for duty in the fourth floor press room at the Houston Police Department's 61 Reisner Street headquarters. Before noon I had lost about $25 in a poker game that was interrupted by the killing of a bank president who had tried to stop a robbery with his personal sidearm only to die in a hail of gunfire as he chased the robbers down the street.

The morning delivery *Post* had hired me specifically to become one of its night police beat reporters. New hires usually covered the cops for about a year before promotion to assignments with less gore and more reasonable hours. After my daytime orientation, I began working the night shift of six-to-two,

Sunday through Wednesday. I filed stories directly from a community press room in the police station using a Western Union-style teletype machine.

Houston's economy was large enough to support two daily papers, and I welcomed the challenge of a true competitive situation with the rival afternoon *Houston Chronicle*. *The Post* was owned by the venerable Hobby family, then headed by the matriarch, Oveta Culp Hobby. She was the widow of a former Texas governor and had distinguished herself as well heading the Women's Army Corps during World War II. Her son, William P. Hobby Jr., served as editor of *The Post* but had divided his time just then running what would be a successful campaign to win election as Texas Lieutenant Governor, a position he would hold from 1973 until 1991. To her credit, Mrs. Hobby was a hands-on, news junkie type of executive with a penchant for popping into the newsroom just to see what might be going on. *The Post* served as a flagship for a family media empire that also included ownership of the local NBC radio and television affiliates. Although those electronic outlets generated greater revenues, the daily paper ranked as her professional love. A true matriarch, she considered its stories the diary for her town and its reporters part of her family. She seemed less concerned with how much money the paper made than with how it was done.

My city editor was an easygoing fellow named Jim Holley who had supervised the reporting six years earlier on a series of articles that won the paper its only Pulitzer Prize. That saga still ranks among the most exciting of the Pulitzer Prize archives as *The Post* uncovered a web of corruption in the neighboring City of Pasadena, an industrial enclave along the Houston Ship Channel. At one point the paper hired a bodyguard for the reporter who eventually claimed the national investigative prize under Holley's supervision.

As the night police reporter for *The Post*, I shared the police station press room with my counterpart from the *Chronicle*, a reporter my same age named Tim Fleck. He later would earn fame as a local political commentator in the 1990s. But back in those days we occupied the lowest link on the food chain at our respective publications. We usually played several games of chess each night while waiting for news to break by monitoring the six individual radio speakers that broadcast conversations between police cruisers and central dispatch. Once an hour we would walk the halls visiting detectives in the homicide and robbery divisions to ferret out stories from them. Back in those days, reporters enjoyed an amicable relationship with cops, and we were usually welcome in their offices. Often we served as witnesses on confessions, and I sometimes participated in lineups when detectives needed extras to fill the slots around the usual suspects. On one occasion a witness actually picked me as the perpetrator in some case only to hear the detective sigh: "Unfortunately he has an iron-clad alibi."

We also had extracurricular duties for the dean of the police reporting community, a colorful TV reporter named Jack Cato. His Mustang fastback was packed with police monitors that covered every channel, and he often just cruised the streets like a news cabbie rushing to a scene for film before anyone could haul away the body. In addition, he also owned a soda machine on the fourth floor of the police station and assigned me to keep it full or refund money to cops who lost their change when it didn't work. He benefited from a remarkable relationship with all the cops, and you could always hear him coming down the hall: "Hey, how's the family? Have a cigar? Had that baby yet?" Cato's political savvy paid off later when he was elected in the 1990s to serve as Harris County Treasurer, a position he held until his death in 2006.

So, I was paying my dues, spending every night trying to make sense of a cacophony of radio conversations on the wall—listening specifically for the red light codes of "DOA" or "officer down" or any other cry with news potential. Usually once a night we'd hear something interesting, interrupt our chess game, and drive to the scene of a crime. Back then, the cops usually allowed us to walk around the dead bodies with them as long as we didn't intrude or offend.

The big story from my one year of night police duty occurred in November of 1972 when I fielded the report of a DOA at an upscale address in Houston's posh River Oaks section. The call came blaring from a police speaker early one Sunday evening when I was alone in the press room. As a result, I was the first reporter to arrive on the scene of the murder of Dr. John Hill, a plastic surgeon who would become immortalized in Tommy Thompson's best-selling true crime book *Blood and Money*. Hill had been suspected in the poisoning death of his first wife, the daughter of a wealthy Houston oil man. He was facing a second trial in the case when intruders shot him dead in the doorway of his River Oaks mansion.

I finished that one-year tour of night police satisfied I had made the right move coming to Houston. The stories just seemed to keep growing larger and more exciting. As a reporter in Houston in the 1970s, I felt like a dog abandoned in a butcher shop.

TEN

Mid-1970s

The larger community of reporters in Houston was closer to my own age, and I had no mentors to help me navigate the rivalries of this more political environment. Reporters can be among the most egocentric of professionals, and back-stabbing ranks as a natural hazard of the job. We could work together as a team, have some beers, and laugh about outsiders. But once the *Post* presses rolled, we were as competitive among ourselves as with our rivals at the *Chronicle*. The hidden side of every newsroom resembles something out of *Wild Kingdom* as the reporters cautiously circle each other while looking for weaknesses. It's a rough place for anyone with thin skin, but that same natural system also works more efficiently than pay hikes at producing special stories. Peer pressure pushes almost everyone to reach while also holding them in check against abusing their power.

Of course, no system is perfect, and, despite the fear of social scorn, every newsroom produces its share of laggards content to slide by on one end and overachievers willing to risk exposure for an exaggerated scoop on the other. Overstepping the public trust with exaggeration generates more vicious peer contempt than goofing off. Goof-offs pose little threat to reporters vying for a chance to cover the big one. Like jackals attacking a wounded lion, however, reporters move faster than management when they see a chance to bring down a prima donna from their own tribe by uncovering a fireable offense such as plagiarism or invention of a source. And it's no coincidence that the well-publicized scandals of plagiarism and fictionalized copy at major news institutions in recent years were sparked primarily by opportunistic whistle-blowing peers rather than any quality control system designed by management. I watched journalism's version of this natural selection process unfold in its basic state during the 1970s at *The Post*.

In the tradition of all the night police beat reporters before me, I spent much of my time that first year plotting a plan to escape it. Although the beat offered many moments of excitement, night police overall resembled fireman's duty that involved hours of waiting for something to happen. But night police ranked as the standard first stop for new reporters, forcing them to learn about the city by rapidly driving its streets and testing their ability to get facts straight. I learned quickly that success in this business springs not from talent as a writer but from credibility as a reporter. The writing part of journalism is less than 20 percent of the job. If a story is compared with a journey, reporting is the selection of the destination and the mapping for the trip. Writing is just the vehicle used to go there. You may be driving a Porsche, but, if your destination is just a McDonald's, you're still only eating fast food.

Over the next few years I worked a variety of beats at *The Post* that kept me outside the newsroom itself. I covered county government and civil courts, working from the press room at the civil courts building downtown. I also created a state prison beat on a part-time basis, convincing editors to let me spend one day each week looking for stories in Huntsville, seventy miles north of Houston, where the Texas Department of Corrections had its headquarters and primary unit known affectionately as "The Walls." I also worked general assignment for a while, just hanging out at the city desk and taking any stories that might come along. Eventually I nabbed one of the glamour beats, assuming the criminal courts mantle in 1977.

During those years between police and courts, I developed a reputation as a trustworthy reporter who could handle a wide range of stories, from the serious to the silly. One of my major assignments began the night of July 24, 1974, when a south Texas drug lord named Fred Carrasco seized control of the Walls prison unit in Huntsville. Aided by henchmen Rudy Dominguez and Ignacio Cuevas, he grabbed eighty hostages using pistols smuggled inside a ham. Taking refuge in the prison library, they whittled their hostage roster down to a more manageable eleven that included the system's chaplain, educators and some other inmates. Aware that Carrasco was reputed to have murdered more than a hundred persons running a drug empire along the border, prison officials prepared for the worst and began negotiating a solution to what would become, at eleven days, the longest prison hostage siege in US history.

The national press quickly joined us locals at the TDC headquarters in Huntsville, covering the grounds around the stately, dark bricks of The Walls like some invading army. Various news organizations pitched tents on the grassy prison grounds for use as shelter while waiting for the standoff to play out. The duty involved hours of monotony broken by two or three daily briefings that allowed the prison staff to share their latest exchanges with the inmates.

Our mood turned somber and serious on the Saturday evening of August 3 as we sensed something set to happen. Word spread through the press corps that a vehicle of some sort had been moved into the unit, and we waited silently for a showdown. We would learn later that prison officials had teamed with the legendary Texas Rangers and hatched a plan to offer the inmates transportation out aboard an armored car. As the inmates and their hostages moved from the library to the car, lawmen hoped to knock them down with high pressure water hoses and avoid a bloodbath.

But Carrasco feared a trap. Before leaving the library, he and his sidekicks taped together chalkboards and textbooks to build what became known as their "Trojan Horse" to shield them as they and the hostages walked through the door and down a ramp to the armored car. When the hoses failed to topple the horse, the shooting began. Within minutes, two of the hostages lay dead beside Carrasco and Dominguez. And Cuevas would spend the next seventeen years fighting the death penalty, with the state's top criminal appellate lawyer, Will Gray, winning appeals for Cuevas on three convictions before Cuevas finally received a lethal injection in 1991. I did not know it then, but Gray was destined to play an important role in my relationship later with Catherine Mehaffey.

My previous work developing the prison beat paid off the morning after the siege when I got an exclusive interview with the system's bedraggled director, Jim Estelle. With most of the deadline work completed just after the shootout and unable to sleep, I had wandered over to The Walls from our offsite motel room sanctuary to find the prison grounds deserted, the tents emptied, and the grass littered with coffee cups and other debris. Concluding no one was around, I prepared to leave when a car drove by. Estelle sat behind the wheel, all alone, and he spotted me. He pointed a finger toward his office window and nodded. While he parked his car, I entered the administration building that stood just a few hundred yards from the last night's carnage. We talked for two hours about the event, the burdens of responsibility, the realities of crime and punishment, and the myth of rehabilitation. When we were done, I had a page one story. And Estelle had the rest of his life to punish himself for all the tragic things that went wrong.

I wish I could say I nailed the best story from the Carrasco siege with my interview of Estelle, but another reporter trumped that the next day. He cornered the local justice of peace who had authority in that rural area to declare the cause of death for Carrasco and Dominguez. His decision: Suicide.

"Suicide?"

"Yep, suicide," said his honor. "Everybody knows it's just plain suicide to go up against the Texas Rangers."

ELEVEN

Mid-1970s

As a general assignments reporter at *The Post* during the 1970s, I polished a reputation for versatility. I showed I could handle soft features, hard-breaking news and investigative challenges. The paper sent me to spend a weekend in a Texas nudist camp. I covered a Ku Klux Klan rally. I sat with blind children at a circus. I attended an underwater wedding held in a tank on the front lawn of a church where a skin-diving minister married a skin-diving couple who wrote their "I dos" on an underwater slate. I stood in line for the movie *Jaws* and wrote a feature about the people willing to wait to see a movie. I covered explosions. Every day was a new adventure. I joined a prison inmate as he left The Walls after serving a sentence for marijuana possession and experienced his first three days of freedom with him. I won a statewide enterprise reporting award for work on a series of stories exposing the use of electric cattle prods by a local police department to extract confessions.

In late 1975 I received an unexpected phone call from a recruiter for the weekly tabloid scandal sheet, *The National Enquirer*. He said he had read one of my *Post* features about the tactics of bill collectors headlined "Wolf at the Door" and thought that I might be *Enquirer* material. Still a bit confused over whether I wanted to be "*Enquirer* material," I nevertheless joined him for breakfast. As a result I used four weeks of vacation in January 1976 living in the Lantana, Florida, Holiday Inn and earning about three times my *Houston Post* salary on a "tryout" with *The Enquirer* to sample the tabloid experience.

My sojourn at *The Enquirer* proved to be one of the most interesting escapades in my journalism career. It also served to invigorate my imagination when I returned to *The Post* after learning that I probably was not *"Enquirer material."* Or, maybe I would have been had I not gotten caught in the middle of an internal political squabble between the paper's British and American editors. At the end of my "tryout" working for one of the American editors, the paper offered an extension with no guarantee of a job. Since I had exhausted my vacation time, I declined, choosing instead to return to a sure thing at *The Post*.

Contrary to what might be the popular perception, I found my *Enquirer* colleagues to be the most professional group of journalism heavyweights I had ever encountered. The staff included many burned-out mainstream stars who sought a high-paying change of pace. One example was a former political writer from *The Chicago Tribune* who greeted me with a smile and said, "Can you believe this place? I just got back from Rio doing a story on a bleeding statue of Christ. What a hoot!" That list also included *The Houston Post's* Pulitzer winner, Gene Goltz, who, I was told, had been assigned to stake out the Jackie Onassis apartment in New York City. What an image for me: Gene Goltz on the Jackie O nightshift waiting for her to step into the street so he could scream embarrassing questions. The *Enquirer* remains an incredible commercial success, providing mostly entertainment but also, I found, a good deal of important information buried behind its facade of outrage. As such, the paper carefully monitored its sales demographics, and it was well known that any time Jackie O's face appeared on the front page, sales soared off the charts.

The current star on the staff, however, was a former *Boston Globe* reporter about my own age who took me under his wing. Jeff had done a story the month before that sent sales to a record for the year. Crashing Frank Sinatra's birthday party and being physically evicted by Old Blue Eyes himself, Jeff had written an unforgettable piece on celebrity rage that shared the experience of having the legendary crooner spit in his face. Beyond the smokescreen of celebrity coverage that paid the bills, however, Jeff offered an anecdote demonstrating the way the paper actually developed solid stories of general interest that even the nation's most prestigious publications would want to have. Searching through obscure historical journals, Jeff had uncovered an academic treatise by some anthropologists who had analyzed some old stone tablets discovered in New England and linked them to ninth-century Iberia to show that the Spanish had reached the New World some five hundred years before Columbus. He wrote a story and presented it to his editor who smiled and said: "Something isn't right."

"Huh?" Jeff asked.

"These tablets," the editor continued. "I don't believe they came from Iberia."

Jeff shook his head and asked, "OK, where are they from?"

The editor just sighed and pointed toward the heavens.

"Of course," said Jeff. "I should have known."

He then spent the next week calling so-called authorities on UFOs for their reaction to discovery of these tablets. Finally, a former astronaut agreed these had to be from outer space. So his story ran with a headline: "Tablets from Outer Space Discovered in New England?" His first paragraph featured the astronaut as a primary source on the meaning of these tablets. Then, the rest of the story cited the anthropologists and their theory on Iberian origins. Anyone with half-a-brain reading past the first paragraph would glean information of anthropological significance and likely chuckle at the UFO link that had attracted their attention in the first place. Jeff's point had applications anywhere in the news business. Every editor or publisher has their own agenda. But it is possible to compromise and finesse your assignment so that somehow everyone is satisfied with the result, and, most importantly, the readers receive the information they need to carry on with their lives.

As a stimulant for finding scoops, *The Enquirer* employed a bounty system. It paid a hundred-dollar fee to anyone—staffer, reader or kook—who suggested an idea that eventually became a published story, even if someone else ended up writing it. Many staffers spent their weekends sitting in the local library pouring through arcane medical and scientific journals, seeking overlooked footnotes on potentially exciting breakthroughs and discoveries that might turn into articles of public significance. I got caught up in the frenzy for generating story ideas, and, when I returned to Houston, I put it to work at *The Post*, listing all sorts of ideas for local stories that might turn into something there.

I didn't have long to wait for that habit to pay off with what would be the strongest story I ever reported, one that would see me nominated for a Pulitzer Prize. That adventure began when I convinced my editors at *The Post* to let me research a story on old men in Texas prisons. I didn't really know what I would find. But roaming around the geriatrics ward at TDC's hospital behind The Walls in Huntsville, I struck up a conversation with an addled eighty-three-year-old con named Gene Winchester who couldn't even remember why he was there. Checking his file a little later to get the facts, I saw that he had received a fifty-year sentence in 1918 for murder. I did a quick calculation and realized he'd actually been locked up for fifty-eight years with no mention in his file of additional crimes. I showed the discrepancy to the prison bosses and waited several days for an explanation.

When it arrived, that explanation revealed a more interesting problem. Winchester had killed another inmate in 1920, and, instead of charging him in that crime, the prison simply shipped him off to the state mental hospital in Rusk, where he sat until 1968. He returned to TDC that year as part of a clearance at the hospital, and the state's attorney general had decreed he would not receive credit for the forty-eight years in Rusk. Not only had Winchester been lost in the system for several generations, he still had several more to serve. Although the state had locked him up since 1918 on a fifty-year term, official records showed he had served only ten of those years. I had exposed a bureaucratic mess with no apparent solution that triggered cries of outrage from legislators and penal reform advocates. It also drew a phone call from a woman who claimed Winchester as her "Uncle Gene"—a family icon believed to have died in prison forty years before.

Eager to take Winchester's story further, I buckled down and negotiated his release by brokering a deal between the Social Security Administration, the Board of Pardons and Paroles, and a nursing home south of Houston. The Board agreed to release him on parole while Social Security determined him eligible for special benefits. The nursing home offered a room. Within a month, I was back in Huntsville covering the release of Gene Winchester. He worried me a bit when I asked him about his plans only to hear him say with a sickening grin: "Goin' to find me a woman." I recognized him as a strong and healthy specimen for his age and wondered, *What have I done?*

After arriving in Huntsville fifty-eight years before in a horse-drawn cart, Winchester left with me in a car driving sixty miles per hour down an interstate highway. He had missed everything in the century, including women's lib. But he was destined to live several more years in that home without incident. Winning Winchester's release easily ranked as the high point in my reporting career. Besides the satisfaction of seeing justice properly done and helping an old man land a few years of rest before his death, I also gleaned greater appreciation for my powers as a journalist.

Although I didn't win the Pulitzer, the nomination alone was an accolade that continued to impress acquaintances even more than the awards I actually did collect in the next couple of years to follow, inspired to new ambitions by my experience getting an old man out of prison.

Unfortunately, however, I would soon become more widely known for something else. Just once now, I would enjoy walking into a bar and hearing someone say, "Yeah, you're the guy who was nominated for the Pulitzer on that Winchester story." Instead, I usually only hear, "Yeah, you're guy who got messed up with that Mehaffey bitch."

TWELVE

Late 1970s

Early in 1977 I received the assignment most responsible for placing me professionally on a collision course with Catherine Mehaffey. That's when *The Post* made me its criminal courthouse beat reporter, a job I had wanted since first arriving in Houston. Although the issues and basic elements were the same as I had seen covering courts in Flint, the system in Houston magnified the challenge and the adventure the way shopping in an urban mall would dwarf a trip to the neighborhood convenience store.

On its most basic level the physical demands of the beat were daunting. Just as in Flint, I was responsible for reporting all the important criminal court action in the county. While Flint's Genesee County was small enough to conduct its business in one building among six judges, Houston's Harris County system operated in multiple buildings with at least thirty separate judges dispensing justice every day. That system had just been expanded to reflect Houston's oilpatch-boomtown atmosphere and the crimes that entailed. Besides the regularly appointed and elected judges, the county also employed a number of part-time, or what it called "visiting judges," to handle additional cases and keep the treadmill rolling. As a result, it was nearly impossible to monitor all the courts like some omniscient chronicler of current history. Some days I would pass a room that had served as a broom closet just one week before only to find inside some retired judge from West Texas sitting as a visitor while a prosecutor, defense attorney, and a defendant haggled over a plea bargain. In addition to the courtrooms, I also had to monitor general activities of the district attorney's office, grand jury proceedings, and the defense attorneys who moved through the building while also tracking broader, big picture issues of crime and punishment.

In that era, one of the biggest issues on my plate involved the death penalty which had just been reinstated by the U. S. Supreme Court after a ten-year hiatus. The Texas Legislature had moved quickly to fashion a new capital punishment statute designed to meet the parameters established by the high court and put Texas back on the execution hit parade. Those high court parameters had established crucial elements for bringing capital charges and selecting juries. Prosecutors in the past had enjoyed great leeway seeking death as punishment for crimes as far-ranging as rape to murder in the heat of passion without premeditation. But the new rules required accusations of more substantial transgressions. They limited capital crimes to murders committed in the course of another felony, such as the armed robber who kills the store clerk or the rapist who leaves his victim dead. Also included were murders done for hire or the murder of a peace officer in the line of duty. Despite those limitations, Houston, in those days, became fertile ground for capital crimes, and the Harris County District Attorney's office quickly established itself as the nation's most aggressive grim reaper.

Although Texas would not resume executions until 1982, I caught the first wave of the tsunami caseload in the late 1970s as Harris County began holding trials to line them up for the gallows. I considered it my duty to try and attend as much of every capital case as possible on my watch, but sometimes that proved impossible. One week, for example, Harris County had five different capital trials under way simultaneously. I ran from courtroom to courtroom trying to keep up. Most of these cases needed only a minimal amount of actual trial time, but each one lasted for weeks because jury selection took so long. The attorneys interrogated potential jurors individually at great length to determine if they actually would have the courage to send anyone to Death Row.

Another important issue concerned the county's system for providing defense lawyers to impoverished defendants, a category that covered about 90 percent of the courthouse-accused. While many jurisdictions created public defender bureaucracies to handle that role, Harris County had its own unique and controversial system of appointment by judges from the ranks of the county's criminal defense bar. Often I saw judges simply shout in a crowded courtroom for an attorney to step forward and take a case. Another judge occasionally collected business cards from all lawyers hanging around the courtroom, shuffled them, and then dealt from the top of the deck to his clerk, matching an attorney with a defendant as each case was called.

And there always were plenty of lawyers hungry for the assignments that generated fees based on a schedule established by the county: $250 for an appearance in court, five hundred dollars per day for trials, and so on. Although they belittled the fees and compared them derisively with grander sums they bragged they could have been making on car wrecks or divorces, they always lined up there like dock workers at the union hall waiting for a job. Many built a substantial portion of their practices on the foundation of daily appointments. Often they could grab an assignment, negotiate a plea, and collect $250 before noon, leaving the rest of the day free for those car wrecks anyhow. While the drama of trials captures our imagination, the overwhelming majority of criminal cases are resolved without them, often quickly with a deal. If this plea-bargaining system did not exist, the courts would grind to a smashing halt on the burden of the caseload. To begin each auction, prosecutors review the quality of evidence brought by police against an accused and weigh that against his likely defense and other mitigating factors like his looks or lack of a criminal background. Charged with burglary, a defendant might be facing a maximum sentence of ten years in prison. But the case can be disposed that morning if he agrees to plead guilty to trespassing and takes a year in jail. Often that's exactly what happens.

I wrote some memorable stories on this appointment system by annually scrutinizing the total bills paid out by the county for the past year and identifying the lawyers milking it dry. Their services definitely were needed, but, my stories in April 1978 and June of 1979, showed that some of them were earning more as appointed defense attorneys than the judges and other high ranking county officials actually on the public payroll. The highest earners rarely handled cases that went to trial. Moreover, my stories exposed a system in which many judges routinely assigned cases to the same small club of private attorneys working only in their courts, creating a de-facto public defender system at their personal disposal. Some judges explained their motives by touting the diligence of the lawyers working exclusively for them and bragging about the painstaking research on background checks before completing the rosters. Fair enough, I said, and included that defense in my stories. But I also knew that the most effective defense lawyers likely won that reputation by moving cases through the courts as quickly as possible, leaving the system open to charges it served the interest of the judges rather than indigent defendants. I also imagined that most of their painstaking background research likely had occurred in saloons rather than libraries. Since I watched the system work on a daily basis, I was confident that most of the time it accomplished its goal of providing justice for indigents and the public, too, at a reasonable taxpayer cost.

But anyone could recognize this system as rife with opportunity for cronyism or abuse, and Catherine Mehaffey would be no exception when she eventually entered my life a year later.

THIRTEEN

Late 1970s

Each capital murder trial in those early years of the new process promised its own special twist. Early in my tenure came the trial of "Sleeping" Billy Wayne White, who, at age twenty in March of 1977, became the youngest killer sentenced to death to that date from Harris County. I gave him his nickname and made him an international celebrity.

Billy had capped a short but illustrious juvenile record by killing a sixty-five-year-old woman who ran a furniture store with her husband. Billy shot her dead while robbing the couple in their store, killing her in front of her husband without provocation and for no reason anyone could fathom. No one could figure why he left the old man alive to testify at his trial, either. Billy had no defense and presented no witnesses. His court-appointed attorney, Leroy Peavy, emerged as his only hope. I discussed the case with Peavy before trial and eagerly awaited the event. It was to be Peavy's first death penalty defense, and he planned to put capital punishment on trial. He boned up for weeks, gathering all facts ever used against capital punishment. He knew Billy would never win an acquittal on the evidence. But Peavy hoped he could turn jurors against the system itself and convince them to sentence his client to life in prison instead of death.

I watched as Peavy began his impassioned plea. But I couldn't hear him clearly. Another sound was drowning him out. I looked around for signs of a broken air conditioner or some other mechanical malfunction and saw nothing. Then I spotted Billy at the defense table. While his lawyer begged for his life, Billy had laid his head on the table and gone sound to sleep. Billy wasn't just dozing. He snored like a big dog just home from a run in the park. Jurors poked each other and pointed at Billy while Peavy continued, pretending to ignore him. The lawyer resembled a singer who forgets the lyrics but continues to hum with the melody because the show must go on. Once Peavy completed his summation, however, he succumbed to his own disgust and that only made things worse. Taking his seat beside Billy as the prosecutor rose to offer the state's final argument, Peavy tried to nudge Billy with an elbow and jostle him awake. Billy raised his head, glanced at Peavy, and then waved him away with one of his hands while clearly mouthing the words: "Fuck off, asshole."

The jury deliberated all of thirty minutes before sending Billy to Death Row, and the wire services picked up my front page story to share it with the world. I felt sympathetic for Peavy as the hard-working advocate, but he seemed unfazed the next day. He smiled and told me he would appeal the conviction on the grounds his client suffered a sleeping ailment and could not assist with the defense. So, for two days in a row, Sleeping Billy made front page news in Houston and around the world. The State of Texas eventually executed Billy on April 23, 1992, after exhausting all appeals.

About a year after Billy became the county's youngest immigrant to Death Row, eighteen-year-old Anthony "Bo Peep" Williams dislodged him from the record books. Bo Peep earned his nickname from the neighborhood where he had gained a reputation for peeking around trees and corners while hiding from other kids who generally wanted nothing to do with him. One night in 1977, Bo Peep was cruising through a bowling alley parking lot when he saw thirteen-year-old Vickie Lynn Wright walking to her sister's car. Vickie was really excited because this was the first time her parents had ever let her accompany their older daughter to bowl. She had left something in the car and went outside to retrieve it. But she never made it back inside. Bo Peep grabbed her, took her in the nearby woods, raped her, and then beat her to death with a two-by-four he'd found in a trash pile.

He had no defense for his crime, either, and faced an overwhelming collection of physical evidence. But his appointed lawyer also did his best, presenting witnesses to show that Bo Peep lacked the mental faculties to accept responsibility. The night before a psychiatrist testified in court, I received a copy of *National Geographic* magazine and read the cover story about a research gorilla with a verifiable I.Q. of eighty-two at the Yerkes Primate Center. The next day I stared at Bo Peep in the courtroom and listened while that psychiatrist estimated his I.Q. at seventy-five. I thought about that little girl who had paid the ultimate penalty for leaving something in her sister's car. I thought about the older sister who likely would never forgive herself for letting Vickie run to the car alone. I thought of the parents in the hallway crying throughout the trial. I thought about that gorilla at Yerkes who probably had spent his day showing off his eighty-two I.Q. by moving wooden blocks around on a table while scientists recorded grades. I wondered: What are we supposed to do? Then I had to leave the courtroom because I realized I was fighting a nearly irresistible urge to grab Bo Peep around the throat and stomp his ugly face.

I would see Bo Peep again in 1987 on assignment for *Time Magazine* shortly before his execution that year on May 28. *Time* was researching a broader story on the death penalty and assigned me to interview three residents of Texas's Death Row. I picked the subjects myself and included Bo Peep in that group because I had never been able to shake him from my mind. On Death Row, Bo Peep had found religion. But he remained adamant about his innocence. Another Bo Peep had killed that girl, he told me. He had been there, too, but he hadn't struck the blows. Those came from the other Bo Peep, the bad one who always got him trouble. And I wondered again: What are we supposed to do?

Daily the courts beat offered more difficult lessons on cruelty and violence than I had ever experienced covering police. While the police beat exposed me to the gore at crime scenes, trials provided the final review with all the pieces in place—excuses and whining from the defendants drowning out the cries of the victims as each case presented a neatly finished story to digest. Every time I thought I had heard it all, I would arrive at court to hear something worse, and it hardly came only from the capital trials.

One assault case, for example, involved a strip club bouncer convicted for beating a customer into a vegetative state, overreacting to his resistance when evicted from the club. Prosecutors wheeled the customer into the courtroom on a gurney where he lay in a coma like an organic Exhibit A while jurors heard testimony from witnesses. The bouncer went to prison, and the customer never left the nursing home.

Another case involved a mother who had intentionally infected her own child with feces to keep her sick and bedridden in a hospital because the mother was infatuated with physicians. The mother suffered an obsessive psychological disorder known as Munchausen's Syndrome by Proxy that forced her to constantly seek the excitement of hospitals while pretending to be a victim of unexplainable illness to her child. A jury convicted her of injury to the child.

Although odds usually favor the state, some sensational cases did end with acquittals. In 1979, prominent attorney David Berg won acquittal for a woman accused of killing her lover, cutting his body into five pieces, and burying him in an orange grove. He convinced the jury that the dead man had been a monster who beat his client regularly, read books on Satan worship, and even rooted for the Nazis during a television movie about the Holocaust. At Berg's victory press conference I couldn't resist the urge and asked in front of the cameras: "Is it true you were paid an arm and a leg?"

Two of the biggest cases on my watch did not involve capital murder. First came the 1977 trial of two Houston cops accused of murder in the drowning of an Hispanic laborer named Joe Torres. They had thrown him into a creek after he resisted arrest for being drunk. Even before the trial, the incident had swallowed the city, pitting its Hispanic community against the police department, and spawning a riot. The two cops hired top legal guns Mike Ramsey and Bob Bennett, who had the trial moved to Huntsville seeking an impartial jury. The trial was held in an auditorium at Sam Houston State University's criminology school, allowing students to fill the audience seats and witness real justice in action. Reporters sat at a table on the main floor, right beside the defendants taking notes. I lived in a dormitory room at the school for about three weeks, sending stories back to the newsroom every evening.

In the end, prosecutors could not prove that the cops had intended Torres to die when they tossed him into the bayou. The cops admitted losing their tempers and beating on Torres. But they said they meant to cut him a break by releasing him instead of taking him to jail. They were surprised he didn't survive. Prosecutors Bert Graham and Ted Poe argued the cops probably didn't want to take Torres to jail where his beating would be discovered. Nevertheless, they couldn't sell all the jurors on a theory of murder-by-drowning, and the jury compromised with a verdict of negligent homicide. I thought that decision pretty fair after hearing all the evidence, but Bert considered it the first case he ever had lost. The sentence of one year's probation on the misdemeanor charge only incited new animosity among Houston's Hispanics, and the Torres case remained a sore spot for years.

I couldn't know it then, but Bert was destined for an important role ahead in the explosion of my relationship with Catherine Mehaffey.

Between October of 1978 and January 1979, Houston hosted one of the sensational trials of Fort Worth industrialist and millionaire T. Cullen Davis. A leading Fort Worth citizen and socialite, Davis had been embroiled in a high stakes divorce case that reached a crescendo when someone entered his Fort Worth mansion and killed his estranged wife's boyfriend as well as her daughter from a prior marriage. Police focused on Davis as the killer and took him to trial in 1977 with a hung jury as the result. While waiting for a second trial on the murder, the case took another bizarre twist as police arrested Davis again, alleging he had tried to hire a hit man to assassinate the judge in his hotly-contested divorce case. Because of Davis's standing in Fort Worth, prosecutors wanted to move the Davis cases elsewhere. So, they showed up in my courthouse seeking an impartial Houston jury to hear their charges of conspiracy to commit capital murder in the plot on the judge.

The Davis trial in Houston gave new meaning to the phrase "legal circus." The millionaire had a high-priced defense team headed by legendary Houston attorney Richard "Racehorse" Haynes, who had just won the mistrial for Davis in the first murder trial and eventually would succeed in clearing Davis on all charges. But the Fort Worth prosecutors boasted strong evidence in the alleged plot on the judge. It had begun when police character David McCrory visited police claiming Davis had hired him to kill the judge. Detectives enlisted McCrory as an undercover operative and told him to continue with the plot while they secretly monitored his negotiations with the millionaire. They persuaded the targeted judge to feign a death pose in the trunk of a car with ketchup splattered on his body for a photo used by McCrory to collect his fee from Davis. They wired McCrory for sound and took film of him meeting with Davis in the parking lot of a Fort Worth diner. Essentially, they had captured the conspiracy on film. Jurors needed only to watch the screen and listen to the tapes. But Racehorse had other ideas.

After Percy Foreman and with the possible exception of Foreman protégé Dick DeGuerin, Racehorse still ranks as the most colorful criminal defense attorney ever in a city that seems to breed them. His nickname stemmed from high school football in Houston where he excelled as an undersized but aggressive linebacker. Pacing back and forth behind his line waiting to move for the kill, young Richard's coach compared him with a racehorse and the name stuck. It also became a great handle for a criminal defense icon in Houston, and Racehorse had achieved that stature by the end of the 1970s. Handsome, eloquent, and witty, he enthralled jurors with his language and knowledge of the law.

For Davis, he conducted a clinic on how to drag out a trial until no jurors remember the evidence or why they even are there. He questioned all witnesses relentlessly, asking the same questions dozens of different ways. Even as the judge overruled his questions on objections from prosecutors, he hammered away. He attacked McCrory head on, questioning every word uttered on the tapes and challenging his unsavory background. On the defense, he called multiple witnesses designed to paint Davis's estranged wife, Priscilla, as the cause of the trouble. The parade included an old boyfriend whose motorcycle had left oil stains in the Davis driveway. Outside the courthouse one day, the biker sold custom T-shirts that displayed pictures of Davis and Racehorse sitting beside a chimpanzee above the slogan: "What price justice, Racehorse?" Although overpriced at ten dollars, I bought a couple as souvenirs and took the biker out for a few beers. The defense finally climaxed with testimony from Davis himself claiming the plot had been McCrory's idea. He said he had gone along with the plot as a self-appointed undercover agent gathering evidence against McCrory and just hadn't had time to deliver his case to police. Racehorse painted Davis as the victim of a prosecutorial scam motivated by their failure to convict him in the murder. The jury hung up eight-to-four for conviction, and Fort Worth's prosecutors decided against retrying that case, choosing instead to move ahead on the original murder. Eventually, that ended with an acquittal in Fort Worth.

To outsiders, the job of covering something like the Davis trial likely appears to be more fun than work—just sit around the court, listen to the excitement, and have a few laughs. In truth, it ranks as a good example of the kind of grind reporters face behind the scenes. For starters, the days ran long. After sitting through eight hours of testimony, I then had to digest it into a written version for the next morning's newspaper—a job that usually kept me writing at the courthouse until nine or ten each night. Moreover, turning the day's action into an understandable story required sideline interviews with members of the legal teams or, in some cases, the judge, who often agreed to chat off the record. Since the court had not imposed a gag order, Racehorse and one of the prosecutors usually held impromptu press conferences in different corners of the courtroom after each day's testimony. In addition, I had to oversee the work of another reporter dispatched to cover the rest of the action at the courthouse while I focused on that trial.

In short, I recall the Davis trial as a marathon that worked me harder than any other story of my career. In contrast, the courthouse slowed to a state of boredom a year later, in the fall of 1979, when Catherine came into my life. For me, she would provide proof for the old saying about idle hands and the devil's workshop. I would often look back during the later days of our fatal attraction to realize that, had I met her a year before, I would not have had time for Catherine's shenanigans.

The same week the Davis trial ended at the courthouse, George Tedesco's bludgeoned body was found in his condo across town.

FOURTEEN

Late 1960s

I've always believed the demands of covering that Cullen Davis trial drove the final nail into the coffin that had become my second marriage. It also underscored the connection and conflicts between my professional and domestic lives. But I also realize that my general attitude about marriage and relationships likely doomed them from the start. Whenever anyone asks why I was married twice, I usually smile and say: "I guess I'm just not the marrying kind." I'm only half joking about that line, and I am completely serious when I add: "I consider both of my marriages successes."

Why do people get married? My answer to that question evolved over the years to reflect the events of my life. Before my first marriage in 1969, I thought people should get married if they fall in love. After my first divorce in 1973, I revised that theory. People should get married, I decided, if they find someone really rich, or if one of them gets pregnant. Then, when my second marriage ended in 1979—and I was broke with two children—I revised my philosophy again. I concluded the only real reason for marriage is to commit adultery.

As a teenager, I had planned never to marry. I was so committed to that plan that the thought of sexual activity terrified me for fear I might impregnate someone who would saddle me with a kid. I had positive role models for marriage in my parents. Although they fought occasionally, the institution seemed to work well for them. It provided security for my mom and a guarantee of companionship for the old man. But it just didn't appeal to me. It simply looked like a tremendous bore. I was determined to get out in the world, out of St. Louis, away from the family business, and fulfill some fanciful dreams of adventure. I saw marriage and family as an anchor that would hold me down. Most normal folks likely would describe that view as anti-American, sacrilegious, antisocial, or all three, but I really didn't care. My religion was agnostic, and my goal was to experience life.

Eventually, however, in failing to stay unmarried, I did learn that marriage and family constitute a special sort of adventure—one of life's experiences I am glad to have survived. As a result, I do consider both of my marriages as successes that provided the kind of emotional education unavailable through any alternative experience. I still recommend it to all my younger friends nervous about taking such a serious step. "Try it," I tell them. "If it doesn't work, you can always do something else. It won't be the end of the world."

I know that Domestic Gary began to emerge during my junior year of college. But even with hindsight, I don't really understand how the first marriage happened, and I bet my first wife would agree to some confusion about that as well. The best explanation might just be because there was nothing else to do. We met at the start of my junior year at Mizzou in 1967. She was a freshman just hanging around her dormitory when I called looking for another girl I had dated the year before. Classes hadn't even started yet. She answered the phone and said she couldn't find the girl I wanted.

"You'll do," I said. "How do you look? Want to come out to a party?"

She hesitated only a heartbeat, then answered with a confident: "You'll like me. Let's go." She was destined to become wife number one.

When I introduced her to my roommates, one of them noted her uncanny resemblance to the 1930s flapper cartoon character Betty Boop— flashing doe eyes, infectious smile, puffy cheeks, a football helmet hair cut, and, most importantly, an attitude of independence. It didn't hurt that she also packed a pair of thirty-eights. Of course, Boop automatically became her nickname. And as we became better acquainted, she found a way to humor me by playing a little game with Betty Boop's trademark buzz phrase: "Boop-oop-a-doop." If I asked nicely, she would say it for me and shake her hips like the cartoon. It could have been pretty corny, but she managed to pull it off, creating another level of comfort with her.

Boop entered my life at a particularly unsettled point, and I've always given her a lot of credit for my career. In the beginning, I wanted to do well for her. She provided motivation. I wanted to impress her. I was showing off for her. And in the process, I proved to myself how good I really should be.

At the start of my junior year I stood at a personal crossroads. I had burned out on school. I was just starting my journalism curriculum after two years of preliminary coursework, and it was proving pretty much of a basics bore that would not trigger my excitement until later when I actually started reporting. I seriously considered dropping out and heading for Vietnam.

Boop did not arrive in a loveless vacuum. I had endured at least three serious relationships to that point. A high school sweetheart sat heartbroken in St. Louis, and a Mizzou co-ed had broken my heart by dumping me the year before to stick with her high school boyfriend. Then, there was a girl named Pixie attending one of the girls colleges in Columbia. Everyone should have an old girlfriend named Pixie. She was still in the picture at the start of the year, and for a while I juggled her with Boop. But Boop won out with her reaction when I told her I had decided to go steady with Pixie. She laughed in my face. So I broke up with Pixie and went steady with Boop.

Just as our relationship grew tighter, my best friends started peeling off to lives of their own. Suddenly one day, I looked around to realize my entourage had boiled away to myself, my last remaining roommate, and Boop. But Boop was two years behind. I realized I had started thinking in terms of "us" when I noticed I had decided I needed to resolve the future.

So, in a drunken haze one night at a party, I slobbered something like, "We should get married." I expected her sarcastic laugh again, but instead I got a wink and a nod. She, too, had reached a point where she wanted something new for a lifestyle. I had already agreed to take that job in Flint, and the options seemed clear. We either got married or broke up. Marriage suddenly looked like a pretty interesting adventure of its own.

The next week found us making wedding plans with her astonished father in Kansas City. He didn't look that thrilled, and I guessed he had always imagined his daughter as a college graduate rather than a newspaper reporter's wife in Flint, Michigan. My sympathy for his plight grew even larger a few years later when I calculated we probably got divorced before he had finished paying for the full-blown church ceremony of June 8, 1969.

FIFTEEN

Early 1970s

With my student deferment gone and Vietnam looming just ahead, Boop and I approached our move to Flint with a fatalistic view. We figured we'd go up, learn about sharing a life, have a good time, and keep an open mind about the future. We packed everything we owned into a trailer and pulled it to Flint one sunny day in June behind the black 1966 Mustang I had bought with money saved from my part-time jobs. She wanted to continue school up there, working at that point toward some kind of a degree in psychology. But we learned she would not qualify for the affordable Michigan resident tuition until we had lived there a year, and we couldn't afford it until then. But she didn't seem all that upset and found a job in a shoe repair shop just around the corner from *The Flint Journal*. We rented a furnished apartment just outside Flint and drove back and forth together each day in that Mustang. We settled in to wait on the draft.

Those times in Flint formed the kind of idyllic salad days on which many couples usually build their lives together. We struggled some financially but learned to live within our means. And many times when I have needed to find peace in the midst of some later life hassle, I have retreated in my mind back to that time when the world stood filled with promise. Just as she had at Mizzou, Boop became one of the "guys"—a mascot at *The Flint Journal*. Several nights each week, staffers would gather at a bar beside the shoe shop to blast away the stress, and she fit right in. By the time we left in 1971, she had become so engrained that a fellow reporter felt obliged to include her in the final scene of a farewell movie he'd prepared for my departure party. He ended that film by telling the crowd, "Here's the real reason we tolerated Taylor these past two years." Then his film cut to a long shot of Boop walking away from the *Journal* building, twisting her ass in a miniskirt, and looking back over a shoulder to wink.

But our relationship had started to change in a subtle way even before we entertained thoughts of leaving Flint. The catalyst came in the surprising form of my draft lottery victory, the one that placed my birthday so far from the front that we could finally plan on a long-term future without an interruption for the draft or Vietnam. We suddenly had to face a troubling question: Had we really expected a concept as serious as long-term? We should have been overjoyed with the lottery as a deliverance, and, on the surface, we appeared to celebrate. But we never discussed the doubts. For the first time, however, I got scared about commitment, and I believe she did, too. Those doubts stormed to the surface as we questioned our next moves. Buy a house? Have a baby? Buy furniture? Get into debt? Meanwhile, we privately confronted the more basic question each on our own: What did we really want with our lives? In lieu of an answer, we just marched along.

Boop enrolled at the Flint campus for the University of Michigan while I focused on my job. She seemed pointed to the future. Then I came to a conclusion that I needed to move on to a bigger challenge in a place with a better climate. Although she wanted to finish school, Boop agreed to relocate our shared life adventure, provided I found a place interesting enough to her. Houston worked for both of us.

Once again we couldn't afford the out-of-state tuition in Texas, so she had to find a job and wait a year to become a resident. This time, however, she wanted something more interesting than shoe repair and found it teaching in a school for retarded children south of town. We bought a second car for her and began our lives again. I worked nights at the police station while she worked days in the school. After a year, we woke up one morning to discover we really didn't know each other anymore. Boop had the courage to be the first to voice a doubt, and it took me by surprise.

"There's a problem, Gary and I don't know what it is," she said one day in December of 1972. "But this just isn't working any more. Something has to change."

Despite our liberated view of the world on the surface, we still clung to those Midwestern values that considered divorce an unspeakable word. *But what was wrong with me?* I wondered. My self-esteem flushed down the toilet, and I decided to give myself a thorough character exam. In the end I determined the problem: In my focus on the future, I had become a square. I was an old man at the age of twenty-four. I didn't even listen to rock music any more. And who knows how I performed in bed? All these things, I decided, would have to change.

By the time Boop finally left in March of 1973, I was prepared for the end. We had been to a party the night before. We woke up on Sunday and made love. Then she told me she planned to rent an apartment that afternoon. I chuckled as I remembered a teasing comment from a friend at that party. When he asked Boop to name her favorite song, he said, she had looked at me and sighed: "I Can't Get No Satisfaction."

She really busted me up for a while, but I recovered. And I quickly became grateful she had the strength to stop our charade. It worked out best for us both. Although we were married for nearly four years, I still look back on that relationship with the sort of memories reserved for a high school romance. In many ways we functioned more like brother and sister. But we crossed a bridge into the adult world together and learned the value of helping each other along.

Her candor with me helped me get my life back on track. And she was one reason I had a promising career. *What if she never comes back?* I asked myself. *What if she'd never come at all?* I replied. I confronted the demons of possession and dispatched them with development of a new philosophy: We can only expect from another person what they already have given. Anything more is gravy.

In my personal makeover, I grew one of the earliest beards seen at *The Post* and won the nickname Junkyard from my colleagues who often heard me joking about the lyrics from the Jim Croce song about *Bad, Bad Leroy Brown* being "meaner than a junkyard dog." They said it seemed to fit my new persona. I developed a social life again. And I got my reward about a year after the split when one of Boop's friends told me Boop had been complaining only half in jest about our divorce. Boop had told her, "I dump a guy because he turns into a stiff and then what happens? Three weeks later he's cool."

But it couldn't have happened if she hadn't dumped me. I realized that. I also realized I harbored only one regret about our marriage. I had practiced fidelity. I thought wistfully of all the attractive women working that courthouse in Flint. But I had been true and turned them away. Many times again when I have needed to find peace in the midst of some later life hassle, I have retreated in my mind back to that time in Flint, when the world stood filled with so much pussy that eluded my grasp. There has been more to finding my "happy place" than recalling idyllic times with Boop. Besides my beard, I had grown a new attitude about fidelity—never again. Everyone should have secrets they can take to the grave. I wanted some of my own.

SIXTEEN

Mid-1970s

A series of timely trends converged in the 1970s to transform those years into the decade of what I call the Great American Boomer Bacchanal. Future historians should look back at the '70s and recognize them as the years when the so-called sexual revolution peaked. For starters, on the scientific front, birth control pills and intrauterine devices had removed one of the great fears of unprotected sex by providing secure methods for contraception. With enhanced antibiotics licking the threat of serious venereal diseases, scientific advances appeared to have rendered the condom obsolete.

Then, on the moral and social front, the largest population bubble in U.S. history had entered its most active and experimental sexual age, as troopers in the first generation of the World War II Baby Boom reached their mid-twenties. Each old enough to have sampled first love, most were just completing initial attempts at marriage. With many divorced or wishing they were, innocence had vanished. Fears of singles-bar serial killers would not become a deterrent until the exploits of Ted Bundy splashed across television screens with his trial in 1979. And the threatening reality of AIDS as a serious sexual disease scourge would not emerge until the early 1980s.

In short, getting laid in the 1970s was about as difficult as getting sand on your feet while strolling a beach. So I emerged from my first marriage in March of 1973 and quickly enlisted in the revolution. For about four months I stayed single, and at times it wore me out. I moved into an apartment complex known as "Heartbreak Hotel." The place catered to short-timers suffering breaks in relationships, and everyone enjoyed nursing their sorrows together. Two of Boop's girlfriends also assisted my transition, and, finally in September, I rented a more suitable one-bedroom apartment in Houston's Bohemian Montrose section—a neighborhood that better reflected my fantasies of a bachelor pad inhabited by the big city reporter.

Seeking self-improvement and still curious about fulfilling my potential as a writer, I signed up to take a few night courses at the University of Houston in creative writing and literature. Oh yeah, this program also included the potential for meeting some new women, and that's where I met wife number two. Let's call her Cindy. A tall, dishwater blonde with a shag hair style, she was described by some back then as resembling the actress Diane Keaton. Just twenty-one, Cindy was trying to finish a degree in English. She worked days as a secretary for a physician who performed hand surgeries. She was married to an accountant who had wooed her when they were students at the University of Texas in Austin. He'd graduated, landed a job at a firm in Houston, and they had relocated the year before. She had about a year left on her degree program.

Cindy was quiet in class and never spoke to me. But she had a girlfriend in the class who did, and the girlfriend arranged for us to get together. The girlfriend was nursing a crush on our professor, a mid-thirties guy then separated from his first wife. One night about a week into the class, the four of us ended up at the professor's apartment to drink wine and debate the meaning of life. Of course, things quickly deteriorated—or maybe escalated—and we discovered more immediate meaning in the physical. Within a week Cindy had assumed control of my sex life, or at least the central core of it, and then we returned to discussions on the meaning of life.

Her life was in shambles. The husband was a bum. She was struggling to find her own focus. She wanted to leave but just didn't know how. They had gotten married in school because she thought she was pregnant. When they discovered a false pregnancy, her husband rebelled and treated her poorly, like a man who had been tricked. She suffered no physical beatings, but he didn't respect her, talked down and *blah, blah, blah*. It all sounded like some script from soap opera central, and I listened through my reporter's skeptical ear. I figured the husband probably had an equally sad tale, but I wasn't there to make judgments. I was there at first to get laid. I also discovered the risk of having sex with another man's wife in his bed added an extra level of excitement. We never came close to discovery, but, then again, my tenure as her extramarital lover didn't last that long. I mentioned once or twice she'd be welcome to stay with me while sorting things out. So, one Sunday night, she showed up at my door with a suitcase in one hand and her cat in the other. I let her inside, and thus began a wild but rewarding rollercoaster ride destined to last six more years. Neither of us made any promises to the other.

Coincidentally, Cindy also had grown up in St. Louis, leaving there her senior year of high school when her dad got a job as a professor at Texas A&M University in College Station about ninety miles northwest of Houston. Her St. Louis high school had been just a few miles from mine. So we decided to take a trip down Memory Lane to St. Louis during Thanksgiving weekend and stay at my family's home. I introduced her as my new roommate and got a stunned look from my dad that translated: "I thought this only happened in San Francisco or Tanganyika." My little sister told me later she had been expecting a total skank but was pleasantly surprised with Cindy's demeanor. My mom said, "I thought maybe you'd move back home after your divorce." I could only shake my head in wonder. My only regret about the trip occurred when my high school girlfriend visited on the off chance I had come home for the holiday. She, too, had just recently divorced and obviously desired her own trip down Memory Lane. Unfortunately I couldn't figure any way to sneak off. The week was just too short.

So, Cindy and I started playing house, and it was different from my marriage to Boop. Cindy worked all day and attended classes at night with an eye toward graduation. I quickly recognized her as an extremely driven and ambitious woman, uncertain of what exactly she wanted to do in life but determined to make it meaningful. I respected that. We operated fairly independent of each other, and she started to grow on me. We took a trip together to the Yucatan Peninsula in Mexico, sharing rickety old buses with peasants and their chickens, hiking around the Mayan ruins, and then staying a few days on a Caribbean island off the coast called Isla Mueres. We rented hammocks and slept on the beach. It was all very third world and certainly exotic to be tramping that area before Mexico's resort-building boom occurred. We were good for each other at that time in our lives.

But I'm not sure either of us ever saw our relationship then as a long-term proposition. I know I didn't. I needed some time to recover from my divorce and reconstruct my future around a vision of myself as a loner again. She needed a sanctuary for finishing school without the distractions of a disintegrating marriage. Our relationship provided a vehicle for both goals. Looking ahead with a fresh attitude, I began to entertain visions for solitary travel. A friend had just returned from a year's sabbatical bumming around Africa, and I wondered if it wasn't time to move along from *The Post*. Cindy and I both knew a turning point of some sort lay just ahead if we could only sort through the fog and map a path. That turning point arrived, but not in the way we expected.

About a month after I covered the 1974 prison siege in Huntsville, Cindy wanted a serious talk. I expected her to ask about our future. I figured she had reached a conclusion for herself. When she told me she was pregnant, I was stunned. She had stopped taking the pill and switched to an IUD. I guess it just hadn't worked.

"I'm not having an abortion," she volunteered defiantly as we discussed our options.

OK, I thought, if she is going to have the baby, I will be a father. There's no way to change that. But I never had entertained any desire to raise children and had fought every way possible to prevent it. Her condition ranked among my worst nightmares.

Commit the crime, gotta do the time, I thought to myself, laughing a little. Would I really consider conception a crime? And the time? That would be a twenty-year sentence for me at the least. Should I run? Should I just pay child support and turn the kid into a monthly bill without any larger constraints on my life?

Nope, I decided more quickly than I believed possible as I reviewed my options. Here is a new adventure, I concluded: fatherhood.

Discussing things further, we backtracked the days to determine where this might have happened. When we pinpointed the date, I shook my head.

"Remember that night you came to Huntsville during the prison riot, and we slept in the tent behind the prison administration building?" I asked.

"Shit," she said. "That means…"

"It means we made that child on the lawn at the Texas Department of Corrections while I was covering a major news story. This kid will be a real legend at the paper."

It was worth a good laugh before we went to bed with the sobering thought that the mysterious maw of parenthood stood gaping before us, ready to swallow us whole.

SEVENTEEN

Mid-1970s

If the news of Cindy getting knocked up during the prison riot wasn't enough to generate gossip at the paper, our "wedding" set a new standard for chitchat.

"First things first," I told one of my colleagues at the paper, outlining my strategy for transformation into a family man.

"Reminds me of *Lady and the Tramp*," he replied. "Cindy takes a junkyard dog and turns him into a real show animal."

I had saved about fifteen hundred dollars and decided to start with the purchase of a house. Unsure of how long our relationship might last, I thought it best to accumulate some assets. Within a week I found a little bungalow in Houston's gentrifying Heights neighborhood, just north of downtown. A purple, one-story stucco structure about fifty years old, it had been converted to a duplex and needed work. But I was surprised I had been able to find a place where I could afford the payments. I managed to buy into that neighborhood at an opportune time for a price of fifteen thousand dollars with seller financing by a little old lady who had owned it for years. I spent a few days painting the interior and had carpet installed. Then we moved from the apartment into the house.

Cindy had seen an obstetrician and started on her vitamins.

We ticked off our to-do list and decided the only thing left was to get married. I was covering county government at the time and worked at the courthouse. So I told her to come over on September 18, 1974, and meet me at noon in the offices of Judge Larry Wayne, a friend who served as justice of the peace for the downtown precinct. He had acquired a nickname of "Marryin' Sam"—after the character in the *L'il Abner* comics—because his chambers stood just down the hall from the county office that processed marriage licenses, providing couples a convenient location for one-stop nuptials. Wayne led all the county's justices in wedding fees, earning more from performing marriages as a sideline than he did from his judicial salary. Cindy showed up over the lunch break wearing one of her early maternity outfits, and we walked inside his office, license in hand.

"The time has come," I told Wayne, who took one look at her and started laughing. He escorted us into his office and began to mumble some ceremonial nonsense before I cut him off.

"We'll just take the five-dollar job."

He looked a little surprised but then signed the bottom of our license without any elaboration.

"OK, it's done," he said, handing the certificate back to me. "It will cost you thousands now to get out of this."

We emerged into the hall to find the county government reporter from the rival *Chronicle* waiting outside. She had followed me after I quietly left our press room to make sure I wasn't working some secret scoop. When she realized I had gone down on my lunch hour to get married, she didn't know whether to laugh, cry, or scream at me. Somewhere in Wayne's office she had found a package of rice and started tossing it at us in the hall. More than thirty years later I would run into an old editor from those days who greeted me in fond remembrance as "the reporter who got married on his lunch break."

Cindy laughed about this cavalier and unromantic approach to matrimony, but I always suspected she was hiding some pain. When breaking up five years later she confided she never felt we had any kind of marriage, just a partnership. And, she wanted to be courted. At the time, however, she probably was more than a little frightened about the pregnancy, and those first few weeks she seemed in a daze. She was probably just satisfied that I was making an attempt to take care of us and seemed willing to let me take the lead on just about everything. But, let's face it. I had a good job, had put us in a house, and I was even smiling about the future. I figured plenty of unmarried pregnant women should wish they had her problems.

I had even helped her find a new job. OK, so she was using her English degree to transcribe autopsy reports in the Harris County Morgue! But, it would turn out to lead into a couple of much more important positions for her, thanks to her personal initiative. She was destined to parlay that job into a caseworker's post with the welfare office investigating food stamp applications. And from there she would go on to become an important child welfare case investigator assigned to the main county hospital, Ben Taub.

In the beginning, however, we both just settled in to wait for the baby. About the only thing really upsetting her was the suspicion that her supervisor at the morgue intentionally assigned all the dead-baby cases to her for transcription as a way to tease. But she could take it. Those days became an interesting and relaxing period for both of us. Besides feeling the baby move and picking out names, we attended the *Lamaze* natural childbirth classes that were all the rage back then. I learned how to be the coach and practiced those special breathing techniques until I almost wished I were the one who was pregnant. Besides helping her breathe, I planned to take photos in the delivery room and capture the moment for posterity, and, I figured, also for the kid's prom date to see eighteen years down the road.

We made other plans for life after the delivery, too. If she had any desires to be a stay-at-home mom, Cindy never expressed them. No, she was too driven to take more than the minimum time allowed and had just started the more challenging job at the welfare department. She wanted to move her career forward as fast as possible. So we found a day care center about half-a-mile from our house with a suitable baby nursery and made a reservation. The cost nearly cancelled any financial advantage from her job, but that didn't matter. We believed each of us had to continue growing and felt comfortable the baby would do that, too, in the neighborhood nursery school.

So, on April 25, 1975, the moment came, and we hustled to the hospital. As Cindy's labor pains increased, I deployed my most inspired *Lamaze* drills.

"Breathe," I demanded, huffing and puffing for her to follow. She responded as we had practiced for a while, and I continued to coax the best of natural childbirth from her. "Breathe. Hoo, hoo, hoo, hoo." Suddenly she stopped responding. She raised up on her elbows and looked into my eyes. I knew she wanted to tell me how wonderful I was. She pulled about three inches from my face. And then she snarled: "Get me a fucking shot."

So much for natural childbirth. But that shot finished the job as our first daughter, Little E, entered the world. And I got plenty of shots of my own, capturing every angle with *Kodachrome*.

EIGHTEEN

Mid-1970s

Cindy's later characterization of our marriage as more a partnership than a romance now seems right on target. We had launched the partnership with a deal to have a child and becoming good parents stood as our business mission. We never shared a joint checking account and Cindy continued to use her original last name, which had been restored after her divorce. She bought a wedding band, she insisted, to help keep the wolves away and make life easier in the workplace. I never wore one myself because, I insisted, a ring would irritate my finger. Our wedding featured no flowers or reception and, most importantly, no vows. Our honeymoon occurred at the hospital when Little E was born, and the photos of her birth were the closest we had to a wedding album.

But I still argue that our partnership included plenty of romance. It might not have been the traditional hearts and flowers variety. But dictionaries define romance as the pleasure experienced with someone you love. They also describe it as the feeling of excitement or mystery from a particular experience or event. I can look back on those years as a period filled with excitement and mystery, a period good for all three of us.

As inspirational as Boop had been in launching my professional life, Cindy proved indispensable in pushing it to the next level. By giving me Little E, she offered a new motivation to excel. Besides providing the inspiration of the baby, however, Cindy also pushed us positively in other directions. We had hardly finished our work on that first house, for example, when she decided we needed to cash out and move up. I grumbled. But, after learning we had prospective buyers offering twice our initial purchase price, I had to agree. I could take credit for establishing our real estate beachhead in Houston's Heights neighborhood, but Cindy deserved high marks for pushing it forward.

By 1976 we had sold the first house and used the profit to buy a larger old house that needed some work. I spent weekends stripping six coats of paint off a built-in buffet to discover the original wood had been a gorgeous Philippine mahogany. I built a loose brick patio in the backyard. We started dabbling in antiques. We also bought a rental beach house that year on Galveston Island's west beach, about seventy miles south of Houston along the Gulf of Mexico. The house had been the oldest on that strip of beach, and, over the years, a community of more modern rental dwellings had grown up around it. We had hoped to make enough from summer rentals to allow us to use the house in the winter, but we found no summer vacationers wanted that place. We did manage to adjust and find regular tenants who could cover our payments so we could maintain the place as an investment likely to appreciate. At work for me, 1976 also had been the year of my Pulitzer Prize nomination. And Cindy had taken the next step in her career, landing a spot as a child welfare caseworker investigating allegations of abuse and neglect for the county.

Despite our hectic work and investment project schedules, Little E remained the center of our lives, the glue that really held us together. We read books on parenting theories and shared the joys of watching her rapid development from infant to child. I'm still convinced her early transfer to day care four weeks after birth sparked more rapid development. Parents don't receive final grades on their decisions until twenty or thirty years after they've been made. Based on the success she's become as an adult, Little E now makes a persuasive argument for early day care. But she also gave me a new dimension and purpose of a more immediate nature at that time. Although I lost a lot of sleep with her nighttime restlessness, I actually came to enjoy the sound of Little E's cries because it meant I could spend the next hour rocking her back to sleep in the wicker rocking chair we'd bought for that purpose. For the first time in my life I felt in balance because she gave me a link to the future. I felt suspended in time by her in front and my parents in the past. She kindled an interest in researching my family history, and I started spending some of my few free moments reviewing old census reports at Houston's extensive genealogical library. She walked and talked at an early age, and, as she grew, I took great delight in trips to the park on Sunday mornings, infant swimming lessons, and Dr. Seuss at bedtime.

So, Cindy and I decided Little E needed a sibling. This time we planned it. About the time she started to show, my dad in St. Louis suffered a stroke— a big one destined to sideline him from life. He needed my help so I took a leave of absence from *The Post* in the summer of 1977 to spend a couple of months restructuring his life. My youngest sister was only fourteen, and my mom could not handle all the stress. In addition, he still owned that lawnmower repair business, which, by then, had grown into the largest in the city with about a dozen employees. When I came home for this extended visit, I brought Little E along so Cindy could concentrate on her new pregnancy without the dangerous hassles of also minding a two-year-old. More than that, however, I knew it would give my dad a chance to spend some precious time with his granddaughter, and it turned out to be an experience he revered.

"It's just like you came back again," he said, noting the resemblance between Little E and photos of me as a child.

Although she was barely two, Little E was talking like a chatterbox and had begun to demonstrate the spunk and gregariousness that would mark her personality. Her outbursts ranged from compassion to high comedy. One day she tumbled down a staircase and gave us a shock. An athletic little kid, she simply rolled across the floor at the bottom and started laughing. But five minutes later she spotted my poor old dad hobbling around near the top of the stairs on his cane and showed she obviously had taken note of his decrepit condition.

"No, granddaddy, no," she screamed with the plea of a protective mama bear. "You stay away from those stairs."

During that summer of 1977, we forged a special kind of relationship.

By late August I had everything stabilized in St. Louis. The business was up for sale. My dad was getting around better and fortunately had not suffered much mental damage at all. He was destined to live another seven years before eventually succumbing to cancer. But his working days were done. While living there that summer I had bought a small 360 Honda motorcycle for transportation. So I put Little E on a plane and took my own little trip back to Houston. I mapped out a relaxing backwoods route through the Missouri Ozarks, Arkansas, and East Texas that would take five days. As I rolled along those deserted country roads, spending nights in isolated motels, I thought about my life and found it sweet. Fatherhood had not become the burden I had feared. And Cindy's January due date on our second child was just ahead.

I had no way to foresee the catastrophic turmoil that lay just beyond the horizon.

NINETEEN

Late 1970s

After that sabbatical to assist my dad, my domestic "partnership" with Cindy in Houston shifted to a higher gear of growth and prosperity. I returned to cover the criminal courts in what would become my most productive period as a newspaper reporter. Meanwhile, Cindy moved up the hierarchy at the child welfare department. We were making a solid living from satisfying and interesting jobs while building a good home for a family that increased by one on January 18, 1978, with the birth of our second daughter, Shannon.

Cindy had been so convinced that the child in her womb was male, she had agreed I could pick the name if it emerged a girl. We hadn't been able to agree on names to that point, but I shrugged off the compromise in anticipation of a boy. Her doctor had gauged Shannon's activity level in the womb and also predicted a male. Even in the delivery room, the doctor kept saying, "Here he comes." Cindy was smiling, after having this time taken her shot a little earlier, and I was snapping pictures. The doctor and nurses took the child to the side to count its fingers and toes, and, then I heard the doctor say: "Oops. This is a girl. Do you have a name?" It was my turn to smile as I told them, "Shannon." Cindy just stuck out her tongue and laughed some more.

Behind her façade as the joyful mother, however, Cindy was starting to develop some personal anxieties. Although I could notice them, there wasn't much I could do. She was growing restless with personal ambition and started grasping impulsively at projects designed to move both of us along at a faster

78

pace. Some of these projects worked to our advantage while others just left her more frustrated.

For starters, she decided we needed a more valuable, bigger house. Once again I resisted only to relent after learning we could double our money again thanks to appreciation of values in the Houston Heights and the sweat equity generated with renovations. So we sold out and bought another old house nearby. But this time we bought a two-story that needed no serious repairs. It also included a garage with an apartment on a second floor. Suddenly we were landlords with two tenants—one in a beach house in Galveston and another at the end of our driveway. In less than four years we had parlayed a fifteen-hundred-dollar investment for a fifteen-thousand-dollar bungalow into a two-story home worth seventy thousand dollars with extra income from apartment rental.

We had moved Little E into a Montessori school that also had a nursery so the infant Shannon could go there, too. The price tag was steep, but the educational results worth the money. Little E continued to blossom both socially and intellectually in the Montessori environment designed to promote an early appreciation for the concept of learning. Cindy had responsibility for taking them to the campus and picking them up after work because my schedule usually kept me at the courthouse later in the day.

But I would have had trouble carrying them around anyway, since an oversight by her had limited my transportation options to that little Honda motorcycle I had bought in St. Louis and ridden through Arkansas to get back home. While driving my car one day, she had failed to notice the heat lamp burning on the dashboard. By the time she returned to the house, a leaking radiator had warped my engine. I left the hunk of junk parked on the curb for six months until some guy came along and offered a hundred dollars to drag it away. I rode the motorcycle exclusively in Houston for a year but never really enjoyed it like some others might. I never felt comfortable enough with speed to be a safe motorcycle rider. I could not employ velocity to enhance my balance and always risked collisions from behind by moving too slowly. I never chanced riding that bike on Houston's freeways. But I still cultivated the image of a renegade, parking it outside the courthouse each morning after riding downtown wearing a jacket and tie. I finally managed to upgrade in early 1979, when I bought another reporter's beat-up old 1973 Chevy Vega for two hundred dollars.

By 1978 Cindy had been promoted to one of child welfare's most stressful but crucial posts as the primary caseworker at Houston's largest public hospital, Ben Taub. She literally worked at ground zero for child abuse and neglect investigations with responsibility for reviewing the circumstances of any child posting to the emergency room. She worked closely with the physicians as well as the cops and daily saw the worst that Houston had to offer in brutality to children. Often her work dovetailed into mine, as I covered many of those cases in court. Sometimes she tipped me to stories as we discussed our day's experiences over dinner. More often, however, our discussions deteriorated into a depressing game of "Top It" as I shared the latest gore from a murder trial only to be trumped by her account of some kid beaten half to death. I was extremely proud of the work she did and still consider that job to be among the most important anywhere in the country.

But she wanted more. First she enrolled in graduate school at night hoping for a Master's of Social Work that could propel her into administrative or executive contention. She dropped out quickly in 1978, however, after finding the demands on her time too daunting. I couldn't retrieve the girls after school, and she couldn't get to class. By summer of 1979, she was determined to try again. This time she enrolled in night law school. We made arrangements for a babysitter and tried to juggle our schedules, but I knew my late hours would remain an issue. I couldn't know an even bigger issue sat boiling toward a climax. Besides trying to balance law school with work and motherhood, Cindy had launched another secret project vying for even more of her time.

"So, how was your weekend?" I naively asked Little E when I arrived home one Sunday night in August after a trip to Fort Worth.

"Terrible," she snorted. "Uncle Al was here all weekend."

"Uncle Al?" I asked, looking at Cindy for an explanation. She just shook her head and tried to look firm. I sensed another one of those inevitable turning points in the air.

"We need to talk," she said, confirming my suspicion. After ushering Little E to her bedroom, I learned that Cindy had been working a little too closely with one of those physicians at the hospital. She had been close enough to have quietly sustained an extramarital affair for the past year.

"A year?" I asked in shock. I wondered how I could have missed it. Then I realized her tension and her scramble for improved status through law school or grad school had all been designed as part of a grander plan for an image more suitable to a doctor's wife. For a moment I thought maybe she had brought him to our house that weekend as a final gesture before ending it and confessing to me, so we could start anew. Then I learned this final gesture had been for my benefit. I was being replaced. The realization left me too stunned for anger, and she stood resolute.

We were finished. We just needed to separately reassemble the pieces of our lives in the most civilized way possible. Unfortunately, Catherine Mehaffey would enter our lives soon to help, and the result would prove anything but civil.

TWENTY

1960s

"We need a man."

A dark-haired young woman had written that plea with her finger on the car window in the frost. It was a cold December night in 1964, and I spotted her note as soon as I had backed my 1954 Ford sedan into the space beside her at Chuck-A-Burger in St. Louis. Some guy and another girl sat in the front seat of her car while I had two of my high school pals in the front seat with me.

"Am I man enough?" I asked, rolling down the window.

"Let's take a look," she said, as her message disappeared with her window.

I hopped out and gave her one. She opened her door and said, "You'll do."

I climbed in beside her, and we had a chat. I learned she had been stood up that night, and they had been cruising the drive-in restaurants for adventure. She looked cute enough and appeared to be two or three years older than me. They had driven all the way from the town of St. Charles, about thirty miles away on the other side of the Missouri River. After about five minutes, they invited me to ride back to St. Charles with them for a little party.

"Hey," I told my pals after excusing myself to secure my car, "I need you to find another ride out of here and park this thing on the street over there with the keys under the mat so I can find it fast if I need it."

"Taylor, you are fucking nuts!" one of them quickly advised. "How do you know where they're going to take you? And why do you need to go with them? Just follow them in your car."

"I don't know," I said. "It just feels OK. The guy said he'll bring me back here. If I get in trouble, I'll figure something out."

My friend should have been right. But I was seventeen and invincible. She was cute and wanted me in the back seat of that car. So off we drove. As an event in my life, it had little consequence. I didn't even get laid. We spent most of that night in the living room of some house in St. Charles with her mother asleep in a bedroom and the other couple making out on the couch beside us. I'm sure I could have turned that meeting into my first sexual experience if I hadn't been so shy about it. But her most aggressive move of the night occurred when she scrawled that note on the window. Mine came when I hopped into her car. The guy drove me back to Chuck-A-Burger about three in the morning. I found my car and went home.

Nevertheless, I recall that incident often as a harbinger of things to come when I try to analyze my third personality as the charming rogue—the one destined to keep me poised on the edge of trouble for most of my life. I've never been embarrassed to admit the things I've done and actually consider the Rogue to be a pretty interesting guy. He's usually been smart enough to cooperate with the professional, recognizing the truce as essential for survival. In my mind I've taken calculated risks more often than not, based on an unexplainable belief that if I do get into trouble, I'll figure something out. It explains why I could not feel too much self pity when Cindy unceremoniously ended our partnership in August of 1979. And it explains why I was the kind of guy willing to tempt the devil in a relationship with an obvious threat like Catherine Mehaffey. It's because I am the kind of guy who will climb into the back seat of a car with a complete stranger and take off for St. Charles, certain only of the fact I believe I'll get home one way or another.

I believe we each have a rogue. Some just keep theirs bottled better than others. Introducing mine—and letting him confess his sins—should prevent the uninitiated from feeling too much sympathy for the domestic Gary who got side-swiped by Uncle Al. After meeting my rogue, others may even shake their heads and whistle about my later adventures with Catherine: "He had it coming." I'll admit I had something coming. But I also would stop to remind those more judgmental souls to consider the words of that cinematic philosopher-king, Clint Eastwood, in his classic western, *Unforgiven*: "We all got it comin'."

Likely born from a combination of boredom and over-active imagination and, of course, my own narcissistic flaw to routinely become the center of attention, my rogue emerged most prominently about our junior year in high school. Anyone looking only at the academic side of my high school record would find an ambitious, hard-working stiff focused only on scholarship. At the same time, anyone looking only at the other side of that ledger likely would ask: "How come he's never been in jail?" With several of my pals I pulled so many pranks, I ask that question often myself. I rarely missed a week in high school without hitting some stranger with an egg or a water balloon. We operated like hunters on weekends and evenings, seeking prey among the unsuspecting masses arrogant enough to believe they could move around town unmolested. One night while cruising for victims, I pulled alongside a car that was waiting to turn left at a light. In the front seat sat a man and his wife dressed in evening clothes, obviously headed out on the town. When my light turned green so I could go straight, the rogue took one of our loaded water balloons and popped it through the open passenger side window of their car. The image returns to me in slow motion, when I close my eyes, and again I can see that plump balloon sliding across the dashboard. I see the looks of horror over their shoulders as it slams into the window and breaks unleashing a wall of water, and drenching them just as I drive away.

"Jesus," the rogue told my sidekick, as we raced through the intersection and away from the scene of the crime. "That looked like a wave from the ocean. I had no idea those things held that much water. I hope they don't have a wreck."

Another time, the rogue got me suspended for two weeks from riding the school bus because he clobbered the local police chief in the head with a snowball from inside the bus while the chief directed traffic at a busy intersection. Enraged, the chief chased down the bus, curbed it, and ordered all the kids outside.

"I could have been killed out there, do you understand?" he roared to a line of teens, each fighting hard to stop giggling. "I am going to find out who threw that snowball, and he's going to be sorry."

In an early example of the rogue's ability to cooperate with the professional, we realized the chief probably was correct. Somebody would snitch. So we derailed the investigation by visiting the police station that night, admitting our role, and apologizing. By then, the chief had cooled off and had a little laugh about it himself. Because I had come forward, my principal decided on leniency. Instead of suspending me from school, he simply suspended me from riding the bus, which had been required by the distance of my house from the school. That should have effectively prevented my attendance and triggered failing grades. But then, for some unfathomable reason, he said I could drive my car to school and park it in the lot during the suspension.

The punishment made no sense, but it underscored my confidence in the power of a balanced life. That snowball shot stands as the only time I ever confessed to any transgression, and then I only did it as a strategy for survival. It became the foundation for my philosophy on secrets we take to our graves. Everyone should have some of those. I know I have plenty, and I have managed to elude exposure on many aspects of my secret life because my professional and domestic images cover my tracks. I also knew where to draw the line between malicious shenanigans and serious criminal behavior. I had little trouble making good grades, and I earned my own money to pay for my car. My parents could never believe some of the things I would do behind their backs. Every drug dealer has a mother who loves him. So, why wouldn't mine turn a deaf ear to the monkey shines of the rogue they had spawned? More important—I never asked for money.

One of my pranks did result in the only failing grade of my high school days. But, even that episode reinforced my view that a balanced Renaissance Man can always enjoy a secret life as a hooligan. On this occasion—in the last semester of my senior year—I took advantage of a substitute teacher for our math analysis class. An unsuspecting, over-eager rookie, he played right into the hands of me and one of my cohorts named Ken. Over the years, Ken and I had carefully honed a fake-fighting routine so well known in the school that classmates had learned to ignore it. We could have been stunt performers in the movies. This sub had been in our class about ten minutes and was writing furiously on the blackboard, when Ken started the action.

"Hey, Taylor, I'm not taking any more," he yelled, standing up beside his desk at the back of the room.

"That's what you think," I shouted, lunging in his direction. By this time the sub was spinning around at the blackboard and knocking chalk to the floor. I got to Ken and ran my left hand across his cheek, meeting that palm with my right to produce an echoing *Thwack* with the illusion of a sweeping slap across the face. Ken's role involved a pratfall backward over his desk and into the wall of the room. The sub froze at his desk, and I'm sure he couldn't understand why the whole class started clapping. But they had seen all this before. Ken got up and took a bow. I did the same and returned to my desk. The episode was far from complete. Our teacher returned from his sick day enraged. He ordered us to move our desks into the hall and said we could not return to class until we had copied the trigonometry tables.

"I'm not doing that," the rogue spoke right up, adding, "I'll sit in the hall and read a book if you want but I'm not copying those tables."

"You have an *A* in this class right now. But I can make it an *F*."

"Go ahead, make it an *F*. But I'm not copying the trig tables."

So I sat in the hall reading several books during his class for the rest of the year. The rogue's recreational reading list for that period included paperback classics like *Candy* and *Tobacco Road*. Ken sat there, too, for a while—until he finished copying the trig tables. Then he left me alone. I wasn't concerned. My grades had always been so strong that one *F* wouldn't hurt my final standing. Already accepted at Mizzou, I didn't need anything from that teacher or his class. Even he had said I had learned math analysis well enough to post a grade of *A*. Surely, I thought, the knowledge itself is basically what we need.

That teacher approached at graduation with a serious smile across his face as I stood reviewing my final report card. He extended a hand.

"No hard feelings," he said. "I just hope you learned something from this."

"Yes sir," said the rogue, suppressing a laugh. "Yes, I certainly did."

TWENTY-ONE

The 1960s

The rogue's Tom Foolery only escalated in college where I became the central focus in a legendary incident known as the Francis House Feces Case of 1966. That adventure forced me to wrestle deeply with the concept of honesty and became the foundation for another personal philosophy establishing what I call my law of ultimate resolutions. That law seeks to answer the dilemma: When can you lie? Using that law as our guide, the rogue determined I can lie whenever the punishment for telling the truth would realistically threaten our survival, and as long as we are sure the lie will succeed.

To those who would call that an excuse to do whatever you want, the rogue responds that he has found he only rarely has again encountered those circumstances, as long as he is honest in his assessment of survival. Few confrontations in life truly threaten your survival. It also is more difficult than many might think to lie successfully about anything for very long. Sooner or later, you always get caught, and usually you are better off when exposure comes sooner, before the first lie creates an impenetrable web of confusion. So, for me to lie, I must be certain my life is on the line and believe my lie is solid enough to save it.

I won't lie to get ahead. Only in self-defense.

The Francis House incident began innocently enough one Saturday night in October when I was sitting around my dormitory room with three pals discussing our lack of plans for that night. My high school sidekick Ken had become my roommate, and we were joined in our discussion by two fellow residents of Francis House who called themselves Surf and Doeda. We were feeling liberated because all authority figures from the dorm had left for the weekend. That list included our official personnel assistant or P.A. as we called them. These student-employees received complementary room and board to live amongst us in the public housing facilities and function much like dormitory cops, keeping the peace and snitching off delinquents to the housing dean. Also missing that weekend were all other elected Francis House leaders, except for me. And I only served as the house *jock chairman*, running its intramural athletic programs because I had been the quarterback on our flag football squad. So the rogue was feeling like *The Authority* in Francis House that night.

From somewhere in the dark recesses of his troubled mind, Ken suddenly suggested he would like to take a shit down the four-story stairwell of the dorm. He had some disagreements with a couple of freshmen who had rooms in the basement, or what we called the Francis House Grotto. He said he wanted to shit on them. Several minutes later, Ken sat parked with his ass over the rail on the fourth floor grunting like a pig. I stood in the stairs, watching from below, while Surf and Doeda stood guard left and right. We literally had all exits covered. But Ken couldn't do the job. After a couple of minutes he surrendered, jumped off the rail, and kneeled panting with exhaustion.

"Oh, hell," the rogue suddenly said, seizing control and moving up the stairs. "Watch down here, and I'll do it."

I recall the shrill whistling sound of the rogue's turd as it sailed down the well and then *Splat* as it hit the tile floor in the basement. We hustled back to the room and sat around on our beds to see what would happen. What occurred was the most amazing transformation of a building I could ever imagine. It resembled the change that occurs between the minutes before a department store's doors open and the minutes after, on the day of a sale. One second you could hear yourself breathe. The next, all you heard was a roar. I was shocked that such a tiny bit of shit could trigger such chaos.

Of course, the guys from the Grotto found me quickly. After all, I was *The Authority* that night, and they needed help. They were at my door whining about shit in their hall. I started to feel a little guilty.

"I'd better go have a look," I said, and we all went down stairs.

"Yes," I said, "I think that is a pile of shit."

"What are you going to do about it?" one of them asked.

"Clean it up."

Then I went to the janitor's closet to get a broom and dust pan. I cleaned it up and went back to my room as the dorm grew quiet again. But the solitude didn't last. About fifteen minutes later, the uproar began anew. When we heard someone yell, "We got him, we got him," the four of us blew out of that room as fast as we could. In the stairwell I saw a P.A. from another dorm holding an impressionable freshman named Johnnie by the arm with a lynch mob from the grotto gathering along the wall. I quickly learned that, in the excitement over delivery of the first bomb, Johnnie decided to get involved. He had run into a bathroom, filled a pizza box with turds, and tossed its contents over the rail, where they rained down upon the visiting P.A. as he headed up the steps to investigate the earlier altercation. I knew Johnnie as a country boy, just off the farm, but I still couldn't fathom his thought process. I shook my head and shrugged my shoulders as the P.A. led him away.

The next evening I was summoned to the room of the Francis House P.A.—a large, humorless senior named Chuck. He was fuming and wanted to know what happened. I told him somebody shit down the stairwell, and then they caught Johnnie throwing shit over the rail after I cleaned up the first load.

"You know Johnnie will be lucky to stay in school," Chuck said, starting to play me like some cop on a cheesy TV show. "But he's remorseful and admitted what he did."

"It would be pretty hard for him to deny it."

"But he says he didn't start it. He says it was you."

My brain started to compute the options. I knew only my three pals had seen it. I also knew exposure might mean expulsion. I concluded my life was literally on the line. Chuck obviously expected me to break down, fall to my knees, and beg for his mercy. In an instant, I decided to call his bluff. If he wanted my life, I decided, he was going to work harder for it than this. And I knew I could not waiver in my response.

"Nope, Chuck. It wasn't me. I don't know where you'd get that."

He looked startled, and then he grew angry.

"I'm going to prove you did it. I don't feel sorry for you. I feel sorry for that little freshman who has to live with this on his record just because he wanted to be like you."

I just stared at him like I thought he was crazy. Then I walked away with an empty spot in the pit of my stomach. According to dormitory rules, I had the right to a trial before a jury of fellow residents known as a judicial board. But judicial board proceedings were extremely rare as disputes between P.A.s and residents usually settled without trial. And a judicial board's ruling did not necessarily mean resolution. Ultimately, any verdict went to the dean of housing for a final decision. I knew I had to prepare for a full-blown case, and I knew it would involve lying under oath. I had confidence in just about every aspect of this showdown except for one thing: How would they describe this incident in the indictment?

During the next couple of weeks, Chuck trolled the residents with relentless energy. His investigative fury knew no bounds. He was determined to find witnesses. I only needed to check with one. I sought out Johnnie and asked him: "What the fuck were you thinking about?" Then he offered what would become his testimony: "Everybody said it had to be you. They said you or Ken were the only ones in this house with balls enough to try something like that."

As the trial approached, my only concern stemmed from the fear of a set-up. I had made some enemies while running the sports teams, deciding who would play and who would sit. I worried about the possibility Chuck might squeeze someone into lying — and I knew I just couldn't tolerate another liar in the courtroom, even though that might have been an example of universal justice at its best. Those fears grew worse when I learned that Chuck had a secret witness primed for the stand.

The proceeding began with the panel trying to cow me into submission. They demanded my grade point. Although it was a hearty three-five on a four-point scale, they still reminded me that I should be using my time to push it even higher instead of getting involved enough in something like this to face a trial. When they called it the "feces case," I had to suppress a laugh. But they were the ones laughing after Chuck presented Johnnie as the core of his case, admitting he hadn't seen anything but only assumed it. Then I paraded my goons—Ken, Doeda and Surf—who testified they'd been with me all the time. I never asked if they'd seen me shit down the stairwell, so they never had to lie. But then I told the jury I hadn't done it. I said I was being railroaded by an overzealous P.A. That's when Chuck played his trump card.

As his secret witness, Chuck offered a little snit from the Grotto who had a grudge from a football game. He took the stand and offered his evidence. In the week before Chuck left for the weekend, he said, he had overheard me tell Ken, "When Chuck leaves town, the shit's gonna fly." As silly as that sounded, I still felt compelled to clarify the record. I lectured the laughing jurors on the meaning of that phrase as a figure of speech and not a literal call to action.

"I say it all the time," I told them. "Shit's gonna fly. You do, too."

Exonerated unanimously, I stood before the dean of housing two days later to receive his decision.

"I won't overturn a unanimous verdict by your judicial board," he said through a smug sneer. Then he looked over the top of his glasses and added a threat. "But I know you did this. And if you get involved in anything else—any little thing—I will move you out of there."

Although I triumphed in the feces case, he managed to make good on that threat three months later. The second showdown involved a scheme the rogue had hatched to use money from the dorm's highly restricted recreational fees account for a decent party in a barn somewhere with a keg of beer. We persuaded a majority of the residents to transfer those funds into a scholarship for the neediest member of Francis House. The rules we wrote specified no restrictions on his use of the money. The recipient could spend it on books, tuition, housing fee, or anything he needed.

"Hell," I told the group before they voted to approve it, "he might even be so grateful he just spends the whole six hundred dollars throwing a party for everybody."

When Ken emerged as the only applicant in a dormitory of forty men, Chuck smelled a rat and set about frantically working to derail the scholarship. But there was little he could do. We even convinced the director of scholarships to make a special presentation after the start of the second semester in January when Ken would get his check. Reading the fine print, however, Chuck discovered a loophole. I had specified that the recipient also had to reside in Francis House when receiving the award. So, just before the semester's end, during final examination week, he busted us having a shaving cream fight in the bathroom, blowing off a little steam. And the next day, just three days before the deadline for Ken to get the money, I found myself standing once again before the dean of housing, who, this time, had a genuine smile on his lips.

"Can't this wait until next semester?" I asked. "I have two finals tomorrow."

Unimpressed, he ordered us split up and moved to opposite ends of the Missouri campus. And we had to vacate Francis House that night.

TWENTY-TWO

August 1967

"WE WON'T ROB YOU"

I had written those words in psychedelic block letters across an old, brown paper grocery sack so I could tape it to the side of a suitcase. The words were printed large enough to be visible from a considerable distance. I filled in the colors. Black for the "W" and the "B;" red for the "E" and the "Os" in "WON'T" and "ROB;" yellow for the "T" and the "U;" green for the "R;" and, purple for the "W," the "N," the apostrophe and the "O" in "YOU."

Professional Gary had worked eighteen-hour days during June and July in a hell hole, galvanizing chain link fences to save money for his impending junior year at Mizzou. The rogue had allowed it because he knew August belonged to him. Actually, the rogue had owned the whole last year, sacrificing my sophomore grade point average and granting the professional just enough room to survive. The Francis House feces case and our subsequent expulsion from the dorm had just been one of the rogue's many accomplishments the past year. We'd had fun, and I had no regrets about letting him run the show for a while. We had planned an ultimate shenanigan as an exclamation point on the summer, scheduling August to hitchhike from St. Louis to Los Angeles, up to San Francisco, and back across the west just in time for the start of school. Of course, Ken would serve as traveling companion for this adventure that would be our last road trip of life together. His rogue had flunked him out of Mizzou the past year, and all that lay ahead for Ken was Vietnam. He never should have chosen chemistry as his major.

I'm still not sure how or why my rogue had emerged so savagely in the fall of 1966, as I began my sophomore year at Mizzou. Maybe he came out because the professional had caged him so successfully the year before. As a freshman without a car, and, inspired by the intellectual offerings of college classes, I had transformed into a hermit. I had left high school behind and settled in to get an education, driving my grade point to honors college status. My budding domestic had pledged our love to my high school sweetheart, still in her junior year back in St. Louis. She wrote us a letter every single day, confessing her love and always misspelling "sweet" as "sweat." The domestic thought it cute. The professional grunted. The rogue nearly puked. But the professional remained in charge, reading the books, writing the papers, and dominating those freshmen days.

Suddenly, however, as the new school year dawned in September of 1966, my old high school running buddy Ken had joined me at Mizzou after spending his freshman year at a junior college in St. Louis. The rogue had always liked him. We became roommates in the dormitory and I felt something stirring in my gut. Secure in the honors college, where an *F* equaled only a *C*, I had brought my 1962 white, convertible Chevy to campus and things started to change. Before I knew what was happening, the rogue had dialed my girlfriend and dumped her long-distance, sending the domestic sniveling for a standing ten-count in the corner of the ring where my three personalities did battle.

I did enjoy watching the rogue that year, as he nearly forced the professional into early retirement. Of course, the heartbroken domestic was still crying in the corner, unable to protest the rogue's reign of revelry. One week the rogue watched quietly as the professional worked hard to get us the highest grade on the first of three tests in our honors math class. The rogue had not said a word until we visited the professor for the results and learned the score had positioned me for a final grade no lower than *C*.

"So, let me get this straight," I heard the rogue asking before the professional could stop him. "If I never attend the class again or take the other two tests, I can still get a *C*?"

"That's right," said the professor, looking a little confused. "If a *C* is good enough, you have that now."

"Deal," said the rogue, extending my hand and then mumbling some more nonsense about how this would provide me the extra time to handle other challenging course work and get extra credit in those. The rogue knew we wouldn't be wasting all that free time on frivolity like academics. We had beers to drink and two coeds to juggle. The professional started to pout.

The year was looking hopeless to him. So, he just stepped out of the way, surrendering our sophomore year to the rogue.

Under the rogue's direction, I started working nights in a bar, playing poker until dawn just in time for my morning classes, and often finishing a week with no sleep from Tuesday through Saturday. A couple of co-eds recruited Ken and me to drive on a road trip to Fort Lauderdale for Spring Break.

The rogue enjoyed his first taste of forbidden love that Spring semester, too, when I established a liaison with a coed engaged to a guy still living in St. Louis. She visited him at home on alternate weekends while I inserted a girl from one of Columbia's two women's colleges into her spot in the monthly rotation, providing our first experience at relationship juggling, and successfully skulking under the radar as an infamous "other man."

Once that school year ended, the rogue convinced me to spread my wings by finding a new job away from my dad's lawnmower shop. That's how I wound up at Boyles Galvanizing instead of St. John's Lawnmower Service for the summer. The boss at Boyles welcomed me with a smirk and said, "You're going to learn why you want to stay in college, boy." He taught me how to operate some machine that reduced the gauges on long rolls of wire. I would stand beside the machine while the wire ran through a shaver at high speeds. Every fifteen minutes the wire would break and start snapping around like a power cable severed in a storm, sparks shooting from the end. Each time, I would race to stop the machine before the flailing wire could whip around and poke me in the eye. Then, I would fire up a torch to weld the broken strands of wire back together and start all over again. In another part of the building, other workers weaved the coils to make chain link fencing. I regularly worked a second shift helping drag the finished fences through a boiling pool of zinc galvanizing agent designed to coat the wire against corrosion. I wondered about the stench and the fumes as I watched a toothless old man eating Gerber baby food for lunch. I asked him if he had worked there long.

"Sure have," he said. "Ever since I got out of high school about ten years ago."

So the prospect of a cross-country trip by thumb seemed the perfect reward for my suffering in the first two months of this summer, one that would become known as the notorious "Summer of Love." Songwriter Scott McKenzie provided the anthem, inviting all the hippies to San Francisco's Haight Ashbury neighborhood where we'd wear flowers in our hair. He could not yet appreciate the significance of Charles Manson's parole that summer as well. But we all knew the Beatles would make a comeback with their classic Sergeant Pepper album. Ken and I weren't hippies, but we joined the migration anyhow. We just looked like a couple of short-haired, college boys when we stood beside the nation's iconic Route 66 outside St. Louis and stuck out our thumbs, hoping some strangers would take us west. I thought my "We Won't Rob You" suitcase would catch an eye.

Almost immediately, our first ride came with a Mexican headed for… Mexico, of all places! Assured we had driver licenses, he stopped at the first grocery store to buy a small cooler, a bag of ice, and a case of beer. He climbed into the back seat and ordered: "Drive to Amarillo." He obviously planned to turn south from the famous roadway at that Texas Panhandle city, but he passed out somewhere in Oklahoma. We hoped he might sleep right through the stop. Something awakened him, however, and we found ourselves standing beside the highway in the night this time, seeking salvation at two in the morning. It arrived quickly in the form of an old mail truck rehabilitated by a thirty-year-old Bostonian headed west in pursuit of a girlfriend. Riding with him was another hitchhiker, a kid about our age headed home to San Francisco. It seemed the whole world was a-thumb that summer, and the other hitcher, of course, invited us to look him up when we headed north from our initial destination of Los Angeles.

We had secured a couple of places to stay in Los Angeles and planned to hang out there for a couple of weeks before hitching north to San Francisco. My dad's sister, Aunt Francis, had offered a place to sleep at her home in Azusa, one of the Los Angeles suburbs. We also had an invitation from a rich chick named Laura who lived in a mansion in Palos Verdes and had attended one of the women's colleges in Columbia.

We needed only a couple of days to reach LA, even after the rehabilitated postal truck broke down in New Mexico. We caught a lift with a big trucker who carted us all the way there. In Los Angeles, we continued hitching around town and even slept one night along the Santa Monica Freeway when we couldn't catch a ride back to Azusa. Laura picked us up and took us to the beaches. But we didn't even last one night at her house because her dad suffered a nervous breakdown while we were there. We awakened to his screams, "Who the fuck are they? Who are they?" Then Laura carted us back to my Aunt's, where my thirty-year-old cousin had come to visit. She was living in San Jose, just outside San Francisco, so we accepted an invitation to travel back to her house and make it the base for our exploration of Flower Power Central.

Hitching around again, we located our friend from the postal truck and roamed around with him for a couple of days. I recall waking up one morning in a car on a cliff above the Pacific at Santa Cruz to the sound of sea lions roaring above the surf. As unsophisticated rubes from the Midwest, we didn't dabble in the drug culture there beyond sampling a little marijuana, which didn't seem to be as interesting to me as drinking beers. One stranger tried to recruit Ken to join his drug manufacturing business after Ken identified himself as a chemistry major at Mizzou. We both laughed, recalling his grade point, and declined the invitation.

With Labor Day gone and the Fall semester on the near horizon, we started home from San Jose much the same as when we had left a few weeks earlier from St. Louis. My cousin dropped us at a tangle of connector freeways that would lead us to Interstate-80 and the northern route back home. I stuck out my thumb and took stock of my situation. I had sixty dollars cash in my pocket and stood two thousand miles from home, dependent on the fortunes of the road to get me there with no guaranties.

I realized I had never felt so free as on that morning outside San Jose. I didn't know it then, but I would never feel that free again.

Our only anxiety about catching a ride occurred when we risked a detour from the interstate south to Lake Tahoe just to see the place. The summer crowds had cleared, and we found it nearly deserted. I still have a picture someone snapped for the two of us, sitting on our towels on a beach by the lake with my "We Won't Rob You" suitcase in the background, loafers and sleeping bag off to the side. I'm wearing a gray University of Missouri T-shirt while Ken sits shirtless with his best Marlon Brando smirk across his face. We waited several hours for a local in a pickup to haul us back to the highway. Then we shot back to St. Louis, again in record time. The cops in Cheyenne escorted us out of town there with a laugh and warning: "No hitching inside the city." We rode down to Denver and stayed overnight in a YMCA. Then we picked up Interstate-70 for the return through Kansas City back to St. Louis.

At the time I thought very little about the logistics of that trip. Mainly, I felt like a failure because we went all that way and never got laid. I was beginning to fear we would never make it as cocksmen. But we had traveled at least five thousand miles all together, most of that by thumb, and lived for a month on one hundred dollars or less. We'd seen the Pacific and the sea lions, San Francisco and the hippies, Sunset Strip, and the Whiskey A-Go-Go. It would only be in later years that I could come to appreciate the magnitude of the accomplishment itself and the precious nature of those memories.

Back at Mizzou, reality had been waiting to pounce. Ken would be Army-bound within months, and I was destined to meet Boop in just a few weeks with that errant phone call to her dorm. The rogue had enjoyed his time behind the wheel, but the professional decided to lock him in the trunk for a while. Of course, neither knew the domestic stood poised to emerge and lead us in a totally new direction with Boop for the next few years. But the rogue had not retired. He was just in hibernation, dreaming blissfully about the great times he knew were yet to come.

TWENTY-THREE

1970s

If your roommate-lover came home late after a workout at the YMCA, you'd expect to find a gym bag filled with sweat-soaked clothes. Sure. And that's what Cindy figured one evening in early 1974, about six months before she got pregnant. I knew that's what she had expected once I saw the contorted look on her face, after she peeked inside to find my T-shirt and shorts still neatly folded with a pair of white crew socks rolled tightly in a ball. Fortunately, we had a guest from the apartment next door chatting away, or I might have been clobbered with that bag.

"Didn't make it to the gym, huh?" she asked, with more than a touch of sarcasm after our visitor had left. "So what kept you?"

I was busted. Cheating for the first time in my life and caught, I realized lying would just create more problems. So I told her about Maria, who worked as an assistant for one of the elected county commissioners. While out for drinks a few weeks earlier, Maria had confided about her troubled marriage. One thing led to another, and we kissed. Then we went back to the courthouse and had sex on the couch in the commissioner's office. A couple of days later, she introduced me to a little motel just a short drive from the government building so we could enjoy tryst-breaks during the day. The place charged by the hour, and each room had a speaker that allowed the desk clerk to ask after forty-five minutes: "Do you need more time?" Maria had a troubled past that included the defrocking of a Catholic priest a few years before, when she lived in the Rio Grande Valley on the Texas border. She said the experience ruined her faith, and I wondered what it had done to the priest.

Cindy listened patiently and responded without amusement when I suggested the fling had been an attempt at "source development" for news stories.

"You want me to leave?" she finally asked. Although she appeared hurt, she wasn't destroyed. Perhaps she considered it cosmic justice for the cheating she'd done during her marriage and wanted some punishment to soothe her guilt. She also had no alternative living options, having become somewhat dependent on me in those last months of her college plan. I gathered, too, that this had been her first time to assume the position of cheated lover. She didn't quite know how to react, so the emotions were bottled inside.

In that moment, however, several realizations emerged clear to me. First, I really liked Cindy and wanted her to stay. Second, Maria was history. But third, I couldn't be sure this would be my last time in the penalty box for extracurricular activities. I couldn't declare Cindy as the last woman I ever would fuck, particularly at the tender age of twenty-seven. I could, however, work harder at insulating her from the knowledge of any future transgressions. If it happens again, I promised myself, she never will know.

So I made peace with my internal conflicts, and it did not seem that big a deal. Cindy and I both, at that time, fancied ourselves a '70s Boomer couple willing to experiment and push the role of sex as a boundary for relationships. Perhaps she was planning some extracurricular activity of her own, and like as not, she probably had some. But I was more interested in finding a way to disarm jealousy as a destructive influence in my life while discarding the equally destructive view that another person could be a possession. By demystifying sex to the level of a mere physical act, I found the more fundamental aspects of our relationship assumed greater importance. By turning my fears into fantasies, I found I could lick jealousy. I could even become aroused with the thought of some other guy giving her pleasure. My only objection might have been that she hadn't let me watch. She had my permission to mess around. Why shouldn't I have permission from her?

Then again, maybe we actually should have discussed these concepts in greater detail. And, of course, things grew a lot more complicated quickly with her pregnancy and the birth of our first daughter. I never set out to seek adultery, but opportunities always seemed to come my way. It became the new manifestation of the charming rogue as those opportunities blossomed repeatedly after lying dormant while I had built my career and surrendered to the domestic life with Boop.

By the time I had settled in with Cindy, it seemed the domestic, the rogue, and the professional had forged an uneasy truce. The rogue knew he needed the professional to survive and grow, while the professional understood the needs of the rogue. The domestic had his security blossoming with Cindy. So we agreed to release the rogue to prowl on special occasions, as long as he could be discreet. For several years, he succeeded beyond our wildest expectations.

I recall the night before my ten-year high school reunion in 1975. Cindy and Little E stayed with my parents in St. Louis while I ventured out with some old pals. *What have I been missing?* I asked myself as I sat in an apartment watching them roll around on the floor having sex with women from their jobs. Of course, the gals had brought an extra friend who wasted no time getting her hand in my pants while rationalizing with complaints about her husband's unfaithful ways. The eight of us capped that night with an early morning skinny dip, scaling the fence at a local public pool for an encore.

Then there was the time in New Orleans for Mardi Gras when I rendezvoused at Pat O'Brien's saloon with some friends. They had stopped on their drive south the night before at a college, attended some kind of fraternity bash, and left with a college girl asleep in the back seat of their car. She woke up and quickly embraced the spirit of this religious holiday. That night, the men stripped while she draped Mardi Gras necklaces around our genitals. For some still-unexplainable reason I was the only one who got laid. I guess in her heart she was really just the monogamous kind.

During my 1977 sabbatical in St. Louis, I juggled care for my ailing dad and Little E with visits to the apartment of a woman I met while drinking with an old college pal. Ironically, her name also was Cindy and she had attended high school with my Cindy when she lived in St. Louis. As I rode my motorcycle back to my family's house in the early hours of the morning before everyone there would be awake, I couldn't help thinking to myself: *What a small world this is, indeed!*

That year proved fruitful for extracurricular activities. Back at work for *The Post* in the Fall, I spent a month in Huntsville covering that sensational trial of the two Houston cops accused of killing the Hispanic laborer by throwing him into a bayou. While trying to concentrate on testimony from the witness stand, I turned my head to survey the audience of college students attending the trial from Sam Houston State University's school of criminology. One female student caught my eye when she opened her mouth to reveal her teeth and slowly rolled her tongue across the enamel. About an hour later, we were back in my room banging away. A few days later, I hooked up with another coed from the school, and we spent several nights on the water bed at her apartment.

Although Cindy was just a month from delivery of Shannon, we traveled during Christmas of 1977 to St. Louis with Little E for a visit with my parents. I got out one night with the boys again, and that excursion ended at a massage parlor, where one of my friends vanished into the back room with the knockout blonde who ran the place. Instead of leaving, we hung around the waiting room at her invitation for about thirty minutes while she locked up. After breakfast at a Denny's, we adjourned to her condominium and took turns hosing her down while her two children slept in the next room. The next day, I went directly to the St. Louis health department for a venereal disease test and spent an anxious couple of days awaiting the negative results while finding excuses to delay having sex with Cindy.

I could rationalize my behavior by differentiating between the nature of these one-time, special opportunity flings and the destructive potential of a full-blown affair that could threaten our family. I also knew that philandering occurs more as an ego builder than for the physical release, the male culture's version of collecting scalps. No one got hurt, and Cindy never knew. At least, she didn't know until that night in August of 1979, when I learned about Uncle Al. I wanted to lash back, and I also wanted to brag. So, out came a full accounting of the rogue's secret life. I stressed the difference between my flings and her affair, calling hers the extracurricular activity that destroyed our home.

"And you never would have known about mine if I hadn't told you now," I said.

"You say I didn't know," she replied. "But there had to be something telling me we weren't right."

My three lives had converged to create a real mess. Our money was tied in the house, and I didn't have the cash flow to get my own place. I was dumped and driving a two-hundred-dollar car. I was sleeping on a couch at the home of a friend. And I carried my dirty clothes in a brown paper, grocery sack. I called it luggage by Kroger, and that bag came to symbolize my existence during that time. I didn't know I hadn't quite hit bottom or that a special problem-solver named Catherine Mehaffey lurked on the horizon. But pretty soon, despite all this mess, I soon would have only one true problem. Beyond her, I would recall the rest of this simply as bumps in the road.

Part Three:

A Fatal Attraction

TWENTY-FOUR

October 15, 1979

I had no sooner tossed my jacket on the coat rack beside my desk in the courthouse press room to start the day when the phone on my desk began to ring. From the desk beside mine, radio reporter Jim Strong looked up from the morning paper to see who might be calling me so early in the day. I nodded and snapped my fingers when I heard Catherine's voice.

"I guess you've heard about my case by now," she began. Strong drew closer to my desk with a grin on his face. We hadn't seen her in two weeks since that introduction September 28 at the party. He had left a couple of messages with her receptionist, and I had called once. I also had visited the courtroom briefly and seen her testifying in her case to win control of the Tedesco estate as the doctor's widow.

"I just got in and hadn't heard," I told her on the phone. "But I saw you crying on the witness stand."

She laughed out loud and said, "Some show, huh? That didn't even work. The things we do for juries!"

I was more than a little stunned by her cavalier manner. What if I'd been taking notes for a story?

"So, you have a verdict?" I asked.

"They agreed I was his wife, but they didn't give me the estate. So, I lost. And it's worse than that. I guess if you came to court you saw all my old boyfriends sitting in a row. They were there to give me support."

My mind flashed back three days to the scene I had watched through a window in the door from outside the courtroom, standing beside a lower court judge who knew her. He pointed out the gallery of old lovers that included a Houston cop in full uniform and laughed. He also told me his bailiff had testified against her for the family the day before, claiming she had confessed the Tedesco murder to him. He said he didn't believe that would be enough for an arrest. He also snickered at the idea of her attorney possibly handling this probate matter on a contingency-fee basis, as if it were some sort of civil damages case, and the lawyer should take a cut. "Yep," he had said, peering through the glass as she started to cry, "there goes the hanky."

On the phone to me, she continued to joke about the case.

"Weren't they cute? Even Officer Joe in his uniform. He sat right up there and professed his love. And now that I'm not getting any money, guess what? They won't have anything to do with me any more."

Her attitude startled me, but I still had to laugh. She had certainly aroused my curiosity. Then she cut me off and came right to the point.

"I need to put this behind me now and move on with my life. I'm so low right now I really need a change. And it looks like you are my last hope. I think you're a man who could show me the true meaning of love."

Catherine laughed as she said that, of course, making it a tease. I winked at Jim and told her, "I'm willing to try. When should we start?"

"Got plans for tonight?"

"But I'm still estranged," I reminded her. "And you don't like the estranged."

"That was before my boyfriends all left me. Why don't we have a drink tonight?"

"I'll tell you what. I have to drive down to Galveston tonight and collect the rent on a beach house I own. Why don't you ride along, and we'll have something to eat somewhere?"

"That sounds perfect. That's just what I need, to get out of this city for a while."

So, about seven that night I was parking my two-hundred-dollar, 1973 Chevy Vega in front of a relatively new, ranch-style house on Houston's far west side for my first date with Catherine Mehaffey. She was renting a bedroom there from a long-time friend who owned it. She assured me their relationship was strictly business. The arrangement did sound a bit strange, but I figured I'd learn more when she wanted to share. As we started walking toward my car, she broke out laughing.

"What is that? Is that your car?"

"I know it needs some work, but there is a story here."

She stopped and pointed to a 1979, burgundy-colored Cougar parked in the driveway and asked, "Would you be offended if I want to take my car? You can still drive."

Her invitation came as a relief. I feared the Vega would not even make it to Galveston, and her new Cougar looked pretty comfortable. I would have bet it even had air conditioning. I nodded and went to my car, taking the grocery bag of laundry from the back seat.

"I need to store these somewhere," I explained. "I was going to do laundry later, and the car has no locks."

"Your clothes? In a grocery bag?" Her laughter had the tone of a woman who had just caught her puppy trying to climb onto a table. She took the sack, placed it inside the front door, and said playfully, "Maybe we can run a load when we get back. We can't have you wearing scruffy clothes. How will you ever find any new girlfriends?"

Of course, this all had been part of the courting strategy designed for her. I had hoped to generate pity, wash a load of clothes, and maybe even get laid while the washer ran. So far, I thought, she was falling into all my traps. While I started her car and backed out of the driveway, Catherine popped a new Billy Joel tape into the dashboard. She caught me peaking at one of her breasts, exposed behind her red blouse as she leaned forward to work the controls.

"Don't wreck my car," she teased with a grin. "You can take a closer look later when you're not behind the wheel. It's still pretty new and about all I have left now. This probate case cost me plenty and kept me from working for a long time."

We stopped for gas, and I filled her tank. Then we hit the freeway for the sixty-minute drive south to the island. The ride gave us plenty of time to get acquainted. She said she wanted to talk about me, but, somehow, the topic always shifted back to Tedesco and the terrible things people were saying about her. She was convinced the Tedesco family private eyes were following us down the highway and kept turning to look.

"Now tell me," she said, "where did you get that car? You said there was a story."

"It's just temporary. I bought it from another reporter for two hundred dollars after my wife burned up my other car."

"She burned up your car? I'd like to meet her. Sounds like your divorce is more out of control than you say."

"No, not like that. She drove it with a radiator leaking and ignored the red warning light. It warped the engine."

"So that's why you left her?"

My turn to chuckle.

"The picture on you is becoming clearer by the minute," she purred. "Here you are, racing through the streets in a two-hundred-dollar car with your clothes in a paper bag, after confessing to eight affairs in fours years, and you're just trying to find out: 'What happened to my life?'"

"It's actually an amicable split. We're even using the same lawyer."

"Ah, yes, and don't a lot of them start that way? But the amicable divorces usually lose their charm. My advice is to get your own lawyer."

"I already have one. She's using mine."

"That will change."

She sounded rude, but she had only voiced a thought I had harbored anyway. I was drawn to her dark sense of humor and the mystery of her questionable reputation. After working as a reporter for ten years, I had stopped judging people by their reputations. I always wanted to keep them in mind, of course, but I also wanted the facts and tried to approach everyone with an open mind. Aware that I knew more about her than most new acquaintances, she worked hard on the drive down to plead her case. Six feet tall and 200 pounds with dark hair and a full beard, I considered myself an attractive enough guy to merit some of her self-serving pitch. I figured she craved a physical relationship for the short term and didn't want to scare me off. From what I knew of her past, however, I also expected some secret agenda might unfold at any time and reminded myself to remain on guard. I wasn't foolish enough to believe an attractive, intelligent blonde would view me as merely a sex object or trophy material.

I found her engaging and charming—in a brutally dark sort of way. I had trouble believing many of her comments were on the level. As she joked about the Tedesco matter, I kept thinking, *She must be kidding! She's testing my limits.* I developed a quick fascination for her sick brand of humor and realized it only reflected my own. I wondered, *It's so bad I enjoy this, something must be wrong with me.* Then I reminded myself, *That's right. Something is wrong with me. I better just face the fact that maybe we were meant for each other.* Ironically, I didn't really find her all that physically gorgeous as some others had said and under other circumstances might have passed on a fling. By then, however, the game had begun. Besides, I was horny.

She confronted the Tedesco issues head on, voluntarily denying any involvement in his murder without even being asked. She portrayed herself as an isolated victim of a male-dominated, bullying legal system—presenting an image guaranteed to attract a crusading reporter dedicated to afflicting the comfortable while comforting the afflicted. Her theory had some merit. Back then, lady lawyers were still fairly rare and female criminal practitioners almost nonexistent. Yet there she worked, banging around the courthouse like one of the guys, seeking court appointments, and getting her hands dirty in the very bowels of the machine. I knew she had been working the lower level county court circuit, paying her dues in the trenches, and I respected that. She made a passionate case for being a turf-war target of the district attorney's office, as a woman doing battle in an arena reserved for men.

I also found her professional attitude appealing. Regardless of what anyone might say about her, she convinced me immediately she was serious about becoming a top criminal lawyer. In the back of her mind, she already had begun to formulate a plan for us, and my mental alarm signal began to ring as she hinted about it then.

"I think we've both stumbled across each other at the lowest points in our lives," she said, looking over her shoulder to check again for Tedesco detectives. "We should help each other out."

For someone who should have been guarding her comments, Catherine gushed revelations. She blamed her Irish temper for most of her problems and vowed to keep it under control. She said one of her grandfathers had come to America after killing a cop. She bragged about her role as the defender of her brothers, claiming as a child to have beaten up a boy who had bullied one of them. She told me about her marriage to a Navy man and life in Japan. I noticed a theme. In Catherine's relationships, she had always seen herself as both the provider and protector.

When Billy Joel's *Only the Good Die Young* began to play, she raised the volume and told me that song could be her anthem. I listened to some of the words in that ballad about the liberation of a secluded Catholic girl. He sang: "You heard I run with a dangerous crowd, we're not too pretty and not too proud. We might be laughing a bit too loud, but that never hurt no one. Because only the good die young." And, "I'd rather laugh with the sinners than cry with the saints." I noted my age of thirty-two and wondered if I still had time to die young.

As if it were something very important, she declared red as her favorite color, citing her blouse and the car we drove. She said she had wanted to wear red to the probate trial but her lawyer stopped her. Just as I sarcastically wondered why, she returned to Tedesco and unleashed a torrent of complaints about him and the Special Crimes division of the district attorney's office, investigating the case with a focus on her. She mimicked one of her lawyer friends who had called the family's crime stoppers hotline claiming to be a Greek sea captain with inside information on the murder and demanding a reward. She laughed about the scene at his townhome when she scaled a fence to get at his pre-Columbian art from South America—artwork she believed belonged rightfully to her. Tedesco had been involved in all sorts of criminal activity, she said, from smuggling art to running drugs. He had hundreds of enemies who wanted him dead. So, why did the cops focus on her? she asked.

"And who are these special guys from special crimes?" she asked rhetorically. "I guess that's the gang that goes after lawyers. They broke up my relationship with Officer Joe, snatched him up from the middle of the street where he was directing traffic, and told him to forget about me. They'll be talking to you, too, when they find out about this."

I laughed at that. I told her what I knew about the unit. I covered their activities and talked to the prosecutors there on a daily basis. I had no fear of Special Crimes. It had been formed a few years before as part of a trend sweeping the legal law enforcement landscape. It worked closely with the police to help them investigate complicated cases that ranged from public corruption to embezzlement. Only the top prosecutors could join the squad, and they controlled their own team of police detectives assigned specifically to Special Crimes.

"Hey," I said, "you should feel honored to be a target."

She growled a little and then laughed.

"This is a nice ride," she said, checking the rear window one more time. "I'm really starting to relax. But promise me one thing. Believe me when I tell you I had nothing to do with the murder of George Tedesco. Give me a chance."

"Catherine," I said, as we drove over the causeway above Galveston Bay and onto the island, "everybody starts with a clean slate from me."

TWENTY-FIVE

October 15, 1979

Catherine needed less than thirty minutes to start scribbling furiously across that clean slate I had just handed her. That's how long it took to drive to the crummy joint where my tenant worked tending bar, walk inside, get a beer, and begin a discussion about paying the rent. I had long before given up any hopes of ever getting those rent payments by mail. Every time Cindy or I had called, he'd said he just dropped it in the box. After a week with no arrival he'd complain it was lost and send it again. Finally, I realized the only way to collect would be to just show up and confront him.

"Wow," said Catherine as we walked into that dive, which was little more than an old house trailer with a hand painted sign that read Pirates Cove, a couple of tables, and a makeshift bar. "If your tenant works in this place, your beach house must be one of the bargain estates down here. We need to hang out here for a couple of hours. I bet I can find some clients in the Pirates Cove."

"Yeah, the beach house is quite a shithole," I told her. "It's so bad, Cindy just told me to take it. She didn't want to fuck with it any more."

My tenant feigned a welcoming smile, set a couple of beers on the counter, and assured me there had been no need for my trip all the way to Galveston.

"I could have just put a money order in the mail."

"No problem," I said. "I enjoyed the drive. Say hello to my friend, Catherine."

She took a sip of Miller Lite and watched him begin to wiggle.

"So," I said. "That must mean you have the money ready, eh?"

"Well, I have it. But I really need to keep half and pay you later. I have a little cash flow problem right now…"

"You know, I came all the way down here and I'd rather not make the trip again. Is there some way you can pay it now? It was overdue on the 10th."

"I know. But if you'd just waited and given me another week you could get it all. I'm really going to need some of this…"

"All right, give me a couple hundred, and we'll figure the rest of it later."

When he laid two one-hundred-dollar bills on the bar and turned to walk away, Catherine couldn't stand it any longer. She slammed her bottle down on the counter and yelled at him.

"Hey," she screamed. "What are you doing? You have the money, you owe the money, you need to pay him now."

As he turned slowly around to face us again, she turned to me and said, "He has the money, he gives you the money. Don't let him walk on you like that."

"Who the fuck did you say this is?" he asked, hitching a thumb in her direction. "What happened to your wife?"

I just stared at him and then looked at her, thinking how they had just teamed up to chop off one of my balls. I deemed her correct in principle, but I had to question the tactic. I knew I had surrendered to him too easily, but I just didn't want to fight about it. I also knew I had no business pretending to be a landlord. Before I could say anything more, however, Catherine accepted his challenge.

"Who am I?" she snarled. "I am his attorney. And if you don't slap the rest of the money on the bar in the next ten seconds your ass will be in court tomorrow answering an eviction petition."

I started shaking my head, while he stroked his chin. Finally, he asked, "Is she handling your divorce, too?"

This would not be the last time I would get to watch her transform a complete stranger into a seething, enraged enemy. She employed more than the words. She had a true talent for confrontation and a need to antagonize repeatedly. She had wanted much more than for him to pay his rent. She wanted to threaten him and see how much he would take. Her words carried an edge and her green eyes flashed menace as she stared him into backing away. Then, he reached into his back pocket and withdrew two more large bills.

"Forget it," I told him before he could put them on the counter. I figured I had to seize the upper hand, or I'd lose my other ball before we'd even had sex. "It's all right. You can pay it later. Ignore her."

Then I received what I would come to recognize as her special, flashing Medusa stare—a look that insinuated I might not really be a man. It was so ugly I figured our date was over. I just grinned and took a swig of my beer while he walked away. She said nothing else and took a long drink from her bottle, too. I thought she was going to speak again when we got up to leave, and I started to pay for those beers. But he derailed another confrontation by saying, "Don't worry about that. They're on me."

As soon as we walked outside toward her car, Catherine turned to me, and I expected her to order us back to Houston immediately or bitch me out some more for letting him stiff me on the rent. Instead, however, I saw yet another side. As simple as flipping a page, her fury had dissolved to atonement.

"I am so sorry," she moaned, sounding totally sincere. "I was out of line in there. I just don't know what happens to me, why I act like that. I just hate to see anybody taking advantage like that. You are obviously just a really nice guy, and he turned that inside out."

"Don't worry about it," I said, grabbing her arms and pulling her to my chest. "You were right. I shouldn't have let him wiggle out of the rent. But it was still my problem and not yours. It's no big deal. I'll get it eventually."

"I know, I know. I just can't understand it. I'm really sorry. I wouldn't blame you if you throw me in the gutter now and run back to your wife."

She batted her eyes and grinned.

"But I will tell you one thing I believe," she continued. "There are two kinds of people in this world. Predators and prey. You need to decide which one you will be. You either kill or get eaten."

"I'm a reporter. I just sit on the sidelines and watch. Your world sounds too much like *Mutual of Omaha's Wild Kingdom* for me."

"Nobody stays on the sidelines. Sooner or later you'll have to decide. And the sooner you do, the quicker you can get on with your life."

Then she grinned and took another tack. She put her hand on my crotch and asked, "*Wild Kingdom*? Isn't that the show where the animals are always thinking with this?"

Her anger had waned, and we had a pleasant seaside meal at a little restaurant near Galveston's West Beach, where my rent house was located. She was laughing again, and the sexual tension increased over a bottle of wine. Beyond the physical aspects that attracted us, I became aware of something else in the air. I felt that indefinable element each of us probably feels only a time or two in our lives if we are fortunate. Maybe it's pheromones. We were clicking. Conversation was simple, laughter automatic. We might disagree about the most effective way to collect the rent, but nothing would keep our bodies apart.

I suggested a walk in the dark on the beach, and she agreed. Thanks to the state's open beaches law I could just drive onto the beach and park her car. We hadn't walked a hundred yards from the Cougar before we started groping each other in a frenzy of lust. Completely uninhibited, she fell to the sand and unzipped her jeans while I opened my trousers. Our positioning was restricted with our pants lowered just to our knees, but neither of us could wait. We were on the verge of consummating this first date when, suddenly, we were bathed in lights from a car that had stopped beside the Cougar. I raised my head to look.

"Ahh, shit," I muttered, as I saw a lone figure with a flashlight making his way across the sand in our direction. From the look on Catherine's face, I realized she feared an ambush by the Tedesco family, and I had to wonder myself. Then I heard the intruder's voice.

"Are you two all right? I'm with the beach patrol."

"The cops are here," I whispered and did not know whether to feel relief or added worry. We had to have been breaking some kind of law. I hoped they had a simple system for ticketing copulators on the beach. I stood up and buttoned my trousers as the uniformed intruder moved close enough that we could see.

"Have some I.D.?" he asked.

I pulled my wallet from my back pants-pocket and withdrew my press card, a trick I often used to intimidate when asked for I.D. As I presented it, I mumbled, "I'm a reporter."

He read the card, shined a flashlight in my face, and grinned. Then, he said, "If you're down here to cover the sand castle contest, you're about six months too early."

"Funny," I said. "That is funny."

Catherine stepped into the light with her jeans back in place and handed him her business card.

"I'm an attorney," she said. "Were we doing something wrong?"

He grunted while reading her card. Then he said, "Miss Mehaffey? Hmmm, a reporter and a lawyer out for a walk on the beach. Nice night for that. But you might want to be careful. There are some dangerous people around here."

Catherine looked at me, feigning horror, and said, "You didn't tell me about the dangerous people down here."

"Dangerous people?" I asked, wondering if he knew he actually might be looking at the most dangerous person he'd ever seen right then and there. But I kept that thought to myself.

"I just don't want anybody getting hurt out here on my beach," he said, handing back our cards.

"We were just getting ready to go back to Houston," I said. "It's been a long night, you know. I have a beach house down here and I had to collect the rent, then we got something to eat..."

By then, he had turned around and headed back to his patrol vehicle. Catherine started chuckling and mimicked in a whisper, "I'm a reporter, I'm a reporter. I have a beach house, we got something to eat. When is the sand castle contest? And, did you know? I AM A REPORTER!"

"I hope that didn't spoil the evening," I said as we walked back to her car.

"We're just getting started," she said. "Don't forget, we still have some laundry to do."

Then, she added a comment that gave me pause: "Besides, I left my diaphragm at home."

TWENTY-SIX

October 16, 1979

"Look at this. Now that's what I'd call a handsome couple."

Catherine was giggling as she said it while we stood side-by-side in her bathroom, looking in the mirror the next morning. By my calculation we had logged about two hours of sleep after returning to her house, running some laundry, and having sex in her bedroom for most of the night. Between humps, we had swapped stories about mutual acquaintances at the courthouse, and she was proving to be a gossip's goldmine. Gossip for a beat reporter often leads to stories, and she seemed to have the dirt on every judge and lawyer over there. Listening to her, I felt like I had crawled under the chassis of the courthouse machine for a real close look at its filthiest section.

Joking about her diaphragm and the challenge of birth control, she had teased at one point asking, "What would happen if we conceived a child, Gary? What would Special Crimes say about that?"

"Wouldn't be allowed. Couldn't have that."

"Why not?"

"Special Crimes would know that any kid of ours is bound to grow up into a smart alec, and the Lord knows we have enough of those already. So, no, it would not be allowed."

She had cackled and said, "I like that. You're not afraid of those special guys at all, are you? Maybe I have found someone who can protect *me* for a change."

No, I had no fear of the boys from Special Crimes. I knew them all on a first-name basis, and they needed me to tout their cases as much as I needed them to tell me about them. But I was starting to wonder about her preoccupation with pregnancy, and I had begun to see hints of what might be a piece of that secret agenda for me. I concluded there was no harm in viewing me as a buffer that might insulate her from any unseemly persecution by Special Crimes. Reporters were supposed to do that anyway.

I knew we had made a lot of noise overnight, and twice I heard her roommate-landlord rummaging around in the hallways beyond her closed door, obviously disturbed by the loud laughter she never tried to suppress. She identified him as Mike, an acquaintance from her days a few years before at the University of Houston Law School, where she had volunteered her time to student legal services and met him before he graduated. She called him her salvation during the last few months, providing this sanctuary when she had nowhere to stay while pursuing her claim on the Tedesco estate. But he would soon be getting married, she said, and that would leave her seeking a new place to live. He had departed the house for work before we arose, abandoning it to us for showers and breakfast. Sated in more ways than one, we had just applied the finishing touches to our appearances together in the bathroom when Catherine made the declaration about our appeal as a couple.

So, I paused to check it out. At five-feet-three-inches, she stood about nine inches shorter than me with the top of her head coming about to my chest. She wore her shoulder length, naturally blonde hair with bangs in the front and spread out on the sides in curls. She had a petite body, too, weighing I guessed about a hundred pounds. I indeed looked the part of a complementary companion with my dark brown hair and beard—glasses unnecessary thanks to contact lenses I had worn since high school. I had to agree with her observation.

Oh yeah, I said to myself, *we'll turn heads, all right, the first time we show up at the courthouse together—but not because of our looks!*

Before she could put on a dress, the phone rang, and I watched her answer it in bra and panties, then walk around the room having a forceful discussion with someone on the other end. In those primitive days before cell phones, or even cordless devices, she had to carry the rotary dial base in one hand while holding the receiver to her face with the other. I eavesdropped with interest as she paced the bedroom, ordering some unknown party around.

"So you'll be in my office by eleven?" I heard her saying. "OK, you know where the office is? And you know, you better bring the money along and that's cash, five hundred dollars."

Then she laughed aloud and said, "No, a check? Are you serious? No checks. Cash and that's *five* one-hundred-dollar bills. Do that, and he'll be out of jail by two. OK, I'll be there. But don't forget. Bring cash."

I had learned that Catherine actually made the bulk of her earnings as a bail bondsman by abusing a loophole in the rules governing business activities by attorneys. She had even bragged about it during our drive, claiming she had conned some old man into placing a large sum of money under her name as a surety. She gave him a percent of her bonding business as his cut for covering her image as a woman with the funds to back up her bonds. She told me the State Bar of Texas might frown on this arrangement but insisted she only needed to use it temporarily to generate cash. Usually she would refer bonding clients to more experienced lawyers for representation, and then, those lawyers would provide a referral fee, allowing her to profit twice from services rendered on one alleged crime. But she wanted desperately, she said, to leave this bail bonding business behind and create a future as a top lawyer. Once again, I wondered why she would be sharing such information with a reporter, but I realized I couldn't do much with it. My editors had expressed no interest in her unusual probate trial for the Tedesco estate with all its bizarre aspects and allegations. Why would they want coverage about her pushing the rules on bail bonds? Besides, I had to salute her spunky ingenuity and found it intriguing.

We finished dressing, locked Mike's house, and drove toward downtown Houston in our separate cars without making any definite plans for the future.

I arrived at work a little late that morning. But the only ones to notice would have been the five or six "roommates" in my office at the press room on the fourth floor of the Harris County Criminal Courts building. My editors all worked in the main office at *The Post*, about four miles outside downtown, and usually only saw me on alternate Fridays, when I drove over to pick up my paycheck. But I had a professional family in the press room, where reporters from several rival media outlets maintained bureaus for their coverage of the beat. Tucked around the corner from the elevators on a dead-end hallway, the press room harbored barely enough space for the six metal desks stacked around the walls. Besides for Jim Strong and myself, the room served as base of operations at that time for Tom Moran from the rival *Houston Chronicle* newspaper, Sandy for one of the city's all-news radio stations, and Rhia for another news radio station. The extra desk remained available as a floater when needed by visiting members of the working press. Stacks of old newspapers sat in piles around the floor. A single clipping adorned the bulletin board—a ridiculous feature written on an obviously slow news day a couple of months earlier by a *Post* lifestyles editor describing the latest fashion trends at the women's prison unit. In the margin, some sarcastic critic had added a punch line in dark black marker: "All dressed up and nowhere to go?"

My daily routine involved roaming among three or four buildings that housed about thirty courtrooms and finding news stories. I would visit with court personnel over coffee, review docket sheets, chat with attorneys for both sides, and usually uncover more than I could handle in a single day. I would file my stories in the late afternoon, using one of the early telephonic computer terminals. When editors needed me, they called on the phone.

Although technically competitors, the regular tenants of the press room enjoyed a tribal bond that set us apart from the lawyers, judges, clerks, and criminals who also frequented the building. We worked together on some stories, when it was more efficient for a source to hold an impromptu press conference there. So we had an open-door policy on the room at that time.

On this day, I had barely sat down behind my desk, when Chuck Rosenthal of the District Attorney's Special Crimes Bureau popped his head in the door and asked me to step into the hall. He ushered me into the men's restroom around the corner and checked the stalls to ensure privacy before he spoke.

"Are you hanging around with Catherine Mehaffey?" he asked.

His question staggered me. Rosenthal was one of the top dogs in Special Crimes, a hard-nosed prosecutor destined eventually to win election as Harris County District Attorney about twenty years into the future. Since I had not yet sent out engraved announcements about the first date that occurred less than twenty-four hours before, I wondered where he had heard about Catherine and me. My mind flashed back to that Galveston cop and a comment Catherine made as we headed back to Houston. She had warned, "They'll be talking to you, now." I'd laughed it off as paranoia, but this mysterious visit from Chuck immediately raised my curiosity. He ignored my request for the source of his information and came straight to the point.

"I wish you'd think this over before you get too far involved. She is trouble."

"Trouble? Don't you know that's my middle name?"

Chuck ignored my lame attempt to break the tension and offered to let me listen to some of the tape recordings the bureau had confiscated of conversations between Catherine and Tedesco. He said their investigation had uncovered a long trail of battered and broken former lovers with Tedesco as simply the worst example. He said: "You do a good job over here. Everybody likes and respects you. We don't want to see you get hurt."

"Maybe you haven't heard, but I'm not married any more," I began, speculating he might have seen Catherine as an extramarital affair. "I'm not messing with Mehaffey on the sly. She can't tell my wife and destroy the marriage. I'm flat broke. My wife ran up a twelve thousand dollar MasterCard bill and I can't even afford an apartment. I'm sleeping on somebody's couch. Our house will sit on the market for months while I pay child support and the mortgage. So I can't figure out what else Mehaffey could do to me. Would she take my two-hundred-dollar car and my paper bag of dirty shirts?"

"It might not involve money. She usually takes whatever she can get."

"Even if there is nothing?"

He stopped, stared at me, then said, "There's always more than nothing."

"Maybe my soul?" I chuckled at the thought.

He shrugged his shoulders and repeated his offer: "Anytime you reach a point where you want to hear those tapes just drop on by. They're off the record, of course, but I think they would give you a new perspective on Catherine Mehaffey."

I told him thanks, and he walked out the door, leaving me with plenty more to ponder. On one hand, I began to wonder if her claims of persecution might not have merit. How could one night with me trigger a visit from Chuck? On another level, I had to take his concerns seriously. But I had confidence in my final conclusion. I had dealt all my life with all kinds of people and proven my talent as a survivor. I had always been able to find a way out of tight situations. I forecast she likely would play with me for a while, and then go off after some guy with money, finding a superior mark for her talents. Hell, I thought, we might even become long-term drinking buddies.

And I grinned as I thought I knew one thing for sure: No matter what she could do in the days ahead, she'd never get back that pussy from last night.

TWENTY-SEVEN

October 17, 1979

I didn't see Catherine again until the next morning when she used our open door policy to swing into the press room and startle the reporters in there. It marked the first time she had ever come into the press room, and her visit caught all of us by surprise. Then things grew even more bizarre.

She ignored me playfully and stopped first at Sandy's desk, extending her left arm to show Sandy a whopping large diamond ring on her ring finger.

"What do you think?" Catherine asked.

"Is that a diamond?" Sandy said. "Wow."

Until that day, they had never spoken to each other, but Catherine acted like one of the team, part of the press room family. She strolled across the room ignoring me and showed her new ring to Rhia, the black female reporter working for the other radio station.

"You're engaged?" Rhia asked.

Acting as if I were not even in the room, Catherine told her: "This is Gary's ticket out of here."

Everybody looked at me behind my desk in the far corner as if to ask, "What the fuck is this?" Everybody, that is, except Jim Strong at the desk beside me. He just started laughing. Then Catherine whirled around in the open center of the room and acted as if she had just spotted me for the first time.

"Oh, Gary, I didn't know you were in here. Look at this."

Then I received the extended arm with the big diamond on her finger.

"So, congratulations are in order?" I asked. "Who is the lucky man?"

"You are the lucky man," she said. I scanned the room and shrugged my shoulders, waiting for her to elaborate. Finally she cocked her head with a loud laugh, pulled an empty chair to the side of my desk, and sat down. My colleagues turned back to their newspapers and telephones, leaving us to chat—as if we could have had a private conversation in that place.

"Don't you see?" she asked me. "By the time I give this ring back, we'll have the diamond out and a cubic zirconium in."

"Draw on your legal training a moment and answer a question for me," I said, pausing to let her twist her little nose. "Have I now heard enough to make me an indictable co-conspirator?"

"Indicted for what? It's my ring now. I can do whatever I want with it, and I think for safekeeping I might want to have the stone replaced with something less valuable in case the ring is stolen."

I laughed. Once again, I thought she was kidding about this, trying to shock anyone listening with this plan for what seemed to me a blatant scheme to commit a fraud. I told her, "Catherine, I think I've heard about all I want to hear on this plan. My only hope now is to become the proverbial unindicted co-conspirator. You know—the snitch!"

"You don't know enough about this yet to be the snitch."

Although she was giggling, I thought I detected the beginning of a pout, as if I had disappointed her by refusing to immediately pledge allegiance on her caper. She changed the subject.

"We can talk about this longer over lunch," she said. "We're going to Charlie's."

"I'm thinking more like the Hoagie Shop," I replied, rejecting her bid for the most expensive steak joint in downtown Houston. But she stood up and waved me away.

"It's on me," she said. "I made some money yesterday and I want to spend some of it on you. So I insist. Be there at noon."

After she left, Sandy spun in her chair and stared at me.

"Please, Gary, tell me you are not hanging around with her now."

"I've never been one to kiss and tell," I said, shrugging my shoulders as she shot me the finger while turning to dial the phone on her desk with the other hand. I considered Sandy a good friend. She recently had begun dating my long-time friend George, the *Post* assistant city editor who was letting me live temporarily in the living room of the two-story house he was renting in Houston's Heights neighborhood. We had worked together at the paper for eight years, arriving there in the same month. He had accepted the assistant editor's job about a year earlier, after covering a wide range of assignments that included preceding me on the criminal courts beat. Recently divorced from his first wife, George had extended the hospitality of his rent house to me, but I figured my welcome was wearing thin. I already had hatched plans to begin renting a room from Jim Strong at the start of November.

In the last two years of working the courthouse beat, Strong had become an even closer friend to me. Although obviously a very bright guy, he also had a reputation as a loner who had angered many with his acerbic wit. He lived in a house in northwest Houston that was still owned by his ex-wife, who had moved out of the city. She had been an advisor to a number of high-powered, local politicians while he had bummed around on the fringes of mainstream media jobs in the city before they split up a few years before. A burly six-footer with boisterous mannerisms, he said he had been a collegiate wrestler at the University of Texas back in the 1960s. At the courthouse, he worked for a small company called Houston Metro News Service, trying to carve a niche in the Houston media market by providing news content to a number of local music radio stations that had no budget for news staffs of their own. So, he technically worked as the courthouse reporter for about a dozen stations, feeding them all the same stories and taped interviews as part of an independent staff with beat reporters posted at the other key locations around town. More than that, he was destined to play a central role in the tortured drama about to unfold the next few months between me and Catherine Mehaffey.

Our lunch that day should have been a cheerful event. We were still in that early honeymoon phase of our relationship. She had apparently landed a fee on a bail bond and wanted to talk about the future. But I had to spoil things by mentioning the visit from Chuck. I don't know why I told her he had come and talked with me about her. Maybe I wanted to test her reaction.

"That motherfucker," she snorted. "That son of a bitch. They are doing this again. But this is the end. I'm taking care of this now."

I thought she was about to leave her chair and rush over the district attorney's office for a confrontation. Immediately I saw my mistake. Not only had I violated Chuck's confidence, but I had left him exposed to an action where I would be the prime witness. I tried to envision what sort of lawsuit might erupt and realized I had to keep her corralled somehow. I struggled for an escape as she probed for more information on what he had said.

"Oh, you know," I said. "He suggested you might be trouble. So I told him trouble is my middle name."

"That son of a bitch," she seethed, waving off my attempt at humor. "What else did you say? What did you tell him?"

Hoping that humor might actually salvage this mess, I leaned across the table, looked to both sides, then stared into her eyes and whispered, "I told him: 'Chuck, it doesn't matter what you say. Every time I look at her, my dick gets so hard I just can't stand it.'"

She stared back for a moment then burst out laughing. "No shit? Did you really tell him that? That is great."

The ploy cooled her down. She pushed back into her seat still chuckling and began picking at her steak again. Just then, we were joined by one of her acquaintances, another lawyer named Jack. She introduced us and said she wanted him to meet me. Before he could make any small talk, she told him about Chuck.

"They've already been to see him," she said, pointing at me. "Chuck Rosenthal himself. Can you believe that? But you know what Gary told him?"

Jack shrugged his shoulders and looked at me. Catherine urged me on.

"Go ahead, tell him what you told Chuck."

"I told him that trouble is my middle name."

Jack grinned, but Catherine insisted.

"No, no, not that. Tell him the other thing. You know. C'mon."

"OK. I told him that when I look at Catherine, my dick gets so hard I just can't stand it."

Clearly this had touched a nerve. She cackled again while Jack acted as if he wasn't sure how to react. He gave a little grin and mumbled, "Pretty funny."

When they brought our check, Catherine paid with two one-hundred-dollar bills.

TWENTY-EIGHT

October 1979

I still see them everywhere and each time I do, I can't help but stop and wonder what's going on behind the scenes. My heart goes out to them because I remember when I fell into the divorced dad's limbo, and I know how hopeless it can feel. For me at that time, I had no place to take my daughters, outside of McDonalds. At the same time, I had to work at sorting myself out, and that involved rebuilding my self-esteem through self-improvement. Each day I had to work and keep my job because that supported everything. And I also needed a few drinks each day just to help me relax. It was into that arena of chaos that Catherine began to compete with all the other distractions.

Although I've always been a hard drinker, I'm no alcoholic. I know the difference between an alcoholic and a drunk. I can overindulge and have on many occasions. But I've always been able to stop. Fortunately, I am a funny drunk and not abusive. I know because others have told me. Once, I tried to become an alcoholic, years earlier, when I noticed than many great writers suffered the ailment. I drank every night for two weeks. It wore me out. Finally, I just gave up on that idea. Then I went a month not even wanting a drink, and that made me question my manhood.

"What would Hemingway think?" I asked, after ordering an iced tea instead of a scotch. "Sissy?"

So, the drinking during my period of the divorce crazies created no problems. But other activities vied to crowd my schedule. Immediately after

Cindy confessed her affair, I had made an appointment with a therapist and discussed things with him for several weeks. I wanted to learn if I needed psychological repairs. I lasted only a few sessions, describing my attitudes on life and the events that had brought me to his door. Our last appointment had been the evening of October 15, just before I went to pick up Catherine for our drive to the beach house. Although I had some existentialist attitudes on sex and relationships, he told me he considered me true to my beliefs and didn't see anything else I could do to save the marriage. Cindy had made the decision to split up, so she had control. I could have tried therapy for a longer term, but we didn't see where that would lead. In fact, he felt I didn't need any help. Since I was comfortable with myself, I would be difficult to change.

In addition to the shrink, the booze, and the job, I also had enrolled in several classes designed to expand my personal horizons. I had a couple of guitar lessons, rekindling an activity I had abandoned as a teen. I took a lesson on snow skiing, conducted on a huge slanted treadmill. And I signed up for a canoeing class. I quickly concluded I wouldn't enjoy the skiing, and I never had time to practice the guitar. But the canoeing class introduced me to someone who eventually would play a catalytic role in later confrontations with Catherine.

That class took place on October 20, the Saturday of my first week with Catherine. By then I would have been happy just to skip it. But I had committed, and the instructor needed me to balance his boating couples. He put me in a canoe with another novice, a girl named Denise, who was about ten years younger than me. She was an attractive college student looking to expand her own horizons. The instructor had the class working in a polluted body of water through a wooded section of downtown Houston. Called Buffalo Bayou, it actually has been Houston's primary water artery to the Gulf of Mexico, expanded in 1916 at the mouth to create one of the world's largest ports at the Houston Ship Channel. Upstream, however, in the upper-crust neighborhood of River Oaks, Buffalo Bayou accents a picturesque backdrop for landscaped yards and urban greenery.

It should have been a simple trip for a couple of miles along gently flowing waters. But Denise and I started talking. She started swinging her tits around, and the canoe started rocking. Before I knew it, we were in the water, and the canoe was filling up. Denise was laughing, but I felt humiliated. The canoe had sunk, and all the other students had passed us. Try as I might, I couldn't get the canoe out of the muck. So we just left it, and walked out of the woods to a rendezvous with one angry canoe instructor. By this time darkness had fallen, and he had to return upstream to fetch his canoe. I helped as best I could, but he did most of the work, pulling the vessel up a hill through thick trees and bushes to his trailer. I invited Denise to get something to eat, and she accepted. During the meal she revealed that she still lived with her parents, and I knew she was the wrong match for me. I still lived with George. At least Catherine had a bedroom, even if she still lived with Mike.

Through it all, I struggled with my obligations to my girls. Cindy continued to live in our house with them, and I was sure Uncle Al had assumed some sort of quasi-residency there as well. My visitations had to involve trips away from my home since they could hardly visit me on George's couch. Cindy and I had not established any definitive visitation schedule, preferring to remain flexible while sorting out our living arrangements. I was so desperate I agreed to spend a weekend in our house with the girls so that Cindy and Uncle Al could get away. Otherwise, I tried to find places we could go. At just eighteen months, Shannon didn't know what was happening, and there wasn't much I could do with her outside her playroom. I took four-year-old Little E swimming at a Y.M.C.A. and planned other activities. I could tell the separation was tearing her apart, but I didn't know what to do. When she asked me what she had done wrong, I tried to convince her it wasn't her fault. I was overwhelmed by the amount of planning required to make all of this work. I started feeling bipolar with two personalities—one for my kids and another for my new life as a swinging single. And I felt really detached from my former life, as if my daughters had become a distant memory of some other past I had only imagined. Just a few weeks before, they had been as much a daily part of my life as eating or sleeping.

The situation indeed was outside my control. I had made it clear to Cindy that we could stay together somehow, that I could live with her infidelity if she could live with mine. She could have lived with mine, but she didn't want that. She said she had bigger plans and believed she could make a better life for our girls with Uncle Al instead of me. My moods swirled between melancholy and anger, culminating in frustration. But I still believed that eventually the fog would clear, and I would find some way to work this out as well.

I capped that first weekend of Catherine trying to combine a couple of my obligations. I had promised Little E a trip on Sunday—the day after my ill-fated canoeing adventure—to the Alabama-Coushatta Indian Reservation in Livingston, Texas, about a two-hour drive from Houston. Then I invited Catherine along, and we went in her car. It proved an awkward day as I fought to merge my diverging personalities, and I had some concerns about exposing Little E to Catherine so soon. They had a great time together, but I suspect each one had a hidden agenda.

"That kid is ready to rock and roll," said Catherine, paying Little E a high compliment. "I wish I could have one like her some day. You are a lucky guy."

And that night I got Little E's side in a phone call from Cindy.

"I heard all about Little E's new golden-haired princess," Cindy said, sounding a bit jealous. I was sure Little E had exaggerated her description in a childlike ploy to irritate her mother, and I tried to control my glee in seeing her succeed.

"It's all part of the divorce experience," I told Cindy. "You have to get used to these kinds of things."

"I know, I know," she said. "It's just so strange to hear her talk about someone like that after being with you."

"And I know exactly how you feel."

The next weekend I spent at our house babysitting the girls, and I invited Catherine over for that, too. She seemed eager to carve a place in their lives. But events of the next few weeks were destined to make that the last time ever I exposed them to her.

TWENTY-NINE

October 1979

Once they learn about the violence and intrigue that eventually ended my relationship with Catherine, most folks are amazed to learn that the civilized portion of our liaison lasted only about four weeks. They can't imagine how such a short affair could generate the kind of hostility destined to occur. They suggest that four weeks is barely long enough to get acquainted, much less develop a checklist of transgressions to justify murder. But that month from the middle of October until just before Thanksgiving in 1979 proved potent enough to light Catherine's fuse. Our relationship was to continue in some form until its explosive conclusion in January 1980. But those days in late October and early November would stand as the only period of civilized companionship we ever would know.

Civilized, however, did not mean perfectly peaceful. We were still getting acquainted, too, testing the boundaries of the reputations and baggage we'd carried into this thing. The timing couldn't have been more perfect for either of us. She had been right when she described us both at the lowest points in our lives, clutching for any companion to pull the other into the future. Events moved quickly in those weeks as we designed a blueprint.

Although I moved November 1 into a bedroom at Jim Strong's house on Greengrass Drive in northwest Houston, I had been spending most evenings with Catherine and continued to do that until the middle of the month. She was a great drinking buddy, and we usually finished each day at a bar before heading out to the house she shared with Mike. It quickly became easier to leave my two-hundred-dollar Chevy Vega in front of that house and ride each morning into the courthouse area with her. She welcomed my services as a driver, and it gave us plenty of time to talk, revealing other aspects of her secret agenda for me. I also started seeing signs of the problems that lay ahead.

"I need commitment," Catherine said one morning in late October, stunning me with that kind of demand so quickly after we'd just met. But she appeared shocked by my response.

"Isn't it a little too soon to start talking like that?"

"I need it for my career. I need to find someone who can satisfy my physical needs so I can put that part of my life aside and focus on my law practice. That's advice I heard long ago from a law professor on how to succeed. And I'm way behind schedule. This Tedesco bullshit has held me back. I have to get busy."

Without thinking, I challenged her: "Didn't you take a calculated risk that might happen when you went chasing after the estate? You had to know how much time and effort that would take."

She startled me when her voice seemed to change into what I could only describe as a low-pitched growl. It would not be the last time I would hear that sound.

"I…had…no…choice," she snarled in a rhythmic staccato. "It…had…. to…be…done.   And…it…is…not…over.   That…is…why…I…need…. to…know….what….you…are…doing…with….me."

I made a mental note to be careful in the future when challenging her motives on the Tedesco case and peeked from the corner of my eye while driving to make sure she hadn't sprouted fur around her jowls. I let her catch her breath, then offered a response.

"Of course, I know you felt like you had to do that—sue for the estate— and, I understand. But I don't really know what to say about commitment. I have no plans for commitment. For Christ's sake, I'm just getting out of a commitment. I can't think about that now."

Catherine sat biting her lip and gathering her thoughts. She collected herself enough to resume speaking this time in what I could only describe as a businesslike tone of voice, as if negotiating a contract—albeit a strange one.

"So you think you can just fuck me, have your fun, and then go on your way?"

Exactly, I wanted to say. *You've been reading my mind.*

But instead I bit my tongue and just mumbled, "No." Then I realized how surprised I was to learn she might care about something more than the sex. I had begun to think she might be a clinical nymphomaniac, based on our brief time together. And she hadn't demanded much of a courting ritual before dropping down on the beach for our first embrace. I actually had respected that modern, sexually-independent attitude.

But now, I wanted to ask, *it turns out you're just another old-fashioned girl?* I bit my tongue again and all that emerged from my mouth was another, "No, not at all."

"Nothing is free," she said before I could start talking myself into an even deeper hole. "You need to remember that nothing is free."

What are you, a prostitute? I wanted to ask. But my mind quickly predicted her likely reply: *Aren't we all? The only difference is that some of us charge more than others.* To that, I might even have to agree. And I realized she did not appear prepared to accept exposure to my wit and charm as payment enough for the sexual delights she considered so valuable. I understood I was running a considerable tab in her view and knew our day of reckoning could prove expensive. I wondered if she was charging interest. So I whined for pity.

"Catherine, I need some time. I'm really confused right now, and I really enjoy your company. You make me laugh. But I can't be making any commitment decisions yet. If you tell me you need to find someone who can give you commitment, then you'll have to look for someone else."

"You can't tell me you love me?"

After just two weeks together, she was talking about love? Questions bombarded my mind, but I didn't have time to sort them out. Catherine awaited an answer.

"Of course, I love you," I replied, feeling guilty the second the words left my mouth. I had only said that to three other women: Cindy, Boop, and my high school sweetheart. And, I had always struggled with the phrase. After much soul-searching over the years, however, I had learned to shrug it off. I considered it meaningless, the same as handing someone an open-ended contract. Each person has a unique definition they consider universal. I asked my high school sweetheart for a definition one time, and she told me it meant I should be willing to die in her place. After hearing that definition, I made a mental note to never ask *that* question again. I had survived two marriages without a serious dissection of the phrase. It could not have been any more ridiculous for me to tell Catherine after two weeks than it was for her to ask. To me, it was like answering yes when your kid asks, "Are we almost there?" Besides, it seemed like she wanted to hear it from someone—maybe anyone. But I decided to follow up with a bit of humor.

"What if I said you're just a piece of ass?"

Catherine hesitated while mulling that over. Then she grinned and replied, "As long as you say I am *your* piece of ass, that's all right. I like that."

"Good. I would hate to stop fucking just to start making love."

THIRTY

October 29, 1979

As my move into Jim Strong's house approached, we were discussing the details in the press room when he asked about Catherine.

"I'm reminded of times I went camping with my dad," I said. "Did you ever put a stick into a fire and try to see how long you could hold until the flame moved up and burned your hand?"

"Of course," he said. "Who hasn't? But I was always an expert at throwing the thing down before it reached my hand. How about you?"

I shook my head, chuckled, and turned back to some notes on my desk. Catherine had insisted again that I meet her for lunch at Charlie's that day. She had said she wanted to introduce me to someone important. So, I was reviewing a mental tally of the items revealed so far on her secret agenda of reasons for maintaining an interest in me. Besides our physical attraction to each other, I believed she had revealed several ulterior motives. She considered me a buffer that might protect her from overly aggressive investigators in the Tedesco murder. She had told me she felt safer on the arm of a reporter who would expose the police and Special Crimes if they took liberties on the case.

Catherine also had said she intended to appeal the verdict on Tedesco's estate and needed to develop a respectable relationship with me so I could testify on her behalf if she won a new trial. I just grunted when she said that, considering it pretty farfetched to believe she'd get a new trial and maybe even sillier to think I'd present as "respectable" after cross-examination from Tedesco's lawyers in front of a jury. But I realized her hopes for a retrial could moderate her behavior. If she thought she needed me as a positive witness, she would work harder to behave.

Then, there also had been her discussion of a need to separate the professional and physical sides of her life. I had concluded Catherine viewed me as a prime candidate for domestic slavery. *Would she call me her bitch?* Trying to see myself from her point of view, I realized I did have the look of a desperate creature begging for rescue from the two-hundred-dollar car and the luggage by Kroger. I knew she saw me as a puppy she could easily control and manipulate, after some short period of breaking. But none of this bothered me. I considered myself unbreakable. And, I thought I might enjoy playing the role of a kept man for a while. I also rather relished my new image around the courthouse as the latest foil for our most notorious femme fatale. I had prosecutors warning me off the scent, and the whole scene had provided sanctuary from gossip about Cindy's soap opera. Catherine amused me with her constant parade of schemes and Machiavellian maneuvers. In my mind, our relationship had become much like a game of chess. I hoped to lull her into a state of overconfidence by accepting her portrayal of me as a chump. And, I firmly believed her mercenary nature would force her to drop me anyway, as soon as a more lucrative target entered her life.

"You need to think seriously today about the things I am going to ask you to do," she said firmly as soon as I joined her at a table in Charlie's. Bringing me to a place that required jackets for lunch was this city's version of taking a mutt to a dog show. I had a tie, but it was loosened at the collar. My khaki trousers and frayed herringbone jacket contrasted sharply with the three-piece suits scattered about the darkened dining room. A waiter in white stood nearby just itching to scrape cracker crumbs from the tablecloth, should any fall from my mouth.

"You have some genuine opportunities, thanks to me," she began. "Our future depends on it."

Not that again, I thought, taking a sip of ice tea. I grinned and told her, "Our future is now." But I don't think she understood my double entendre.

"That's right," she said. "Our future *is* now, and we need to get going. I want you to help us make a lot of money."

"How does that happen?"

"You need to use your influence with the felony judges at the courthouse to appoint me to defense assignments for indigents. I've done that for misdemeanors, but I have to start getting felony assignments—the big cases. I want to defend on a murder case."

"I can't do that, Catherine."

"You can. You go to every court, every day. They all want publicity. They all want you to help them. Nothing is free. I could have a $250 assignment every day just pleading somebody out on lower charges. You'd get your share. How about 10 percent? There might be larger cases with more money involved. You'd get 10 percent of anything you bring me."

"I can't do that, Catherine."

She applied the Medusa stare. Then she placed her face in her hands, and I thought she was going to cry.

"I can't take money on something like that, Catherine," I said, as she peeked over her fingertips. "But I'll tell you what I will do. I will take you to Judge Route's courtroom and introduce you to his court coordinator, Edd Blackwood. He has an open door policy on appointments. You see him, tell him your background, and he'll find something for you. If that works out, he'll give you something else. I saw him one time take business cards from about a dozen lawyers, shuffle them up, and then deal out representation to a whole room full of defendants."

She started laughing and said, "You would do that for me? And, if that works out there, you'll help in some other courts?"

"But I can't take any money from you. It would be a conflict in my journalistic ethics," I said, then quietly questioned that comment as I considered the hypocrisy of preparing to eat a $150 lunch on her tab. I didn't elaborate for her, but I would have no problem introducing her to Edd, who had become a good friend during our time together at the courthouse. He was a law school dropout who had joined the sheriff's department and then moved on to court administration. Later on, in the 1980s, he would become a successful Houston bail bondsman. In 1979, however, he was always asking me to find new lawyers to audition for court appointments because his judge, Thomas Route, liked to spread the appointments around. Other courts would be more difficult because most judges preferred to work exclusively with their own cadre of lawyers.

Just then her "important" guest arrived and sat down at our table. He was a former prosecutor named James who required no introduction. I had known him from the courthouse but hadn't seen him in months, since he had left the district attorney's office and started his own private practice. We made small talk for a bit, finished our meal, and then Catherine came to the point.

"James is here because I want him to take your case."

"My case?" I asked while James continued to sip coffee. "What case do I have?"

"Your divorce case. You have to take charge of that thing now before you lose out."

"I have a lawyer."

She waved her hand around as if scolding me and said, "No, you can't have one lawyer for both of you. Too much is at stake."

Then she looked at James, who offered his first observation: "You have a very valuable house, Gary. You have some mitigating factors in your favor for protecting that investment."

Flabbergasted and growing angry, I looked him square in the eye and said, "What the fuck do you know about my house or my mitigating factors?"

"I've been in your house," he said. "We went through it with the Realtor just to see what you have. Catherine asked me to assist."

Then she added her advice: "Don't ignore the adultery. I think you could get those kids if you do this right. Let James help you."

I pushed my chair back from the table, wiped my mouth with my napkin, and started shaking my head.

"Let me get this straight," I said. "You two toured my house with the Realtor. Then you discussed my mitigating factors. And now you think I'm going to fire my lawyer and hire you to handle the divorce?"

They just stared at me. I paused a few seconds and stood up to leave.

"I'm finished here," I said. "Thanks for the lunch."

Before I could leave, James bolted from his chair and said, "No, no, I'll go. I have to be in court anyway. You two should talk about this."

As he walked away, I sat back down and stared at her.

"You crossed the line here," I said. "Even if I wanted to fire my attorney, there's no way in hell I'd ever hire that slug."

"You know what," she began. "I don't need your bullshit. You humiliated me in front of someone I need to impress. I was trying to help you, and you just don't see what a big problem you're making for yourself."

"You don't need *my* bullshit? I don't need *this* bullshit. Why don't you find a new boyfriend who'll take it?"

Our relationship should have ended right there. But it didn't. The waiter refilled our coffees, and we sat in silence for a few minutes staring at our cups. I didn't leave, and she just sat planning her next move. Finally, she said quietly, "I just wanted to help you because you have been so good for me."

"Thank you. But I really would appreciate it if you will stay out of my divorce. It's my business. If I fuck it up, that will be my cross to bear. I'm sorry if I got too rough with James, but he just caught me by surprise. I felt violated, like a burglary victim, to hear about that slug crawling around my house behind my back trying to figure out if I would be worth his time."

"All right," she said, giving me an encore of her humility performance from that night at the beach after ripping my tenant apart. "I'll try to keep my mouth shut. But you know, I can't stand to see anyone taking advantage of you, and I think that is happening now. You're just a nice guy who needs someone to stand up for you."

As we finished the meal and prepared to leave I realized I had a couple more items to add to her secret agenda. And these appeared more threatening than the rest. She wanted me to help her generate income through my job at the courthouse. And, she obviously had decided I might be worth more than she initially had thought.

Finally, I was starting to get nervous. I realized Catherine was moving to take control of my life.

THIRTY-ONE

November 1979

Although I moved into Jim Strong's house on November 1, paying him a hundred dollars monthly for a bedroom with a closet, I continued to spend most of my time with Catherine at Mike's place in far west Houston. And, in the weeks before Thanksgiving we spent a lot of time with Strong as well. I recall that period now as similar to the lull later in my life before Hurricane Alicia in 1983: peaceful, but punctuated here and there by a few ominous clouds.

One Saturday the three of us drove to Galveston to walk around the older sections of the historic city rather than visit the beach. We had a charming lunch and shopped at the huge Army-Navy surplus store in Galveston's Strand district. Strong had fun teasing Catherine about her reputation, offering to purchase old World War I gas masks and showing her a box of grenades.

"Use these on your next job," he said. "There will be no witnesses."

She took it all in stride, enjoying the attention from her colorful aura. On the way out of town we noticed a sign for a fortune teller in the window of an old house and stopped to have our palms read. I've never been a believer in the occult. But that experience proved downright spooky. The Gypsy woman read Strong's palm and jabbered about his need to fulfill his potential. After searching Catherine's palm, however, the laughter died as the old woman refused to share anything about it and insisted on refunding the two dollars that Strong had given her. Then, when the woman felt my hand, she looked into my eyes and refused again. I demanded a reading.

"You are in very great danger," the old woman said.

Strong repeatedly has sworn over the years that he did not set that up or pay the woman extra for her dramatic presentation. Catherine laughed it off, speculating that the old woman probably played that game routinely as a way to generate repeat customers and had just picked us at random for her pitch.

On another Saturday night, Catherine complained about an infected mosquito bite on her ass, claiming I was to blame. She said the bite had occurred while servicing my lust during our tryst on the beach and later got infected. She insisted I take her to an emergency room and pay any expenses above what her State Bar of Texas medical plan would cover.

"You got what you wanted, and now I'm the one who has to suffer," she muttered.

We walked into the emergency room at Houston's Memorial Southwest Hospital to compete with the usual Saturday night crowd of blood and gore waiting for service. Unmoved, Catherine strolled forcefully to the nurse's station with her complaint of a bug bite on her ass and demanded immediate help.

"Listen," she lectured the nurse. "I am a lawyer. Do you understand what that means? My time is too valuable for this. I bill at the rate of two hundred dollars per hour. I have clients who depend on me right now. I don't have time for this. I have to be available if something happens. So get me a doctor right away."

The nurse yawned in the middle of Catherine's tirade, then shoved a clipboard in her direction and told her to fill out the form and take a seat. Catherine repeated her demand a few minutes later while returning the form, but the nurse just pointed back to the chair. During the next three hours Catherine pitched her case repeatedly to the same nurse who continued to yawn and point her back at the chair. Catherine watched in horror as the nurse ushered patients with broken limbs and bloody faces into the rooms ahead of her bug bite on the ass. Each time she demanded her turn and each time the nurse pointed at the chair. I had a hard time holding my laughter.

Finally, her turn arrived. She insisted I accompany her into the curtained examination cubicle, telling the doctor, "I insist on a witness." Then she pulled a pen and a notebook from her purse and asked for his name.

"We'll need this information in case there has to be a malpractice suit," she said. I started laughing but he was not amused. He grunted when she added, "I am a lawyer, and I know what happens in these hospitals."

Then he prescribed an antibiotic and sent us on our way.

Just as she'd promised, Catherine refrained from debating my divorce case or making comments about my marriage. We grew better acquainted and went to old movies like *Casablanca* and *Red Dust*. We saw some fresh releases, too. Catherine embraced a line from the police murder drama *The Onion Field*, chuckling as one of the characters chided another who had expressed a conscience about his actions: "Guilty is just something you say in the courtroom when your luck runs out."

Whenever we encountered some old pal of hers while crawling the bars, she'd introduce me and then demand I repeat what I had said to Chuck when he warned me about her. That, too, became one of her favorite lines.

We spent a lot of time together alone at Mike's house while he was out making arrangements for his wedding. She took pride in her cooking skills, preparing a variety of dishes from Greek salads to shrimp scampi or something as simple as hamburgers. She told me about her affair with the cop named Joseph and how sexually charged it had been to watch him unbuckle his Sam Browne gunbelt, then hang it over the bedpost before climbing beneath the covers with her. Of course, she kept a .32-revolver on the table beside her bed and said she had a .22 stashed somewhere, a memento from her father.

"I need to be prepared," she warned. "You never know when the 'Tedescos' are going to kick down the door here and come for me."

Tedesco remained a common theme in her conversations. No day passed without a mention of his name or the names of other lovers from her past who had suffered their own particular punishments for alleged transgressions against her. I felt like a confidante to someone truly living on the edge. She ridiculed that court bailiff who had testified against her in the estate trial and boasted about destroying his marriage.

"That's how low I had sunk, to have sex with a slob like that," she said. "And then, he wouldn't even pay for my abortion. All I needed was two hundred dollars, and it was his bill to pay. Nothing is free. But he didn't pay and look what happened. He's out on the street, his family is gone, and he has nothing. Even at that, if I saw him and his kids in the desert begging for water and I had a little in my canteen, you know what I would do? I would pour it into the sand in front of his face and watch them all die of thirst."

She asked one time to watch me masturbate and I obliged. She said she'd never seen that before.

"You should have asked me years ago," I said. "Thanks to you, I now only have to beat off twice a week."

She adopted that line as well and started sharing it with other friends any time we met some.

"Gary says he only has to jack off twice a week now that he's met me," she would say with a girlish giggle. Then she would order: "Tell them how you handled Chuck."

I kept my word on the defense appointment opportunity and asked Edd Blackwood to check her out. I figured he would toss her a burglary plea, but then he shocked me by assigning her to defend a murder case against an Hispanic gang leader named Blackie that would probably go all the way to jury trial.

"Hey," I asked him, "you didn't do that for me did you? That sounds like a complicated case."

"Nah," he said. "She checked out OK. She's got some experience. If she can't handle it, we'll pull her off and reassign it."

Then, one Saturday after a bottle of wine with shrimp scampi, she ran out of things to say. Candles danced in the darkened dining room of Mike's house, and she sat quietly as if considering the moment. She reached across the table and took my hands.

"Gary, I want you to listen to me. What if I were to tell you that I did kill George?"

"Huh?"

"What if I told you that we had a meeting that night to talk about our divorce case? We were talking in his garage, and I was making him angry. He was vicious when he got angry. He was a dangerous, little man."

She paused, looked down at the table, and then returned my stare.

"What if I told you he started to make threats, and he doubled up his fists. And I couldn't take another beating from that man. I was not going to take another beating. So, I looked around for a weapon, and I saw the leg of a bar stool against the wall. He came for me, but I was too quick. I jumped out of his way, and I grabbed that chair leg, and I hit him in the head. When he fell, I hit him again and again and again. I couldn't stop. I kept beating him until I was exhausted, and then he was dead. What would you say if I told you that?"

She left me speechless. I shook my head and tried to guess her intention with this confession—if that was what it had been. She stared, awaiting an answer.

"I don't know what to say. What do you expect me to say?"

Catherine laughed then and said, "I just wanted to see the look on your face."

"How did I look?"

"I think I scared you."

It could have been a performance. If it was, I thought, she should get an award. I would have sworn from the tone in her voice and glint in her eyes that she had been there.

As shocking as that confession had been, it couldn't top another comment from Catherine in those days as our relationship approached the Thanksgiving holiday mark. She drew my undivided attention one evening when she mumbled and tossed off another riveting remark:

"I think my period is late."

THIRTY-TWO

November 1979

Already troubled in my mind, our relationship began its full transition into a war zone on the Sunday night of November 11 when Catherine and I returned to her house after a weekend trip to Austin in her car. We arrived about eight to find her roommate Mike waiting to have a chat. He took her aside to speak privately for only a few minutes while I relaxed in Catherine's bedroom. Then he climbed in his car and left while she joined me wearing a serious look on her face.

"We've been evicted," she said with a giggle.

"We?"

"Well, I am evicted now because of you. He said either you go, or we both go. You know what I told him?"

"I'm afraid to guess."

"Ha! I told him, 'I'll never give him up, even if I have to sleep in the gutter.' Ha! He said he can't stand your car parked in front of his house all the time."

"I can park it down the street."

"He also doesn't like the noise all night long."

For a moment, I saw this development as perhaps an opportunity to accomplish the inevitable and put some distance between us. She had grown too possessive, and I had spotted a few danger signals. But she wouldn't have it.

"Maybe we should cool things for a while," I said. "I'm over at Strong's now, and you're back in business. We can…"

"Wait a minute," she cut me off. "You're not dumping me over this. You don't dump me."

"Well, you can dump me. I'll tell everybody it was your idea," I said, thinking, *as if anyone could care.*

"I can't stay here after this. I've told Mike to fuck off because we're leaving. We'll be out in a week. And you better find me a place to stay. There has to be room at Strong's. We don't take up much space, and that stooge is out running around all night anyway, isn't he? No, you got the pussy, and now you have to make this right. Nothing is free."

I should have been offended, I guess, by that tirade, but instead I found it amusing, and I realized I wasn't quite ready to break away. She had played the guilt card, blaming me for her eviction. Although I did not agree with her contention, I let it slide without an argument. I checked with Strong, and he immediately agreed to let her bunk with me for a while until she could find a more permanent solution, mumbling something about being a little lonely over there and looking forward to the excitement Catherine might introduce to his life. It would take him only eleven more days to adopt a dramatically different attitude. By then, however, we would have passed a point of no return, with Strong poised to experience more excitement than he ever could have imagined.

I tried to move Catherine in drips and drabs, using the cars. Like me, she had no large pieces of furniture. Besides the two pistols, her prized possession was a Sony color television set I figured had come from a burglary client as payment for a bond. But I didn't ask specifics. She mostly had clothes she did not want wrinkled. Left alone, I would have tossed her whole closet in my Vega and sorted it out later. But she demanded more respect for her clothes and threatened to serve me with a dry cleaning bill for any wrinkles. For a woman who allegedly had the power to mobilize an army of felons for burglaries on a moment's notice, Catherine really had trouble finding anyone to help her move. So the burden fell on me. But, as she reminded me several times during the week, "Nothing is free."

As it turned out, however, she was not the only one in my life who was moving. I had gotten Catherine well resettled into Strong's house and prepared to have a meal at home on the evening of Monday, November 19, when the phone rang and she answered. Cindy, on the other end, asked for me. Catherine handed me the receiver then perched nearby, hanging on every word she could hear.

"I called to tell you I have moved out of the house," Cindy said.

"That doesn't make much sense," I replied. "We're still making house payments so somebody should be living there. Now I'm paying rent here, and you're paying rent wherever you are. Where are you anyway? What's the address?"

"I can't give it to you."

"What's going on?"

"I just can't give you this address. Al doesn't want you to have it."

Uncle Al again, I thought. I looked at Catherine and popped my eyeballs out to make her laugh. She didn't. I figured that Al now had persuaded Cindy to join him in a new love nest somewhere that wouldn't have the smell of me in the walls. And I was willing to bet they had used a moving company to handle my furniture. But I got a little upset about Cindy's reaction to my request for the address. So I offered a compromise.

"Well," I said, "why don't you tell me the new address for my children? Al can't object to that, can he? I think the lawyers would order you to do it."

Cindy chuckled at that and, for a moment, sounded conciliatory. She said, "It's a little house in West University Place…"

Then, suddenly, I heard a pop, and the telephone line went dead. I stared at the receiver in my hand, looked at Catherine with a shrug of my shoulders, and hung it up.

"I heard a strange sound and now the phone is dead," I told her.

"I can't sit still about this any longer," she said. "Cindy has moved out of your house and won't tell you where she lives? It is time now for you to hire a real lawyer and go after that bitch."

Although I wanted to tell her to mind her own business, I found myself warming to her rant. Cindy had angered me with everything from her unexpected relocation to her obstinate attitude on the new address. I agreed that Catherine had a point and decided to listen. But, of course, she instantly pushed her wise counsel beyond the limits of reason.

"And, I think it is time to unleash the clients," she said, sounding like a gang leader with a mob at her disposal. "Cindy needs a good beating. Nothing drastic but just something to get her attention."

Before I could respond, the phone rang again and I answered.

"Gary," Cindy began, her voice shaking for some as yet unknown reason. "Do not try to find us. I will try to straighten this out as soon as possible. But if you come over here somehow, there could be trouble. Something is going wrong. And you already have enough trouble with your new girlfriend."

"Oops," I told her, "I think you just stepped in a bucket of shit with that remark. I can tell you, she's the last person on earth you want in your face right now."

"Be patient, that's all I can say." And she hung up.

"Bucket of shit?" Catherine asked.

"Yeah, she told me I have enough trouble with you without biting off some more at her house."

I could feel the steam pouring out of Catherine's ears.

"Now I *am* going to call the clients—"

"No, you aren't doing anything. It's not your fight. Stay out of it."

She sat quietly for a moment, gathering her thoughts, then made a fist and pointed a finger at me.

"You know what I think now? I think you are going to give me a share of your house when it sells. I think I deserve it for all the bullshit I have had to suffer."

I couldn't help myself and started to laugh.

"You think this is funny?" she asked. "I'm serious. You owe me."

Yeah, yeah, blah blah blah, I thought, tuning her out. I had reached a point where I could not really tell how serious her threats might be. *Are you for real?* I wanted to ask. But I didn't want to spend any time on that debate, as dangerous as it might be to underestimate her potential for havoc. Instead, I focused on Cindy and my daughters. Something suddenly seemed twisted on that side of my life, and I felt concerned. I figured I would hear more soon enough, but I could not help but be anxious.

"Please give me a break," I finally told Catherine in an effort to shut her up. "I'm getting confused here, and I need to think about all this before I make any moves. You can lay off for a couple of days, can't you?"

She scowled but nodded and let it drop.

THIRTY-THREE

November 21, 1979

It took Cindy just two days to elaborate on her mysterious phone call, and, when she did, it brought the stew of my relationship with Catherine into its first hard, dangerous boil. Shortly after noon on the day before Thanksgiving, Cindy popped her head through the press room door and motioned for me to take a walk. Strong saw me leave our shared office but said nothing. The courthouse was deadly slow that day before the holiday, with many of the courts in recess. Cindy asked to go someplace private, so I took her to a vacant courtroom where we talked in the dark. She was quaking like a little dog that had just been caught messing the floor. She was terrified, and this was the first time I ever had seen her this way.

"I want off this treadmill," she said, trembling as we sat along one of the attorney tables in the dim light. "Al is crazy."

"What are you saying? Now you don't want the divorce?"

"I can't take any more of this. You don't know how crazy he is. He wants to control everything I do."

"You want us back together?"

She nodded, looked at me, and said, "He shot the telephone."

I didn't quite grasp her remark and tried to envision that in my head. I squinted with my eyes, then stared in an expression of disbelief.

"He did that, Gary! He shot the telephone while I was talking to you. That's why it went dead. That's why I didn't want you coming anywhere near the house. There is a hole in the phone. You can see it if you want to."

Although I genuinely felt sorry for her, realizing that her dream love affair had turned into a nightmare, I started to laugh at the image in my mind of a doctor pulling a pistol from his white coat and drilling a telephone while Cindy had the receiver up to her ear. I had never even seen Uncle Al so I had to improvise for his face. But Cindy I could conjure. I imagined her eyes popping out and her feet jumping off the floor when the gun discharged.

"Sorry," I said when she scowled at my involuntary reaction. "I don't know what to say. Where were the girls?"

"They were in bed, but they must have heard the gunshot. I can't stand this any more. He has me so frightened."

Jeez, I thought. *Have we exchanged our marriage for a season pass to theatre of the absurd?*

I started to grow angry at the thought of my girls exposed to danger. If Uncle Al could shoot a plastic telephone because I was on the other end of the line, I wondered what he must feel every time he saw Little E or Shannon, knowing my blood and genetic material coursed through their veins.

"We have to fix this," I said. "You can't allow him near the girls."

"I know it, I know," she started to cry. "He's gone. I told him to leave. But I'm so confused. I don't know what to do. Have we gone too far? Is there any going back?"

I took her hands and said, "Of course. Is that what you really want?"

In the weeks since we had split up, I had thought a lot about what I really wanted. I had decided I could live without Cindy, and I could live as a visiting parent. I could live with the divorce. But I also decided that the girls would be better served with a reconciliation, even if our marital relationship could never be the same. Our home had not been wracked by fighting or become any hellish place to live, as happens in many cases where couples drift apart, making existence unbearable for the children. In fact, we were still having fun as a couple when she had shocked me with her decision to separate. Just as unexpected had been this day's attempt to make up. But I realized I could not hesitate, believing I would figure a way to fix that, too, if we reconciled. What I did not understand, however, was the secret hold of Uncle Al on Cindy—ammunition he carried in his prescription pad. It would be nearly a year before I unraveled the true extent of those powers. On this day before Thanksgiving, however, I was ready to do whatever she wanted if it would ensure the safety of our kids. I thought maybe she had decided she preferred a dedicated partner to a romantic lunatic. Her dilemma sounded familiar, and I knew we had one more dangling problem to discuss.

"You know," I said, "I'm in a bit of situation, too."

"Mehaffey?"

I nodded and said, "This won't be easy. She's already shown some warning signs, and I've about had my fill of her."

"I'm really depressed."

She looked it, too. I realized Cindy was on the edge. I could understand if she felt guilty about the way our marriage had disintegrated and the impact of her decisions on our girls. I wondered if she might be suicidal. So I offered to call my former therapist and see if he could talk with her that night. He had invited us both to come see him, so I didn't see a conflict. And I felt he would already have the background on our situation to allow for a quick consultation. She agreed, I called from the courtroom, and he told me to have her swing by that evening about six.

"Can you pick up the girls from day care and take them to the house?" she asked. "I'll come back after the session."

"Sure. But you'll have to give me the address."

Cindy grinned. Then she took out a pen and wrote the address on a piece of scrap paper there. I folded it up and put it in my shirt pocket as she got up and left.

"Thank you," she whispered as she opened the double doors and walked into the courthouse hallway.

THIRTY-FOUR

November 21, 1979

Catherine and Strong caught me as I left the courtroom after giving Cindy enough time to flee unseen. They had been walking down the hallway checking all the rooms.

"What's up?" joked Strong. "We heard you had a meeting with Cindy somewhere and wanted to make sure you were safe."

Catherine scowled and said nothing.

"Yeah," I said. "She has some problems. Any news breaking around here?"

Catherine eyed me coolly as Strong nodded in the negative.

"Quiet as a tomb," he said, emphasizing *tomb* with a sickening grin.

"Let's get a beer," I said. "I need to talk."

Catherine maintained her silence while we took an elevator down to the courthouse lobby, walked outside, and strolled to the Hoagie Shop in the next block. It was a quiet little sandwich joint that also sold cans and bottles of beer. We often visited the place in the afternoons for the reporter's version of a coffee break. On this occasion, we each grabbed one of those huge cans of Australian Foster's Lager, popped the tabs, and sat down.

"Cindy's doctor boyfriend shot her telephone," I began.

Strong started laughing, but Catherine leaned into the table anxious to hear more.

"I'm not kidding, or, at least, I don't think *she* was kidding," I said. "She's all fucked up."

"Good," said Catherine. "She needs to be fucked up."

"Well," I said, "I have to think about the kids. She has a doctor's appointment at six and needs me to get them from day care, so I guess I'll be busy with them tonight."

"The hell you will," Catherine snarled. Her tone wiped the smile from Strong's face, and he jerked back in his chair. I took a long sip from the beer while she continued her harangue. "I had plans for us tonight, and they didn't include you leaving to spend time with your ex-wife and kids. You'll have to tell her to get a babysitter."

"No," I said. "I need to get them. Besides I haven't seen them in a while."

Now she took a long sip of beer and measured her next reply.

"I don't need this bullshit," she said. I had expected some problems with Catherine but had underestimated the toxicity of her venom. I'd just assumed she'd agree that the kids should always come first. And I didn't know of any plans we had that would interfere, besides the regular routine of having some drinks somewhere and going home. But it instantly became obvious to me, Strong, and several others in the Hoagie Shop that Catherine had lost control. She raised her voice and began to stutter a list of her complaints: "Calls in the night. Visits to the courthouse. Cindy has problems. And, I just don't need this bullshit in *MY* life."

The Medusa stare twisted into just the most visible demonstration of body language that warned she was poised for action. Before I could brace myself, she leaned across the table, knocked her beer to the floor, and grabbed a pen from my shirt pocket. She stood up with that in her hand and slammed it onto the floor where she started stomping on it. I stood up and moved to leave as Strong pushed back from the table and stood up, too. Before I could reach the door, she caught me and grabbed my necktie, pulling on the knot.

Jesus, I thought, *am I going to have to fight her?*

Catherine would not let go of the tie as I tried to move to the door, so I dragged her along beside me. She was screaming orders, demanding that I could not go get my kids. Strong and other patrons watched with their mouths agape. When I stopped moving, she dropped the tie. I knew I had to avoid a physical confrontation at all costs, but I also knew she would grab hold again unless I resumed our debate.

"If you go over to get those girls, Gary, we are through," she warned, as if that would represent her most serious threat. I stood there and stared into her cold, hard eyes.

"I am," I said. "And we are."

Then I turned and walked out the door as fast as I could. But I heard her footsteps behind me, rushing in pursuit. I hustled toward the corner and turned to look over my shoulder at the chaos unfolding on the sidewalk in front of the Hoagie Shop. Catherine had taken an umbrella from its attachment on her briefcase and was smashing it against the brick wall beside the sandwich shop picture window. No one moved to stop her. Strong had retreated to the curb, where he watched this lover's spat with an agonizing look of disbelief. I just wanted to get away, but I had to stop when I heard her footsteps again, moving toward me with the shaft of that shattered umbrella in her hand. I turned and involuntarily raised my arms to ward off the blows I believed would flow from the shaft. By then, however, Strong had come out of his trance and grabbed her from behind. She was sobbing as he held her back.

"What do you want me to do, you bastard?" she screamed and pointed to the curb. "Should I crawl down in the gutter here and beg you?"

"I'm leaving, Catherine. I don't care what you do."

I crossed the street, went to my car, and drove away, truly shaken by her outburst. If I had been watching that scene from across the street as a disinterested third party, I would still have been laughing while phoning friends to share the story. As a participant, however, it had sent a chill up my spine that spread across my shoulders and settled in for the night. Then I wondered if maybe I had been too hasty in counting her behavior out of line. In my life I had never experienced anything similar from a girlfriend or wife, but I knew things like that occurred. I had covered trials that included testimony about temper tantrums like I had just witnessed. Then I remembered, too, that testimony about those outbursts usually had presaged further testimony about murder or mayhem. I wondered how Strong was handling her in the wake of my departure. I thought maybe she would turn to him in the midst of her crisis and out of that comfort might spring a new love affair for my deliverance. Of course, I would move from Strong's house and let the lovers have their way, if only they would ask. Or, maybe they wouldn't even have to ask. But I quickly dismissed this delusion as wishful thinking. And I knew Strong would be fine as long as he was willing to listen to a filibuster of Senatorial proportions.

I also knew I was facing more trouble than I had first imagined. Her secret agenda of reasons for wanting me in her life had just added its most deadly element: pride. I realized she was so threatened by the thought of rejection that she could easily lose control.

What a worthless and destructive emotion is jealousy, I thought. It's the bad mother in any relationship that always eats her young. It destroys judgment and ruins lives.

And I knew I had not seen the last of its unpredictable wrath. From Uncle Al to Catherine Mehaffey, Cindy and I had dug ourselves an ugly hole in what felt to me like quicksand.

So, I picked up the girls from their school and drove them silently to Cindy's new home, where we parked outside to wait for her. I took the innocent eighteen-month-old Shannon in my arms, squeezed her as tight as I could, and began to bawl.

"I will get us out of this," I mumbled between sobs while Little E watched from the back seat without a clue about what she should do. *They don't deserve this mess*, I thought as I wept and promised again, "I will get us out of this, somehow."

THIRTY-FIVE

November 21, 1979

By eight-thirty I had given up on Cindy. I had sat with the girls in my old car outside her new house for at least an hour and a half after a dinner at McDonald's. I couldn't get inside, of course, but it looked nice enough. It was a one-story bungalow in Houston's semi-tony West University Place neighborhood, an area that catered to young doctors on the rise in the nearby Medical Center complex and professors at Rice University. I grew worried and tried to figure out a plan. In those days before cell phones, I had no way to reach her. I knew that appointment with the shrink should have ended by seven and feared a catastrophe. Concern about a suicide attempt topped my list of possibilities, so I decided to take a drive.

The girls fell asleep as I cruised the western side of the Loop highway that circles Houston like a wheel around spokes. I don't know what I thought I might see. She was driving our old, mustard-colored Dodge van, so maybe I hoped that would stand out if she had been in a wreck. More likely, I just wanted to think a bit. My drive carried me clockwise around the city until I found myself approaching our old neighborhood in the Houston Heights. I knew I had to do something, so I drove to our house there on Redan and parked the car. I took the girls across the street to the home of our former neighbors and asked if I could use their telephone.

"Where the hell are you?" asked Strong with more than a tinge of anxiety in his voice when I called him at his house.

"Looking for Cindy," I said. "Is something wrong?"

"You better get your ass over here fast. Cindy called a little while ago looking for you. Catherine took the call, and it went crazy. She told Cindy she has the kids over here and that she is now your lawyer. Catherine told her you can't talk with her again, and all conversation must go through her. Cindy's on her way over here now. I don't know what Catherine plans to do, but I'm sure there's going to be trouble."

"I'm on my way."

I left the girls with our old neighbors and pulled up at Strong's just after Cindy had parked her van in the driveway. I climbed out of my car just as Catherine stormed out of the house toward the van with Strong in her wake. I raced to cut her off and stood in her way.

"What are you doing now?" I asked her.

"Let me handle this," she ordered. "Where are those girls? You really need to have those girls."

"You're not handling anything," I replied. She stopped and stared at me. I said, "You need to go back inside. I'll send her away."

She seemed to consider my demand a few moments and then backed toward the house, avoiding a physical confrontation. I recalled the umbrella-smashing of just a few hours earlier and concluded she must have cooled down since then. Taking advantage of this opportunity, I turned and went to Cindy in the van.

"Where the hell have you been?" I asked. "We waited in that car outside your house forever."

She sat in the driver's seat, sipping on a soda from a Jack-in-the-Box and looking no more concerned than if she'd just arrived a little late for someone's birthday party. Comparing my recollection moments before of Catherine at the Hoagie Shop with her retreat in Strong's yard, I contrasted Cindy's dazed appearance with that of the afternoon in the courthouse when she seemed on the verge of suicide. I wondered if I had stumbled into the *Twilight Zone*.

Am I the only one here who missed the guy passing out tranquilizers? I thought.

"I had to take a drive after my appointment and clear my head," she said between sips. "Where are the girls?"

I looked over my shoulder and saw the shadows of Catherine and Strong watching from inside his door.

"They are at Liz's," I said. "What did Catherine tell you?"

"Catherine? She said she's your attorney now and the girls were here."

"Don't believe anything she says."

"I don't. Did you see my new house?"

"Yes. You better go pick up the girls. We can talk later."

"Will I see you this weekend?"

"I'll call you when I can get away."

She finished her soda, tossed the cup onto the floor of the van, and backed out of the driveway. I turned toward the house and almost got trampled by Strong running for his car. He jumped behind the wheel and peeled out, gone for the night. I trudged up the sidewalk and passed Catherine standing silently in the doorway.

"This isn't going to work with us," I told her, as she followed me inside closing the door behind her. I wanted to offer a compromise, breaking up on terms that would not resemble outright rejection. "A lot of things are good between us, but, in the end, all I can see is a bunch of trouble. We're like gasoline and a match."

I could see she was furious and just biting her tongue, collecting her thoughts as she devised a strategy for her next move. I wondered if I would get anger, guilt, pity, or something new. She decided on something new: logic.

"It's a shame about us," she said. "If we lived on a deserted island, just the two of us, we'd have a great life. No Special Crimes, no Cindy, no Strong, no outside distractions. Just us all alone. We'd get along fine. So, why can't we make that happen here?"

Yeah, I thought, *I bet you'd like to have me alone on a deserted island.* I flashed back to her comments on her philosophy of life from our night at the beach: Everyone is either predator or prey? *We could have an eternity of hunting on that island,* I thought. *I'd never get any rest.*

"There will always be distractions, other people," I told her instead. "We have to realize together that we just don't work as a couple. We're only going to hurt each other. I'll help you find a new place to live, and we'll get on with our lives. We'll see each other at the courthouse, say, 'Hi,' and move on down the hall."

"Bullshit!" She obviously wasn't buying it. "You'll not say, 'Hi' and then walk on by like I am some piece of shit you threw in the gutter. I have to work there. I can't be humiliated by some reporter."

I just stared at her and tried to sort through my options. I knew I would have to find a new place for her to live and oversee a continuation of her move, transferring property from Strong's and gathering what was left at Mike's. I realized it might require some sort of physical confrontation but knew it would have to be done. I decided to avoid any emotional outbursts and let her rant. She needed no encouragement.

"You have ruined my life," she screamed. "I gave up all my friends for you. I gave up the place where I live. I bought you expensive lunches at Charlie's. I spent money on you. I did anything I could to win your love and asked: 'What else can I do? Can I get down in the gutter? Fall on the floor? Kiss your feet?'"

Where does she come up with this stuff? I wondered. Then I listened as the serious threats began.

"Well, you won't get off this easy. You've had everything you wanted, and now it's my turn. You are going to give me some of that house. I think ten thousand dollars is about right. I want ten thousand dollars when you sell that house. And I want you to continue finding me defense appointments. And I want you to pay my rent where I move. On top of that, I still haven't had my period."

"I'm going to bed," I said. "I'm worn out."

I ignored her and walked into the bedroom as if she wasn't there. I stripped off my clothes and crawled under the sheets. I didn't care if she joined me or not. But my action unleashed her savage fury. She raced to a closet and pulled out a suitcase. She opened it, screaming something about getting out of "this house of Strong." Before she could pack anything, however, Catherine apparently had second thoughts and decided instead to destroy the luggage. She smashed it against the walls and the door jam, snarling and shouting in an uncontrollable rage. I began to wonder if this was the last thing seen by George Tedesco, and that thought kept me alert. She gave that suitcase a thorough beating. Recalling it as the brand advertised so tough a gorilla could not destroy it, I thought: *Their competitors might like to look at it now.*

When she finished with the suitcase, she looked around the room and spotted my stereo receiver on the dresser. She yanked the plug from the wall, grabbed the receiver, and came toward the bed holding it above her head. I slid out from beneath the covers, stopped long enough to slip on my jeans, and ran for the front door. As I opened it, I heard footsteps behind me. Expecting to feel that stereo crunch down on my head, I turned in one motion and swung with my fist, timing the move so I caught her in the side of the face and sent her flying. When I saw she had left the stereo in the bedroom, I felt guilty. I had never smacked a woman until that night and never would again. Surely, I thought as I ran into the yard to hide behind my car, I could have handled this differently and not have her eternally on the guilty side of my conscience.

Catherine had risen and come to the doorway calling for me.

"Gary, come back inside. It's cold out there."

She was right. Houston's November chill had arrived, and I stood in the driveway, shivering behind my car in nothing but my pants. Once again, if I had been watching myself from across the street, I would have laughed. With my car keys inside the house, I obviously could not leave. I vowed then and there never to sleep in the nude again. With Catherine in my life, I figured

I never could know when I might have to flee in the night. Just as I was considering that thought, the cops arrived.

"You're really lucky," Catherine told me after they had left, and we had agreed to a truce. "It is rare when the cops come that someone does not go to jail. That's what they do, you know. Take people to jail. It's a good thing I didn't tell them about the beating."

"The beating?"

She rubbed the side of her face, and I saw she would probably raise a bruise. So, I made another vow to myself. Never again would I touch her physically unless backed into an absolute corner. A neighbor had called the cops, and I had told them I would leave the house if I could get dressed and find my car keys—even though I was the one living there. I insisted they stay until I was gone. Before I could dress, however, they had left, and Catherine intercepted me with a new attitude of restraint.

"Don't leave," she sighed. "I am starting to agree with you that this will never work. I can't have this kind of bullshit in my life. I have to get control. Why don't we talk about this in the morning? At least, we'll spend Thanksgiving together and have dinner with my mother. Then we'll see what we want to do."

She seemed like a completely different person from the Catherine of earlier in the day and into the night. I wondered if the visit from the cops had made her more reasonable. I was exhausted and had no place else to go. I believed if she honestly wanted a peaceful end to our relationship, I'd be better off in the long run. So I agreed to stay. But I didn't sleep much that night until I heard Strong return from wherever his night ride had taken him. I figured she would never do anything with a witness in the house.

Despite his late night, Strong awakened early on Thanksgiving morning—early enough to catch me carrying the morning paper in from the driveway. He took me aside and stood three inches from my face.

"Taylor, I want that bitch out of here," he said through clenched teeth that made me wonder what his night with her had been like before I arrived with Cindy. "If you have to pay her rent somewhere else, I will loan you the money. But get her out of here."

"She's going, Jim, she's going," I said. "But it might not be as easy as wishing it done."

THIRTY-SIX
Thanksgiving Weekend, 1979

Our battlefield truce held through Thanksgiving Day without any further outbursts. Catherine and I didn't talk much, but we took her mother to dinner later in the day. I knew I would have to take the initiative and act decisively to accomplish our split without incident, so I rose early on Friday and started checking the classified ads for an apartment for her. I found about half a dozen places in good locations close to downtown, where she maintained an office about three blocks from the courthouse. When I showed her the ads I had circled, she just stared.

"You know you need to live closer to your office and your work," I said, hoping to win her cooperation with logic focused on her ambitions. "You should get that law practice up by living where it's convenient. Don't forget, you have your first murder case to handle, and I want to make sure you do a good job. I'll make some calls and take you around to look at a couple of these places in the Montrose neighborhood.

"I lived in Montrose before," she said, sounding at least a little interested. The neighborhood was Houston's version of a Bohemian community. The houses dated from the 1930s and 1940s, with rental properties catering to an upscale target market of young professionals. Rents were reasonable, and I felt they certainly should have been within the range for someone in Catherine's position. Individual investors predominated as landlords, hoping to launch their real estate empires by subdividing old brick houses into small apartment buildings and duplexes.

Catherine remained uncharacteristically silent during our tour of several potential new homes for her. I hoped she simply wanted to reconcile her paranoia about rejection with the obvious reality of our incompatibility, but I couldn't be sure. I only knew we were making progress. When she seemed impressed with a one-bedroom duplex for four hundred dollars per month at 1723 Kipling Avenue, I talked her into it on the spot. The landlord lived in the older house next door. He wanted the first and last month's rent as a security deposit. Catherine stunned me by taking eight one-hundred-dollars bills from her purse and handing them to him. It was vacant, freshly painted, and ready for a tenant.

"We can start moving stuff tomorrow," I said, as we walked to her car across the lawn.

"I think you should pay half of that," Catherine replied without looking up.

"I'll see what I can do," I said, eager to leave before she had a chance to throw a fit or back out of the deal.

"I know I'm missing a period," she said, but I ignored her.

I had hoped Strong might be around to help move things, since he was so eager to have her out of his house. But he had vanished without a trace, off on some unknown quest, leaving me to cope with her on my own. Some of her belongings still remained at Mike's house in far west Houston, and the rest were at the house of Strong. She also said she had some furniture in storage. We tried moving everything we could fit into my car, but it seemed to take forever. I suspected Catherine was trying to stall, but I remained industrious. At one point on Saturday I even managed to sneak out and visit Cindy at her new house. She showed me the bullet-riddled telephone base and asked me if her rent house was "OK." She insisted she had chased Uncle Al out of her life and was just taking it easy in her new place, waiting for me. Between Cindy and Catherine, that weekend left me dazed, uncertain, and more than a little depressed.

Although Catherine had paid quickly to reserve the duplex at 1723 Kipling, she began dragging her feet on the move. And her solitude made me suspicious. We didn't talk about the future that weekend. I didn't want to set her off. Of course, every now and then she would mumble a subtle threat.

"You remember the court bailiff, don't you?" she asked me. "All he owed was about $250. Now he's lost everything."

I silently reviewed her secret agenda of reasons for wanting a relationship and decided to add another troublesome item: her fear of exposure on a wide range of activities ranging from her abuse of Bar rules on the bail bond certificate to her late night pseudo-confession on the Tedesco murder. I knew that none of it provided the sort of strong evidence that could cause her serious trouble. But I also realized her twisted mind might turn that fear into a rationalization for an irrational act, such as assault or even murder. If she truly had been involved in the Tedesco killing, I reasoned, she indeed would be a dangerous predator—one who likely took pride in the accomplishment of a kill. She had joked about Tedesco and other victims like the bailiff, incorporating them into her resume of fear and wearing their mysterious destruction like a badge of honor. I allowed my imagination to wander and realized: *What a trophy I would make if she could add a notch for me to her gunbelt after just a few weeks together and get away with it.* I wondered: *Am I just paranoid?*

Then I felt ashamed and ridiculous. Here I was at six feet tall, athletic and a relatively strong thirty-two years old living in fear of a five-foot-three-inch female. Of course, she had bragged about unleashing the clients, and, if that threat were true, they would level the field immediately. I also had to sleep some time. I couldn't lie awake to defend myself in case she decided to bash out my brains. I recalled medical examiner testimony about a murder victim assaulted like Tedesco:

His head resembled what you would expect of an egg dropped from a ten-story building and onto the concrete.

Nope, I decided, unpredictability reigned as her source of power, and it would be formidable. I had to stay alert.

Then my paranoia hit a new plateau on Monday night, November 26, when I fielded a call from Strong at our house. I had not seen that guy all weekend. He obviously had skipped out, waiting for her to move. He had returned to work at the courthouse that day, and I had gone back to his house, where Catherine told me she didn't think she could complete the move until the next weekend. Before I could figure my next step, I answered the phone.

"What's going on?" asked Strong.

"What do you mean? I'm trying to get her moved."

"No, there's something else I need to tell you. She called me today and asked me to check on her tonight. She said she is in fear of you."

"She's in fear of me?"

"She said you beat her once, and you might beat her again. She said you've been acting weird, and she may need my help."

"Ahhh, shit," I whispered, while Catherine puttered in the kitchen out of earshot. "That's bullshit, man. I am trying to get her out of here, but she is just not going very easily."

"I believe you," he said. "But I thought you should know, in case she's laying the groundwork for a self-defense story of some kind."

"Can you believe we are having this discussion? It sounds like something from a bad movie."

"What else can I say? You saw the suitcase. You saw the umbrella. She tried to get Cindy over here for God knows what. I think she is capable of incredible violence, and you need to watch your back."

I didn't sleep that night. I lay awake in the bed beside her, watching as she tossed and turned. At one point she woke up sweating and screaming. She told me she had dreamed of hell and wanted a priest. By morning I had decided on a new plan for extracting her from my life. We got up, then drove in separate cars to a little diner where we ate a quiet breakfast. I told her I would see her later and drove off. Instead of going to my office in the fourth floor press room of the criminal courts building, however, I walked across the street to the building where Harris County District Attorney John Holmes had his offices. I took the elevator to the sixth floor where the lawyers of his Special Crimes Bureau kept their desks and files. I asked the receptionist for Don Stricklin, the chief of Special Crimes.

"I need to talk about Catherine Mehaffey," I told Stricklin when he emerged from his office with a curious look on his face. "Would you like to listen?"

Stricklin nodded, ushered me into his office, and closed the door.

THIRTY-SEVEN

November 27, 1979

My decision to enlist Special Crimes in this soap opera would mark a significant turning point in both of our lives. To me, it was a stroke of genius that likely kept me alive. Many others saw it as the desperate act of a fool who had bitten off more than he could chew. Catherine later would say melodramatically that, from the moment I walked through Don Stricklin's doorway, I had entered "the arena of death." I became the Judas in her personal passion play and just the sort of betrayer every underdog heroine needs to justify her future actions. Her own attorneys later would joke about the decision, describing Stricklin as my "father confessor" and asking jurors with a sneer: "Should everyone who has a fight with his girlfriend now report it to Special Crimes?"

The answer, of course, was, "No." But that was precisely the point. Had my girlfriend been anyone but Catherine Mehaffey, I would have expected a horse laugh from Don with a look of, "Who are you kidding? Do I look like a psychotherapist?" Indeed, even though his assistant, Chuck Rosenthal, had personally warned me about her, I remained unsure how Stricklin would receive my visit that morning. I learned a great deal when he hustled me into his office as fast as possible and then asked if Jerry Carpenter could join us. Employed then as a district attorney's investigator for Special Crimes, Carpenter boasted an illustrious background as one of the Houston Police Department's legendary homicide detectives. I had known him when I covered the police beat in 1972. If Stricklin had assigned Carpenter as the bureau's Mehaffey expert, I realized she indeed represented a serious target for Houston's law enforcement community.

Carpenter only added emphasis to that realization when he told me that morning he considered Mehaffey the most dangerous individual he had ever tracked, male or female.

I expected nothing more than a symbiotic relationship with Special Crimes. Although I'm sure Stricklin and Carpenter legitimately wanted to help me, I also figured they primarily wanted to use me to get her. But just as Catherine had viewed me as a buffer between them, I believed I could use Special Crimes as a unique lever in my effort to shed her from my life. I suspected also that they felt a twinge of guilt about Tedesco, a man who futilely had begged the Houston police for help only to be ignored for nearly a year before having his brains scrambled on the floor of his garage. I saw myself as the living embodiment of déjà vu, a Tedesco encore in which they might draft a new ending. In that regard, my knowledge of the system proved crucial. Poor Tedesco just sought help from the street cops at the Beechnut Substation, where they laughed at him and told him to grow a pair of balls big enough to handle his girlfriend. I knew enough to bypass the lower echelon of law enforcement and take my story straight to the top. And the guys at the top proved more than eager to listen.

"I know I got myself into this, and I will have to get myself out," I began with Stricklin seated behind his polished and uncluttered desk and Carpenter lounging to my right in a chair. "That's going to happen, and I expect trouble. But I hoped you would be interested in taking a statement from me before I end up wearing a toe tag, something that might be used in a later investigation or trial—like the victim speaking from the grave. I also want to make sure I haven't inadvertently become involved as an accomplice in some sort of criminal activity she might have under way."

"We're listening," said Stricklin. "Do you mind if I record this?"

I nodded, and he reached into a drawer for a tape recorder. Stricklin and I were about the same age. A dapper, button-down guy, he looked like he might show up if central casting in Hollywood needed a stereotypical FBI agent. He had risen rapidly in the district attorney's office during his six years there and then, as chief of Special Crimes, held what was arguably the third or fourth most powerful job. Later he would win election as a state district court judge. I appreciated his reaction to my tale. He didn't lecture or remind me, "I told you so." He just sat and listened while I spun it out.

And I told it all, starting with my separation from Cindy and my first meeting with Catherine. I told them about the beach and the diamond ring. I told them about her questionable late night confession to the Tedesco murder. I told them about Uncle Al and the telephone. I told them about Cindy's change of plans and the busted umbrella. I told them about the smashed suitcase and how I had hit her when trying to flee the house. And I told them about the last couple of days trying to move her into the duplex.

"She kept saying she wanted a baby and then talked about her abortions and how they affected her outlook on life," I said. "She repeatedly said she did not kill Tedesco. She'd just bring it up out of the blue. She said she refused a lie detector test, but she agreed to answer four questions: Did you kill him? Did you have him killed? Do you know who killed him? And one other I can't recall. But she did not want to answer other questions so the police refused, she said."

Stricklin and Carpenter traded glances and grinned. Stricklin said, "We don't care about a lie detector test with her. It wouldn't mean a thing."

I continued: "She said she sent some clients to take art objects from Tedesco's house because she felt Tedesco owed it to her."

"Did she ever mention a client named Tommy Bell?" Stricklin asked.

"No," I grinned, "that name doesn't ring anything with me."

It was the first time I'd heard Bell's name in all of this. But it wouldn't be the last.

I told them how I'd become depressed the last couple of days and tried to exaggerate that to my advantage by growing nearly catatonic. I told them about the night before: "I'm Mr. Zombie. I lay down in the bed like a corpse." The recollection made me laugh, and I told Stricklin, "Can you imagine playing this tape at a trial where I am exhibit one?"

He didn't laugh, so I continued on: "She's rambling, 'I'm so frightened, I need a priest. I should go to confession.' I say, 'Why, have you done something wrong?' She says, 'So many things.' So I ask, 'Can you get a priest this time of night?' She says, 'No.' So I tell her, 'Maybe we can do that tomorrow.'"

I told them she had given me an ultimatum. She wanted to date through Christmas while I helped her make a lot of money in December using my influence to land indigent defense court appointments. If I did that, I told them, she said she would let it go.

"But now I've decided there will be no payment of money, no weaning, just nothing more," I told Stricklin and Carpenter. "Any contact from this point on will be forced by her."

"You're going to have contact with her," said Stricklin. "Either telephone or personally."

Carpenter added: "If you talk on the phone, you ought to record it."

Then Stricklin advised, "You have no liability to her. But that money is primary to her. If anything, she will look for revenge on you."

Carpenter said, "She thinks you've hurt her and used her."

I thought about my next move, then said: "What if I tell her I've been to Special Crimes, and I've given you a detailed recording, and if anything happens to me, you have it."

Stricklin stroked his chin in thought and said: "In one sense, there's nothing wrong with that. What I do see is that I'd like to know what her next move is going to be."

Carpenter predicted: "She'll go underground."

Just then, Stricklin's secretary entered the room and said that Jim Strong had come to the office and urgently needed to see me. Stricklin told her to have him wait a few minutes.

"Here's what I want to do," I said. "I want to call her from this office and record the call. I will tell her I am not going back to Strong's house until she has gone. I will tell her I am giving her nothing, I owe her nothing. I will tell her this is it, the end of our brief relationship, and that I have given a statement to Special Crimes that could be used if anything should happen to me."

Stricklin nodded affirmation and then offered a warning: "You know, we think she stalked Tedesco."

What an interesting word, I thought. I envisioned a lioness on the Serengeti Plains trailing a herd of zebra. It was the first time I ever had heard anyone use the word *stalking* in regard to human behavior. But I considered it right on the mark. Of course, within a decade the phrase would enter our daily vocabularies as lawmen and legislators worked nationwide to hammer out statutes making such conduct illegal. In the late 1970s, however, stalking prevention fell to the targets—people like Tedesco and me.

"Let me ask another question before we do this, OK?" Stricklin asked.

"Sure."

"Has she ever indicated anything yet about possibly being pregnant?"

"Of course. She says she's missing a period."

Stricklin and Carpenter traded glances, and I could tell by their expressions my cavalier attitude had left them confused. I let their expressions hang a few seconds and then offered my explanation.

"That wouldn't concern me," I said. "I've had a vasectomy, but I never told her. She wanted to handle our birth control so what else did she need to know?"

For the first time since I began covering either one of them, I enjoyed watching both Stricklin and Carpenter laughing out loud.

THIRTY-EIGHT

November 27, 1979

While Carpenter prepared the telephone for taping conversations, Stricklin ushered Strong into his office where I brought him up to date. He told us he had come over from the courts building because Catherine was frantic to find me. He said she had come to the press room and enlisted his help. After Stricklin's receptionist told him I had gone inside Special Crimes, Strong had reported back to Catherine with that news.

"She is freaking out," he said. "I told her you were probably over here working on some story, interviewing the lawmen, but she's sure it's something about her."

"It's always about her, isn't it, at least in her mind," I said. "I guess it's a good thing there's nothing going on in the courts today since we're both busy covering Mehaffey. She's a beat unto herself."

"So, what are you doing over here?"

"Taking out a life insurance policy," I said. He skewered his face in confusion so I explained.

"I gave Stricklin a statement on our relationship. Now I'm going to call her and tape record a conversation where I tell her I'm not going home until she's gone. And if anything happens to me, Don has my statement. If nothing happens to me, nothing happens to her."

164

"If you were talking about anyone other than Catherine Mehaffey, I'd accuse you of being melodramatic. But more importantly, now it looks like I'm the one who will need to get the rest of her stuff out of my house?"

I shrugged my shoulders, and Strong pondered for a moment while Stricklin looked on. Suddenly Strong volunteered: "I need to call her, too, and tape it, so I can make a record. This could get ugly."

Before I could reply, Stricklin jumped into the conversation and said, "That might give us a chance to see what she's thinking. She might talk to Jim more openly. Once you tell her you've been up here, Gary, she's going to clam up. And I can send somebody over to your house with you, Jim, to watch while she gathers her things. Is there much left to move from there?"

I shook my head, recalling only a few clothes and that Sony television she loved so much. But this plan for a tag team approach to Catherine caught me by surprise. Texas law always has allowed individuals to tape their own telephone conversations without informing the other party. Beyond the legal side, however, the practice always raised eyebrows and left the one making the tapes looking like a worm. Personally, I had no qualms about tape recording a conversation with someone who might threaten my life. After telling her about my statement to Special Crimes, I figured she would assume I was taping her anyway. And, if she asked, I would acknowledge.

But Strong's conversation would raise this maneuver to a new level. I figured Stricklin and Carpenter were hoping she'd crack and say something they could use against her. The more I thought about this prospect, however, the more sense it made. I knew I hadn't given Stricklin anything in my statement that could be used directly against her, unless I met a violent end. But I certainly needed to take her emotional temperature so I could brace for the worst. And if that led to her arrest for something she might say, we'd all be better off. I dialed her office, and she came to the phone.

"Where are you?" she asked.

"Special Crimes," I said, striving to sound firm and resolved, without giving her a chance to protest. "I have given them a statement. And now I want you to understand that we are through. I am not going back to Strong's house until you are gone. We'll have no further communication. Nothing more will happen unless you do something to cause it."

Obviously suspecting a recorder was running, Catherine responded with icy diplomacy designed to depict me as a rat.

"So you are up with the boys at Special Crimes making some tapes," she said. "And this is how it ends. Well, that's fine, Gary. You do whatever you think is best."

"I'm hanging up now, Catherine. This will be the last time we speak."

I hung up the phone and looked at Stricklin. He held up one finger for about a minute, then pointed at Strong, who dialed her office number again. What happened next would stun everyone in that room, including the hard-nosed crime dog, Jerry Carpenter. While her conversation with me seemed like a speech to the United Nations, the phone call from Strong would generate comparisons with scenes from a horror show. In fact, his recording soon would be known around the courthouse as the *Exorcist Tape*.

"Jim, Jim, I'm so scared," Catherine said as soon as she heard his voice. She seemed to be panting and filled with anxiety. "Why is he doing this to me?"

"Catherine, I think you've scared him. He's not used to being around your kind of violence."

Catherine rambled in her panic-stricken tone for a while until she talked herself into a higher level of frenzy, one marked by a succinct change in tone. She grew angry and finally bellowed with a sound reminiscent of Linda Blair's possessed ego from the movie *The Exorcist*. Then she started shrieking.

"I've done nothing wrong. Can't you stop him, Jim? He's gone insane. I've got to get away. I haven't done anything. I'm so trapped. He must take it all back. It has to start now. I can't bear it. He's doing it now, he's hurting me."

Strong winced as she raised the volume and screamed: "He got everything he wanted. He fucked my brains out. I'm not a dog. I'm so scared, Jim. I don't know what's happening. I'm starting to hate him. My God, we cannot live here another day. I've never killed anybody in my life. He's panicking. He can't do this to me in Houston. I have to live here, Jim. Couldn't he keep quiet? I'm scared. I've got to stop him."

She took a breath, then continued: "I do have hostility, tremendous hostility. He's got to call me. He's got to come here. He needs to beg for my mercy before this is over."

Beg for her mercy? I wondered if I had heard correctly, and even Carpenter looked stunned.

She continued, "I've never killed anyone but, Jim, he has done so much…"

"Catherine," Jim cut her off. "You need to be careful. If anything happens to him, now—if he gets hit by a bus—they will come looking for you. You need to make sure nothing happens to him."

"A bus? How can I stop it if he's hit by a bus?" she screamed in her demon voice. "He fucked my brains out and then threw me away. He's got to take it all back. He's got to beg for my mercy."

"Calm down, Catherine, calm down. We have to pick up the pieces now."

Almost as suddenly as the hysterics had come, however, she transitioned back to the sympathy-seeking waif. Listening live, I thought I might be witnessing a true split personality in action. But Strong wouldn't cave to her begging about staying longer at his house. They made arrangements to meet there one last time and finally ended the call. Listening to a replay then, I thought I might break a sweat, her voice sounding so surreal and indescribable. Stricklin made a couple of copies for us to keep and placed the original in his file.

"I would advise you guys to continue taping her calls," he said. "There will be more and you need to keep a record. Do you have a tape recorder at the house?"

We laughed. I did not own one, preferring to take notes in a pad with a pen. But Strong worked for a radio news service. He had recorders beside all his phones, ready to tape on a moment's notice for feeds to radio station broadcasts.

When Strong and I returned to the press room, our media roommates were suspicious. They thought we'd been out on a scoop. Instead, I locked the door that never had been locked and said, "It might be best if we keep this locked for a while."

Sandy furrowed her brows, and I could see we needed to provide more details. So Jim took his copy of the *Exorcist Tape* and popped it into his player. He only shared a portion, the part where she screamed, "He has to beg for my mercy." Then he shut it down.

"Oh…my…God," Sandy said, shaking her head. "Taylor, Taylor, what are we going to do with you?"

"Keep the door locked," I said.

"And," said Strong, "if you think that tape is bad, you ought to see the suitcase."

A couple of the other reporters started laughing.

"Love on the rocks," sang one, trying his best Sinatra to even more laughter.

"That's what happens as the world turns," giggled another of my sympathetic colleagues.

Then they all went back to work. They had given my story the five minutes of attention it deserved. But now it was time to dig up something for the next newscast or tomorrow's paper. I made arrangements to spend the night with Edd Blackwood, the court coordinator from Judge Routt's court. His wife was a Houston police officer, and I knew Catherine would not even know where he lived. Then I called Cindy to warn her.

"Gary, I need to tell you something," she said. "Al and I have made up. He's back in the house here."

Clearly, I decided, I would have to do something about the telephone-shooting Uncle Al living with my kids again. But at that particular moment, he ranked lower on my schedule. And just when I thought this day couldn't grow any more complicated, Strong called from his house, where he had gone with an investigator to oversee a peaceful transfer of property to Catherine.

"You know that television she loves so much?" Strong asked me.

"Yes."

"It was stolen property. They ran a serial number or something before she got here and it came back as hot. No wonder she wanted to get over here so quick."

"Where is it now?"

"They took it away and told her they had to process it. Man, was she pissed. They didn't arrest her yet, but I'm sure that's coming soon."

I hung up the phone and laid my head on my desk, unsure whether I should laugh, cry, or get into my two-hundred-dollar car with my grocery sack of laundry and drive west on Interstate-10 as far as it would run.

THIRTY-NINE

November 29, 1979

"There they go," Strong was saying as we sat on stools in a diner in the 500 block of Fannin Street staring through the large plate glass window toward the 609 Fannin Building directly across the street. It was about three in the afternoon and the air was bitter cold outside for Houston, even in November. The wind was blowing. And up the sidewalk on the other side of Fannin walked four men in suits looking very uncomfortable after a frosty, five-block stroll from the courthouse down the street. A raiding party from the district attorney's office, they were led by Don Stricklin, chief of Special Crimes. And they were headed for the law offices of Lloyd Oliver where Catherine Mehaffey also practiced her craft. Stricklin had tipped me about this mission, and I wanted to see for myself. I couldn't believe it was happening. They had enjoyed confiscating that stolen Sony TV so much, they now wanted to see if Catherine had any additional stolen property in her office.

Catherine and Oliver did not have a formal partnership. I never really knew the particulars of their arrangement. They shared a secretary named Rita but that seemed about the extent of it. Lloyd was a fairly successful attorney fond of the Yuppie nightlife and his Corvette. He treated Catherine much like an eccentric younger sister, and I always had the impression he handled her carefully. I doubted they had had any kind of sexual relationship, or he likely would have been in line with me outside Special Crimes seeking help from Stricklin. I even thought it likely he would let it slide if she didn't pay her rent. He might have been trying to stay out of her life and troubles, but now they were both poised to rain straight down on his head, if only for a couple of days. I would have loved to have seen the look on his mustachioed face when Stricklin and his gang stormed into his office looking for stolen goods. They found nothing.

But the raid capped an active couple of emotion-packed days for me. Although technically out of my life, Catherine had kept me so busy I hadn't even had time to mope about Uncle Al, Cindy, and the reconciliation that had derailed my reconciliation. No, Catherine had been calling all hours of the day and night to harangue, harass, and sometimes even make me feel guilty about her current state of affairs. Of course, every time I even hinted to Strong that I might feel even a twinge of sympathy, he would turn on his recorder and play back a portion of the *Exorcist Tape*. He had grown particularly fond of her voice threatening that "someday he's going to look around, and he'll see me standing there. And he's going to wish he'd never done this to me." And always he finished up with the chorus: "He's got to beg for my mercy."

The day before, Catherine had asked me to refer her to a psychiatrist, noting that I had done that for Cindy so I should do it for her. I asked Stricklin if he wanted to suggest a name and Chuck Rosenthal came up with one. The next thing I knew, Rosenthal's psychiatrist had checked Catherine into a hospital. Strong and I wondered how outraged she would become after learning that a Special Crimes psychiatrist had ordered the treatment. But Lloyd had come to her rescue, checking her out of the place after just a couple hours. Obviously aware of my visit to Special Crimes, he apparently felt my battle with Catherine was getting too close to his practice. Then, after Stricklin's subsequent raid on his office, Lloyd decided to bring Catherine along for peace talks that night during a surprise visit to our house.

"I can't have Special Crimes destroying my law office," he said forcefully, as Catherine sat quietly beside him on Strong's couch. Strong excused himself, went to a bedroom, and returned wearing a bicycle helmet.

"In case I'm hit in the head tonight," he said, pointing to the helmet as he sat down in a chair. Lloyd grunted, Catherine winced, and I stifled a grin.

"How can we put an end to this?" Lloyd asked.

"Just leave us alone," I said. "It's done as far as I'm concerned. I can't help because she had a stolen TV."

"It wasn't stolen," Catherine snarled. "It's the finest electronic device known to man, and now the stooges from Special Crimes have had their hands all over it."

"Catherine," I said, "you know that thing came from somebody wanting bail or something, and you just took it without asking questions."

"I bought it," she insisted. "There's been a mistake."

"Let's forget the TV for now," said Lloyd. "I'll buy you a new one. I want to know how we resolve this problem. We need a truce, or somebody might get hurt."

We all looked at Catherine. Finally she pointed at me and said: "You have to take it all back. I want the tape from Special Crimes. And I want you to go up there and tell Don Stricklin you're crazy. I want you to say, 'Don, I'm so sorry. I didn't know what I was saying the other day. I was just so upset because my wife loves some other man, and he shot her telephone. And, now I realize I've taken my anger out on Catherine, who has done nothing. Don, I am the one who is crazy. I take it all back.' Make a tape of that, and then get the other one back, and give it to me. That's what you have to do."

"That's not going to happen," I said stoically. But I was laughing on the inside, impressed with her bluster. In spite of the troubles Catherine had injected into my life, I still enjoyed her tirades, even while I had become the prime target.

"Catherine," said Strong, offering a compromise and looking like a clown in that helmet, "the tape has no meaning until you give it some. It will sit over there turning to mold if you just walk away and forget about it."

"I can't forget about that," she said, looking to Lloyd for support. "I can't have something like that laying around in my past for somebody to pull out and play whenever they want. Lloyd wouldn't stand for that either."

At this point, she had no knowledge of the *Exorcist Tape* made by Strong. She only wanted the tape of my statement about our relationship. I could only imagine her rage if she ever learned Strong had taped her meltdown with Stricklin, Carpenter, and me as an audience. The threats echoed in my head: *He has to beg for my mercy.*

Lloyd shrugged his shoulders on her demand, and I agreed that she had a point. Lloyd wouldn't want the cops to hold a statement like that on him, and, if he thought he could win, he probably would file a suit to order my tape seized and destroyed. But, I figured, too, that he wasn't in the mood for the kind of crusade required to fight Special Crimes.

"This is all so silly," Catherine said. "If we lived in Los Angeles nobody would bat an eye over a broken umbrella. They'd just call us normal."

"Don't forget the suitcase," said Strong. "That's the one the gorilla couldn't destroy."

In return, he received the *Medusa*. To his credit, Strong didn't even blink. And he didn't turn to stone. Lloyd realized his mediation had disintegrated and stood up apparently ready to leave.

"So that's it?" he said, looking first at Catherine and then at me.

"I think we settled it," I said. "There's nothing else to say as far as I'm concerned."

"We'll see about that," Catherine said, and they walked out the door.

FORTY

December 5, 1979

"Gary, there's been a serious mistake," Don Stricklin was saying in an afternoon phone call to my desk in the press room. "That stolen TV? Turns out it wasn't stolen. Our investigator miscopied the serial number while he was over at Strong's. It has to go back. Can you come over to my office?"

"Sure," I said. I pulled on my jacket and headed for the district attorney's office building, wondering why I had been summoned for this. I hadn't reported the television stolen. But I thought maybe there was something else. And I figured I needed to keep Stricklin in my corner. The last week since the visit from Catherine and Lloyd Oliver had been fairly quiet. We had received calls from Catherine at first and tape recorded all of them, delivering the tapes to Stricklin first thing each day. Sometimes she talked so long without stopping that we would take turns sleeping with the receiver on the floor and her just yakking away. I wanted to record any further threats, but she hadn't made any. Instead, she talked about her emotional trauma and apologized for frightening me.

I had to admit her new attitude was softening me. I had started to question my actions, particularly the betrayal to Special Crimes. Although I thought it had been a wise move, it still left me feeling weak and embarrassed—as if I had run to the principal after some bully had grabbed me in the schoolyard. I wondered if I hadn't overreacted to her tantrums and tried to relive them in my mind to determine if they had really been so threatening. She talked violently, of course, but I began to wonder if Catherine really wasn't about 80 percent bluff. One of her attorneys later would describe her to a magazine writer as someone with a "felony mouth and a misdemeanor mind." I never mentioned my second thoughts to Strong because I knew he's just play that *Exorcist Tape* again and show me the suitcase.

A couple of days before Stricklin's call, another of her attorney pals had paid me a bizarre visit in the press room. He had handled her estate case against the Tedesco family and obviously was considering an appeal of the jury's rejection of her claim as the widow. I had only met him briefly one time before, but he sat down beside my desk to chat just like old friends. He said he wanted to share some advice and learn what I might say if I were called to testify about Catherine in a retrial.

"All I can ever do is tell the truth," I told him.

"That's all we would ask," he said. Then he got up to leave while I shook my head.

As I arrived at Special Crimes, I was startled to see Catherine also walking to the door. She had a wide grin on her face and spoke to Stricklin as he opened it. "I'm here to confess," she said with a chuckle.

"I'm waiting," said Stricklin.

"I am the head of all illegal activity in Casablanca," she replied, repeating a Sidney Greenstreet line from that classic film. I smiled, and Stricklin grunted.

"Can't we get it a little closer to Houston?" he asked.

She changed the subject and pointed at me. "I want him to personally carry that TV down to my car and put it inside."

"Fuck that," I said. "I didn't have anything to do with them taking your TV. I don't even know why I'm here right now."

Stricklin shrugged his shoulders and looked at me. "She said she wasn't going to take it unless I got you to personally help load it up. Would you help me out here? I'll even help you carry it down there."

Obviously licked on this debate, I grabbed one end of the 25-inch Sony and helped carry it to the elevator. We followed Catherine out to the curb, where she unlocked her red Cougar and opened the back door. We slid it onto the seat. Stricklin thanked me and went back to his office, after I reassured him I would be all right talking with her on the street.

"Catherine, I know we have had our problems, but I am really sorry about this television fiasco," I said. "I had absolutely nothing to do with it."

"Nothing?" she purred. "You can't really say that can you? Didn't you get it started by running to Don Stricklin and Jerry Carpenter? But I know it happened because I can't control my temper. I know I have to work on that. You're not used to someone like me, a woman who stands up for herself. I understand."

Her eyes sparkled in the afternoon sun, and she tilted her head with a mischievous, cocky grin across her face. I had to agree with at least some of what she had said. I paused, and she stared at that huge television in her back seat.

"Now, how am I ever going to get that into my new apartment? Do you have any ideas?"

Forty-five minutes later I was lugging that Sony into the living room of the duplex apartment I had helped her rent at 1723 Kipling. I sat it down on a chest and looked around. She indeed had been busy. The place had a couch, books, lamps, stereo, and a rug on the floor. She had made it into a home. And she read my mind.

"Yes," she said, "I have to thank you for helping me find this place. I love it. It's so close to the office, and I have so much privacy. Just living here the last few days has given me a whole new outlook on life and how lucky I am."

She sounded like that first Catherine I had met, the ambitious professional in complete control. She had become again the woman who attracted me with her humor and spunk.

"Gary, I have experienced an awakening. I am really going to get my life in order and focus on my practice. You got me that murder case and I appreciate that…"

"Catherine, please, you got that yourself. I just introduced you to Edd. I don't want you telling people I used my position to help you get an appointment."

She waved me away and laughed, saying, "Whatever, whatever. Don't worry about that. You still introduced me, and I am grateful for that kindness. And guess what? I'm going to have a Christmas party right here in this apartment to celebrate my rebirth. I have to show people I'm still in there slugging. What do you think? Will you come?"

"Sure," I whispered, without considering the consequences. After twenty years or more to reflect on the events of this day, I'm still not sure why I did what I did next. I'm sure that Cindy's reconciliation with Uncle Al had left me a little depressed and vengeful. I'm sure the television fiasco had left me vulnerable, foolish, guilt-ridden, and confused about the single-minded behavior of my allies at Special Crimes. I'm sure a lingering spark of attraction had flickered into a small fire within my soul as she talked about her new attitude and the Christmas party. Most of all, I'm also sure I was extremely horny, and she looked exceptionally sexy. Perhaps it was a combination of all those certainties. Perhaps it was something else I'll never understand. But whatever it was, I decided then to give our relationship another try.

"I tell you what, Catherine," I said. "Why don't we get away from everybody tonight? I'll rent a room at the Holiday Inn and we can have dinner there. We can talk about the future and maybe find a way to move forward without killing each other."

"You're serious?"

"If we do that, can you promise me that I'll be safe? Can you promise me that if I fall asleep I will wake up in the morning?"

She nodded vigorously, panting and mimicking a cute puppy waiting for a walk. She put her arms around my neck and we kissed. That kiss was more passionate than ever before. And later, at the Holiday Inn, the sex was hotter than ever before. We had fried shrimp from room service and played with the tails. We split a bottle of champagne. I halfway expected to die that night, but I was beginning to feel like I didn't care. Cindy had hired her own lawyer, and our divorce showed signs of growing contentious. It felt like Catherine was all that I had. I felt like I owed her something for all that trouble. She wanted me to be her escort for the Christmas season. She said we should try it out. That way, she'd have a date for the lawyer parties around town, and she could show everybody I had no reason to fear her. I hoped maybe she would meet someone else in the days ahead and decide to dump me if I exposed her to such opportunities. I hoped we could find some way to separate peacefully, and, somewhere down the line, she could even become a chum who would share some drinks and tell some jokes. I knew I had always managed to get along with a wide range of people. *Why can't I do that with her?* I asked myself. And she assured me that once the holidays had ended, I could walk away if I wanted. And nothing would happen.

"Have you had your period, yet?" I asked.

"Yes, false alarm," she said.

"You don't have to worry about that any more with me," I said. "I've had a vasectomy."

"No more diaphragm?"

And when I woke up the next morning unharmed, I realized I had accepted a new mission with her. I expected another blowup likely would come and considered the idea of a long-term relationship delusion. But I also realized I enjoyed her company in more ways than one. I knew I could have a good time with Catherine during the holidays while I looked for a peaceful solution. I viewed her as a box someone had placed in my hands. When I looked inside, I saw that it held sticks of dynamite. At that point, I had two options. I could throw it to the side and try to outrun the explosion. Or, I could set it down gently somewhere along the sidewalk and just walk away. I was hoping I'd be able to do the latter.

Sure. And monkeys were about to descend from heaven with sacks of gold for everyone on earth.

FORTY-ONE

December 8, 1979

Three days after our reconciliation at the Holiday Inn, Catherine asked for help. She couldn't explain on the phone. She just said to be ready to ride with her somewhere and suggested I wear jeans. It was Saturday night and Catherine showed up about seven in the Cougar with some guy in the passenger seat. At first I hesitated when she told me to hop into the rear. Then I figured, "What the hell?"

"Meet Kenneth," she said. He pivoted in his seat and gave me a big smile. I noticed one of his front teeth was missing, and I could see he probably had a couple of inches on me. He looked like he'd be a rough customer if her plan involved teaching me a lesson with Ken as the professor. I knew he was not one of her attorney pals. But I really didn't feel too nervous. I believed I had bought some time at the Holiday Inn.

"What's going on here?" I asked.

"Well," Catherine purred with a chuckle, "I have to take somebody back to jail. He's a bond client who disappeared a couple of weeks ago. I know he's over at some apartments in Spring Branch tonight. I wanted to take along some muscle. Since I couldn't find anyone qualified in that category, I guess you two will have to do. Ha!"

Kenneth looked at her and started laughing. Then he looked at me.

"So, Kenneth, how do you know Catherine?" I asked.

He shrugged his shoulders and Catherine intervened, saying, "Oh, you might say I've handled some legal work for Kenneth. That about the size of it, Kenneth?"

"That's right, Cathy."

Catherine growled and snapped at him, chiding, "Nobody calls me Cathy. Nobody."

"Sure, sure, I'm sorry. It won't happen again."

I tried to change the subject and asked Kenneth his occupation. He told me he worked as a carpenter. Then he beckoned me forward with his forefinger. I pulled myself over the seat to see what he wanted just as he jerked a seven-inch hunting knife from his cowboy boots.

"Whoa," I screamed, rocketing back into my seat. Catherine glowered at him, but he laughed.

"Don't worry," he said, flipping the blade into his palm and offering me the handle. "You should take this?"

"Huh? We're going somewhere I might need that? If I take your knife, what will you use?"

Kenneth beckoned me forward again, and this time he came up with a .357 Magnum in his hand.

"Take the knife," he said. "That's our last option, anyway. He'll never get past this."

Catherine started shaking her head back and forth and clicking her tongue against the roof of her mouth. I had no intention of even touching the knife for fear of leaving fingerprints on a weapon that might have come from a crime.

"You know, Kenneth," I said, "I think I'll just take my chances. In fact, to tell you truth, if we get in a situation where I need a knife like that, I'll probably just run."

"Suit yourself," he said, and slid the knife back down the side of his boot.

Catherine muttered, "Oh brother, this is going to be some kind of mess with you two. Leave that gun in the car."

I must have chuckled a bit too loudly as I watched Kenneth sulk in his seat like a grade schooler dispatched to time-out because Catherine turned her attention to me.

"And you," she said, glancing into the rearview mirror, "don't try any of your reporter bullshit where we're going because that bullshit is really weak. If we have any problem, they will take your press card, or whatever you have, and just shove it up your ass."

"Yes m'am," I said, saluting. I wanted to reflect a courageous demeanor, but that knife sincerely had me worried. I realized this could grow strange real fast with that yokel in the front seat trying to play hoodlum, and I planned to vanish at the first sign of trouble. We rode in silent darkness into Spring Branch, a suburban community just west of Houston that boasted an enclave of apartment complexes catering to young blue-collar types. I usually got confused trying to find apartments in those things, but Catherine pulled right into a parking space and led us along a sidewalk bordered by crepe myrtles and waxed-leaf ligustrums, then straight to the base of a wrought iron staircase. She pointed to the balcony on the second floor, where we could see lights and activity through the window of an apartment.

"I'm pretty sure that's the one, but I have to check it out," she whispered. If it hadn't been for Kenneth and his buck knife, I would have been enjoying this scene as part of a genuine caper. I had never seen Catherine so serious. Motioning with her hands and speaking in a whisper, she barked orders like the platoon leader on a commando raid.

"Go around back, Kenneth, and set up at the bottom of the back staircase. I don't want him getting away when I come in the front."

Then she looked at me and sighed.

"Taylor, can you just stand right here to make sure he doesn't get past me down these stairs? You think you can handle that?"

Kenneth offered the knife again, and I declined. He shrugged his shoulders and headed for his station, disappearing around a corner of the building. Catherine stared at me with that mischievous grin while waiting for him to set up. Then she tiptoed up the staircase, holding the wrought iron rail and watching for any movement from above. When she reached the landing, Catherine crouched down and peeked into the apartment window where I could see lights and shadows of people moving around inside. I could hear music, too, and suspected some sort of small party under way. Satisfied her quarry awaited inside, Catherine looked back to me, flashed a thumbs up, and stepped to the door. I watched her knock three times and then place her left eye directly on the fish lens peep hole to block anyone looking out. Her speed surprised me when the door opened a crack, and she drove her shoulder into the wood, forcing it all the way. As it swung backward, she raced into the apartment and people started screaming.

What a fucking freak show! I said to myself and moved up a couple of steps, hoping to get a better view of the devastation in Catherine's wake. I could hear frantic footsteps and assumed the bond jumper had chosen flight over fight just as I heard Catherine scream for Kenneth to "Stop that son of a bitch." If I had chosen to make my living as an accountant or an engineer, I probably would have been the kind of guy to walk away. But just as my natural sense of curiosity dictated my profession, it also beckoned me the rest of the way up those stairs, where I wanted a view of that apartment living room. I could see the back door stood open, and I heard the sound of a body hitting the pavement from down the back staircase. In the living room, a small, mixed-gender group of kids in their early twenties sat lounging around on the floor or leaning up against the couch, smoking marijuana.

"Man," said one guy to nobody in particular as I stood in the doorway, "did you see that shit? Who was she?"

"I don't know," said another guy, passing a joint to the girl on his right. "She was fast."

Confident I faced no threat from the stoners inside, I retreated back down the front stairs and headed around the building to see how Kenneth had fared. I walked along a narrow alley that opened into a parking area behind that building and spotted Kenneth right away as he climbed out of a ligustrum bush, looking a bit dazed. Catherine's bond jumper obviously had breeched the perimeter, depositing Kenneth in the bushes, and likely was somewhere in the parking lot fleeing Catherine herself. I looked around, and then I saw them. She had him on his knees, over in a corner of the parking lot between a couple of parked cars. He was pleading, but she stood firm.

"You know who I am," she said, pulling a pair of handcuffs from her jacket pocket. "Run from me, you cocksucker? You are going to the county jail."

This guy looked every bit of six feet five inches tall. Still, he volunteered his wrists and sobbed while she snapped the cuffs around them. She nudged him to stand up and marched him back toward me and Kenneth.

"My brave warriors," Catherine muttered as we fell in line. "What would I do without you?"

"Motherfucker," Kenneth shouted as he shoved the bond jumper. Catherine stepped quickly between them and admonished Kenneth.

"Tough guy, now, huh?" she scolded with a laugh. The bond jumper climbed in the back seat with me and rode sobbing in handcuffs all the way to the old Harris County Jail downtown, where Catherine took about forty-five minutes to surrender him. Then she treated us to a dinner at the Cadillac Bar & Grill.

"Enjoy the show?" she asked as we sipped on beers.

"You know how to have a good time on Saturday night," I replied with a wink. "You always do your own bounty hunting?"

"I never needed to before," she said sternly. "My men usually behave."

I understood painfully well the point of this night's adventure. In one escapade, she had proven that she indeed enjoyed access to goons with buck knives who owed her favors. She also proved she had the power to bring a grown man to his knees. Still bursting with adrenalin a couple of hours later, she took charge of our lovemaking with a cocky, primal aggression and forced an orgasm I imagined her bond jumper felt all the way back at the county jail. I wasn't sure I had even been involved.

FORTY-TWO

December, 1979

I have always been ambivalent about Christmas. In many ways I loathe that time of year. Since the holiday has no religious hold on me, I must consider other reasons to understand it. On one hand, I am revolted by the selfish behavior in the name of the season. Children and many adults lose control when their wishes go unfulfilled. There's no doubt the holiday has evolved into an undisciplined waste of financial resources, as the retail sector feeds the frenzy of material consumption beyond any practical limitation. Even as a kid I dreaded the day itself and felt embarrassed about the presents. I wanted the visitors to leave my house so I could get on with my life of playing ball or reading books on December 26. As a father, I faked enthusiasm so my daughters could enjoy Christmas the way the retailers want all children to do. At the same time, however, I realize the season forms a foundation for sharing and giving, too. I've also enjoyed the parties, particularly those hosted by lawyers willing to spend more on a single night celebration than I earn in a year. By and large, however, for me those days on the calendar have always loomed largely as a black hole in the year, a place where I lose time and just have to accept it. So, surrendering the Christmas season of 1979 to Catherine Mehaffey meant nothing to me. I gave her something I wouldn't have had anyway.

Those weeks between Thanksgiving and New Year's Eve of 1979 sit in my memory as a blur with a few crucial highlights leaping out. Catherine's plan for finally launching her law practice never fulfilled my limited expectations. Her good intentions only reminded me that was the material used to pave the road to hell. For every time she showed signs of accepting the past and just moving forward, she offered a contrary blow that destroyed whatever good will she might have engendered. I began to see more clearly her Machiavellian flaw. Viewing herself as an omnipotent manipulator forced her to plot about everything. She concocted strategies for getting things she wanted and even things she didn't want. The more complex the strategy, the more forcefully she embraced it. I had the feeling I had become the target of some such strategy, a rival she had to defeat. And still, I kept looking for a peaceful way out.

We had a lot of sex that month, often several times each day. It had a calming effect on her, almost like an injection of valium that tended to control her outbursts. I considered her a nymphomaniac at that time and took every advantage I could. Our activity gave new meaning to my view of Christmas as a black hole. I came to see it as a wet one, too.

"Jesus, did you fuck this much when you were married?" she asked me once.

"Of course not," I replied. "Before meeting you?"

I had to admit all that sex helped my condition as well. I had told Cindy I didn't think it safe for me to be around the girls much until I had figured some way to get Catherine out of my life. So, constant sex with Catherine helped cover the melancholy mood derived from constantly thinking about the divorce. That depression probably made it possible for me to answer Catherine's bell as often as she wanted, using it as an avenue for escape from my own predicament.

One afternoon she rang that bell with a phone call to the press room from her office.

"Lloyd had one of his whores in here giving him a blow job yesterday," she claimed. "Today it's my turn. You can be my whore."

"What the hell," I said. "It's a slow news day anyhow."

She left her office door propped open wide enough for Lloyd to get the message as we used her couch to show him he wasn't the only one there with a private life.

Catherine held her Christmas party in her apartment. The place was small, but so was the crowd. She attracted a larger group than I had expected, however. After it ended she asked me to move one of her wooden kitchen chairs back to her bedroom. I set it against the wall by her closet and later would be glad that I did.

We had dinner one night with a lawyer friend and his wife. In the course of routine chitchat, the lawyer asked me about Cindy. He wondered if I had a picture. So, I pulled one from my wallet.

"She's attractive," he said.   Before he could hand it back, Catherine snatched it out of his hand and ripped it to shreds.

"You still carry a picture of that whore?" she screamed.   "Not any more."

While she was in the bathroom, he offered some succinct advice: "Leave town."

When Catherine and I attended the large criminal lawyers party hosted every year at that time by the legendary Mike Ramsey, I accepted a wager from an old friend.

"I bet you a hundred dollars you don't live to come back here next year," whispered Kent Schaffer, at that time a private investigator working his way through law school.

"You're on," I said, shaking his hand.

I also introduced her that night to a younger reporter from *The Post* named Mark. A twenty-five-year-old athletic hunk, he had joined the staff about a year before and also was in the midst of a divorce. I hoped Catherine might catch his eye, and I crossed my fingers when I saw them talking together in a corner of the room. I was sure they'd be seeing each other again soon.

Catherine gave me a baby-blue sweater for Christmas. I don't remember what I gave her. But I do remember what she wanted. She asked me to find a small replica of the creature from the science fiction blockbuster *Alien*. She called it the "perfect predator." I couldn't find one. But I had to admit I really didn't look very hard.

Besides killing her fun with my humbug attitude about Christmas, I also disappointed her with my New Year's Eve superstition of making sure I'm asleep before midnight. We dined that evening on cold-cut sandwiches from a convenience store, drank some scotch, and then went to bed. The decade of the 1970s ended before I arose the next day. For me, the holiday season of 1979 had ended, and a showdown loomed ahead.

FORTY-THREE

January 6, 1980

"Why the hell is that there?" I asked, bolting upright where I had just awakened from a Sunday afternoon nap to see a pistol lying beside the lamp on the table beside the bed. I had only slept a short while after a quick tryst and had fallen asleep on my left side, eyes focused on that table where nothing sat but the lamp as I drifted away. Catherine obviously had taken that pistol from its hiding place while I slept and then laid it on the table where I could see it when I awoke. I wondered how close I had come to dying in my sleep.

"I heard a noise," she said, leaning around the doorway that separated her bedroom from the hall toward the kitchen and the front of her apartment. "I was scared."

I sat up on the bed and rubbed my eyes. I gave the pistol another look and shook my head. I imagined the scene that must have unfolded while I slept:

Catherine paces the floor beside the bed, her pistol in hand. She wonders if she should take her chances now. She knows Christmas and New Year's have come and gone. It will be time to move on separately with our lives. "Did I tell him anything that will ruin me?" she asks herself, trying to remember all he's seen and heard in the weeks since September. And what about that tape recording on file at Special Crimes? What did he tell them that would be so dangerous? "Can I get away with this?" she ponders as she prepares for her statement to the police.

"Shot dead while sleeping half-naked in your house?" the detective would ask. "He raped me," she could explain. "Then he had the nerve to fall asleep there in my bed. I got my gun and watched him, trying to control my anger. He woke up and said he was going to rape me again. I've been used mercilessly by that bastard. I decided to fight back this time. I had my pistol. He started to climb out of bed. I warned him to put on his clothes and leave. But the son of a bitch just laughed. He laughed in my face and said he was going to rape me again. So I shot him. Right between the eyes." "Could that work?" Catherine asks herself. And how would that play around town? "Two men in her life dead, murdered, in the space of a year. Don't fuck with Catherine," they'd all have to say. "She's like the Old West gunslinger with notches on her belt." "But what about that tape at Special Crimes?" Catherine wonders. She considers it further. "That damned tape. What did he tell them? This is too risky now," she decides. "I can pick a better time and make it look like self-defense. I can get away with it, but not now. So I'll just put the pistol down beside the bed and watch him shit his pants."

Paranoia? I wondered, as that scene flashed through my mind. *Or have I become adept at reading her mind?* Either way, I decided I had had enough. I had come to visit that day with plans for the final goodbye, anyway. I could see I had no peaceful, easy way out of this relationship. No new loverboy suckers had emerged to distract her and replace me. The time had come to break this off and take my chances.

"Heard a noise, huh?" I said, realizing she had been standing there expecting a response. "Maybe a rat?"

"Definitely a rat," she said, smiling. "A big fucker, too."

I got the message. I pulled on my pants and walked toward the bedroom door, past the closet on the right and around the chair that I had moved there after her party. I looked over my shoulder to make sure the pistol remained on the bedside table. Then I looked down into her eyes. She looked up and smiled.

"We need to talk," I said, nudging her backward toward the living room in the front of her house. She backed in that direction and sat on the couch.

"How was your Christmas?" I asked.

"OK," she said. "I had a good time this year."

"Do you remember what we talked about the day I brought your television back here, and we went to the Holiday Inn?"

"About our problem?"

"Yes," I acknowledged and continued with a speech I had rehearsed several times in my head that week. "I told you there are times when two people just don't work as a couple. The sex might be spectacular, and there might be pluses. But for some reason, there is still a fundamental problem that should prevent them from staying together. You love someone because of some things and in spite of others. And you have to split because of some things, in spite of others."

I paused, inviting a response and continued when she just sat there staring at me.

"I've given us a good try, and I have helped you get through the Christmas holidays," I said. "But the more I think about it, I have to say we are in that category of couples that will always be in danger from each other. I just make you too angry. I don't know why. But the end result is that I am bad for you. I am preventing you from making something of your life. You are an attractive, intelligent woman. You are funny, like a stand-up comedian. Quick-witted. You need to go out there and use those skills to become a top criminal lawyer instead of getting mad at me all the time and letting our relationship get in the way."

Catherine sat quietly during my presentation, one she obviously had been expecting. I had tried to fashion this discussion in a way that would stress the advantages for her—to give her a reason to accept not just a truce but a permanent armistice without surrender.

"And what about you?" she asked.

"That's another side to it. I have so much bullshit on my plate right now, so many things to straighten out. And I can't do that while we're fighting all the time. There are things I have to do alone. I have a court hearing Wednesday on my divorce, and I have to concentrate on that. I have to make sure my job is secure. We just can't go on. It's time to admit we are fighting a losing battle, and we need to give up the good things so we aren't hurt by the bad."

I thought it made sense. And she just sat quietly, without a response. So I asked, "Will you tell me why it is so important to you that I stay in your life? Surely you can find another lover. What is so special about me?"

"Well," she grinned, "it certainly isn't your two-inch dick."

I laughed and asked, "Then, what?" In response, I believe I received the first honesty I had ever had from her as she ticked off a list of my attractions, confirming my suspicions on a number of points. As a foundation, of course, she said she had found me sexually attractive. Nothing would have transpired further without that. But she also believed I had added much more. She considered me an important buffer on the Tedesco investigation. She also considered a relationship with a reporter similar to an arranged marriage between neighboring kingdoms in the Middle Ages. She admitted she hadn't fully researched all the things I might do for her in my position. But she did know I had helped her get her first murder case and believed I could do more if persuaded over time.

"We are ignoring a lot of opportunities," she said. "I know you will understand that if you just give me a little more time to show you."

"Never going to happen," I said, shaking my head.

"Gary, I also can't remember what I've told you or what you've seen. I can't trust you. I'm worried that you will betray me on something, and I need more time to remember all the things that have happened. All I remember is that through it all, we just kept on fucking."

I laughed at what had become one of her catchphrases the last few weeks. I said, "A good title for the movie, huh? *Through It All They Just Kept on Fucking?* But as far as your fears of me, I can tell you there is nothing I know that can hurt you. I'm certain of it."

She just shrugged, then continued with her list.

"I know I'm going to get a new trial on the Tedesco estate, and I need to neutralize you somehow. I don't believe you could lie in court. It's just not your nature. If you're called as a witness, I am probably in trouble. So I felt I had to make you want to stay with me, so they would never call you to testify."

"I don't know what I can do about that. You need to find a legal argument for making me irrelevant."

"There's something else, too. I'm just humiliated by all of this. I'm terrified you'll be telling jokes, laughing at me behind my back. That's also your nature. But I have to work in that courthouse. I can't tolerate it. Seeing you there would be a daily embarrassment."

"I can promise you that I will never talk about you like that. When I see you in the hall, I'll wink and say, 'Hi.' If anyone asks, I'll just say it didn't work out. I've never been one to kiss and tell."

She scowled at that one, obviously recalling my taped statement for Special Crimes. Then she paid me the kind of compliment that only Catherine Mehaffey could offer, given her Law-of-the-Jungle world view.

"I have been trying to think what kind of animal you are," she said, as I furrowed my brows. "At first, I thought you were a gazelle or a zebra, something to eat. But ever since you went to Special Crimes, I've seen you as something else. You are a leopard. You perch on the branch of a tree, and everybody thinks you're asleep. But all the time, you are peeking out the corner of an eye, ready to pounce when the time is right. That's why I have to keep watching you."

"How about we split with a stalemate?" I asked, wondering if she would understand my comparison of our relationship to a game of chess in which we just simply call it even and walk away. She did but shook her head.

"We're not even," she said. "We won't be even until you go to Special Crimes and take back that tape."

"Catherine, what else can I do? How can we end this? How does it end?"

"When you went to Special Crimes, you entered the arena of death. It can only end one of two ways. You take it back. It cannot end until one of us is dead. What you have done to me is worse than anything by George Tedesco."

I didn't know what else to say. So I stood up and left her sitting on the couch. I walked out the front door, climbed into my two-hundred-dollar car, and drove home to the house of Strong.

FORTY-FOUR

January 9, 1980

A court hearing on Wednesday was scheduled to finalize my divorce from Cindy. In the weeks since Uncle Al had shot her telephone just before Thanksgiving, they had reconciled and she had hired her own attorney. She had assured me that she had Al under control. After discussions with my attorney, Fred Dailey, I decided there was little else I could do but accept the situation with an eye toward monitoring it closely. We had worked out reasonable terms for a fifty-fifty split of all property plus monthly child support payments of $465 to her. She agreed I could have that broken-down beach house. And she said she thought our real estate agent had found someone interested in our house. A sale there would net me about ten thousand dollars—more than enough to buy a new car. Of course, all of these discussions had occurred by telephone without Catherine's knowledge. Cindy cooperated with this clandestine process because she also feared Catherine's unpredictable nature. Catherine had insisted that such discussions should always occur only between the lawyers. She called it the smartest strategy for divorce cases, to prevent anger from disrupting a reasonable settlement. I laughed at the idea of Catherine offering anger management advice.

So, there I stood with Cindy before the judge that morning about nine-thirty, as he reviewed the documents outlining our settlement. He asked if there was anything else to mention.

"I let her collect two hundred dollars in rent from the tenant in our garage apartment," I said while Cindy nodded and the judge looked up.

"You did what?" screamed a voice from the back of the courtroom. We all twirled around to see Catherine standing behind the last row of benches with fire in her eyes. "You gave that bitch two hundred dollars and you never gave me a dime."

Fred leaned over and whispered in my ear, "Is she drunk?"

Cindy left her lawyer's side, walked toward me, and said through clenched teeth: "Get her out of here."

I looked at Fred and then at Cindy and I said, "If I had the power to get her out of here, believe me, I would send her a lot further than the hallway."

Under normal circumstances, our judge might have asked Catherine to leave. In another testament to her reputation for disruption, however, he decided he wanted nothing more to do with any of us and declared a fifteen-minute recess, vanishing instantly into his chambers with robes whipping around his back. Fred motioned for me to follow him into the hall, where Catherine also had gone after realizing she had suffered another of her uncontrolled outbursts. She paced along one side of the hall, obviously upset and trying to figure her next move. As soon as she saw us, she directed advice at Fred.

"Why don't you take better care of him? He needs a real lawyer."

I just looked at her and said, "Please leave." Then I motioned Fred past her, down the hall, and into the men's room.

"I can't believe she won't come in here, too," said Fred. "This is bad. Can't you do anything to get rid of her?"

"Why doesn't that fucking judge lock her up? What can I do? Isn't she in contempt of court or something?"

"That's not going to happen. These family court judges never deal with people like her."

"Divorce court? They've never heard idiots get mad and scream?"

"Ahh, they ignore it. Criminal judges aren't cowed because they send people to jail all the time. Divorce judges hear a lot of anger, but they consider it the heat of the moment that will pass. Best thing is to see what we can do, now. We may have to reschedule this thing. But you have a good settlement on this case, and you shouldn't risk pissing Cindy off any more."

"Fred," I said, "fuck! I'm lost here. If Catherine starts following me everywhere, I don't know what I can do. She is fucking crazy, you know."

He shrugged his shoulders, reminding me he could do nothing himself and left the bathroom. I followed him and saw Catherine still hanging around in the hall. I walked over to her and asked, "What the hell are you doing here?"

"I'm leaving now," she said, and started fumbling around in her purse. She was crying and started mumbling. "I'm sorry, Gary. That was out of line. I'm just so upset. I don't know what I'm doing. I had to be here. I had to come and see, make sure you get divorced. And then, I just lost it. Now I can't find my car keys."

"Huh?"

"I can't leave without my car keys."

"I don't have them. How would I have them?"

She continued to root around in her purse while I looked around the hallway. Over by the courtroom's double doors, Fred stood chatting with Cindy and her lawyer. All three of them glanced at me, waiting for Catherine to leave.

"Can I borrow your car?" Catherine asked, still looking in her purse. "I know I have those keys somewhere."

This did not make sense, I knew. How had she gotten over here? If she walked from her office, why did she need her keys to get back? What is she trying to pull?

"You want to drive my car? The two-hundred-dollar Vega?"

"Give me your keys, and I'll give them back tonight. Meet me at the Cellar Door for drinks after work. Please, just do this for me, and I will leave now. Is it parked in the press space by the criminal court building like always?"

I paused and looked at her while trying to gather my thoughts. I could not think of anything she might do to that car that would hurt me. Kill a pedestrian? She'd be the driver. One of the rules of my life had been to never loan my car to anyone unless my life depended on it. I often had joked, "If Jesus wants my car to attend the second coming, he'll have to provide proof on the first one." I could not recall a time I ever had loaned any car of mine to anyone. But I looked over my shoulder at Cindy and the lawyers, where Fred stood drumming his fingers on the side of a wooden bench and Cindy scowled.

"What the hell?" I said, reaching into my pocket, taking the car key from the latch that also held my door key, and handing it to Catherine. "I'm getting this back tonight at the Cellar Door?"

She nodded and headed for the elevator as I walked back toward Cindy.

"I had to loan her my car to get rid of her," I said.

Cindy started laughing and said, "Mehaffey is driving your car? I'd like to see that."

"I'm glad you get a kick out of that. I hope it comes back in one piece."

"Oh," Cindy continued, "did she promise to take it to a garage and get it into one piece for you?"

"So what are we doing?" I said, changing the subject but glad to see Cindy in a spunky mood. I grinned at the quick recollection of good times in our life together.

"That judge is done for the day," said Fred. He looked at all of us and asked, "Do we still have a settlement?" When we nodded, he said, "I'll schedule a new date." Then he looked at me and asked, "Should we keep it a secret, off the docket? I can arrange that, I think, if everyone agrees."

"I'm sorry about all this," I said, shaking my head. "I don't know what to do."

"Keep it off the docket," said Cindy. "Let's get this out of the way. Gary will figure something out with her. He always does."

Sure, I thought. And monkeys will descend from heaven with bags of money for everyone on earth.

FORTY-FIVE

January 9, 1980

Promptly at five-thirty I walked into the Cellar Door, a restaurant and bar located then in one of the Shell Oil company buildings a few blocks from the courthouse. It had been one of our regular haunts during the past few weeks, and the waitresses knew us by name. I found Catherine at a table with two male attorneys waiting for me. The weeping, helpless waif of the morning had transformed into the life of the party and she cackled, "Hello," as I entered the dimly lit barroom. I had every intention of just taking my key and getting out of there, but her two companions insisted I sit and have a drink with them.

"I hear today was your big day," said one of them, laughing.

"I guess so," I said. "Divorce court. You know the routine."

"Well congratulations," he said, turning to a waitress who spotted me and mouthed "scotch and water?" I nodded and she went to get it while the lawyer yelled, "Put that one on me. It's not every day you get divorced."

"So we all want to hear about it," said Catherine, lifting her glass to her lips.

"Do you have my key?"

"Oh," she said, "sure. You know what? I found my keys right in my purse. I don't know what I was thinking. Let me find yours now."

She started rooting around in her purse again as our waitress brought my drink.

"Here's to your freedom, eh?" said the lawyer, lifting his glass in a toast to me. I really wasn't in the mood for this phony celebration, but I tried to be civil.

"Well, I can't be too free without my car key," I said, glancing at Catherine as she continued searching her purse. The lawyer looked confused so I added, "Catherine borrowed my car. Now she can't find my key."

"I don't believe this," Catherine muttered. "I really can't find your key. I'm not kidding. Where is it?"

"Ahhh, shit," I muttered. "I don't believe this."

"Don't panic," Catherine said. "We'll find it. Just give me a chance."

I made small talk with one of the lawyers about his latest case, and we shared some gossip on a judge. He bought another round of drinks and then another. Meanwhile, Catherine still couldn't locate my key. By seven I decided I had to leave anyway. I stood up and said my goodbyes.

"How can you leave without your key?" Catherine asked.

"I can get a spare," I said. "I know where one is."

"And where is that?"

"Over at Cindy's."

That triggered the Medusa stare.

"I can drive you over there if it isn't very far," said the lawyer who had bought the drinks.

"The fuck you will," she said. Looking at me, she ordered, "You sit here and wait for me. I'll go over there and get it."

Our faux-celebratory mood wilted as suddenly as if someone had opened the tent flap at an Arctic campsite and welcomed a blast of frigid air. The two other lawyers stood moot and watched the confrontation unfold.

"You don't know where she lives," I challenged.

"Wanna bet?" Catherine said, rising as if to leave. I was still standing, and I moved to block her path.

"Catherine," I said, "if you leave this bar, I am going to call Cindy and tell her to call the cops."

The lawyer who had bought the drinks looked at his watch and said, "You know, I think I need to head on home." Then both of them stood and walked away leaving Catherine and me to stare at each other.

"C'mon, Gary," she finally said. "It's my fault I lost them. What am I going to do? Get her down and beat her up?"

"I'm going to make that call anyway," I said, moving away from the table. Catherine responded by reaching out and grabbing my necktie. She pulled me back to the table. I realized I was in another position where I might have to use physical force to just get away. I looked around the bar where patrons at other tables had turned to watch the show.

"Don't do this," I told her.

"You…will…not….call…her," Catherine ordered in a growling staccato.

"You…will…not…go…there," I replied, aping her tone.

She looked around the bar, finally aware that others were watching her provoke this confrontation. She released my tie.

"OK, OK," she said. "Don't worry about your precious Cindy. You know what? I bet that key is up in my office. Why don't we walk over there and look around?"

It already had gotten dark outside. I was sure there would be no one inside her building, unless the cleaning service had not finished its rounds. But it looked like she had me cornered again. Cindy was my only other option, and I was determined to keep her and others out of this final round of battle with Catherine as much as possible. Besides, I would have to take a cab to retrieve my extra key from Cindy. I thought about just calling Strong and asking him to go fetch it. But then, I decided it all sounded like a lot of trouble just to avoid another private meeting with Catherine. I was beaten and worn out. I had just about reached a point where I wanted to say, *Bring it on, bitch! Do whatever you want, and let's see if you can get away with it!* I was ready to call her bluff and see if she really could back up all those threats about the arena of death.

"Yeah," I said. "Let's go on and find it so I can get out of town tonight."

The 609 Fannin Building was just as I had pictured in my mind—dark and foreboding. I had placed my psyche on full-scale red alert, using every bit of peripheral vision to check the doorways and side rooms as we walked down the hall to the offices she shared with Lloyd Oliver. I drew blueprints in my head of plans for action should I be attacked by Kenneth, or that Tommy Bell guy, or anyone else she might have had waiting. But nothing happened. We went into her office, and she took a seat behind her desk. She rummaged around in a drawer and pulled out my key.

"How about that?" she said. "Just like I thought. I'm sorry. I forgot I put that in there for safekeeping. See, you threw that ridiculous fit for nothing."

What is the point of this? I thought. But I just said nothing, continued to look around the room, and held out my palm for the key. She gave it to me and then leaned back in her chair. She pointed at the couch where we had enjoyed that afternoon sex romp and laughed. Then she said, "Hey, why don't we have a drink. One last drink for old times, huh? Will you do that one thing for me? I don't want to leave things like this. I really didn't hide your key as a trick to get you up here. What am I going to do to you, anyway?"

Before I could resist, she got up and took a bottle of scotch from a cabinet behind her, filled two tumblers, and handed one to me. I took a sip.

"I need your help," she said. "I am losing my mind because of the murder of George Tedesco."

"Has something new happened on that? My ears are tired of listening to you. And this day has worn me out."

"You don't want to hear the real story—what actually happened to George?"

"I'm listening," I said, taking a drink of the scotch.

"You aren't wearing a wire, are you? Do I need to search you? Sometimes I think you might have been working for Special Crimes from the start."

"What, as an undercover agent of love? You aren't searching me. Say what's bothering you, or I can go. I'm not that curious any more."

"Sure you are," she said. "I need your advice."

She paused to sip her drink and then continued with her story.

"A week after the murder I got a call from an old boyfriend who wanted to have coffee. He was a younger man, someone I had known right before George swept me off my feet."

I grunted at that description, but she just waved me off.

"Anyway, this boy took me out for coffee. He asked me, 'Are you my attorney?' I said, 'Sure.' He said, 'So anything I say is confidential?' I said, 'Of course.' Then he said, 'I killed George.' He said he had let his anger build while we had been together until he just couldn't stand the way George had treated me. He went to George's condo to confront him, lost his temper, and beat him to death. He said George had pulled a gun on him, but this boy said he was able to grab the leg of a bar stool from above and smack George in the head with it. He said, 'I killed George for you and now you have to help me out.'"

"What did you say?"

"I asked him what he planned to do. He told me he wanted money to leave town. He needed help. So I gave him two hundred dollars. I told him to leave the state of Texas and never come back."

"Where do I come into this? What is your question for me?"

"You know a lot about the law from an outsider perspective," she said, pushing a copy of the legal code of ethics across her desk to me. "Look in there and tell me what you think my obligations are. Now I wish I had never told you about this."

"If this is true, you need a lawyer."

"I've discussed it with a couple of them. They tell me I have no choice but to keep it confidential. But I have to get the investigators and Special Crimes off my back. I have to figure out a way to tell this. Can you help me?"

With that story she now had served up a third version of the Tedesco murder. Initially, she had said she knew nothing about it. Then, that night out at Mike's, she had described the murder in vivid detail, teasing she had done it herself. Now, this night, she had pinned it on some old lover young enough to call a boy. I still wasn't sure which version to believe and certainly didn't know how to advise her on this latest tale. So I improvised.

"Here's an idea. Take a lie detector test. When they get to the question of what you know about Tedesco's death, you claim attorney-client privilege and tell them you can't answer it. That way, they get the test, you don't have to lie, and they know they need to look for somebody else."

She buried her head in her hands and started to cry again. She started shaking her head and muttering, "I can't do that. It won't work. I'm so afraid."

I sat there watching her for a few minutes and reconsidered my idea. It was pretty silly. But it was all I could offer, if indeed that was what she really wanted. I started considering an exit strategy from the building, wondering if she would want to walk out with me.

"I'm really scared," she said. "I can't be alone. These last two nights have been unbearable. Please come with me to my apartment, and this is the last thing I will ever ask of you. Just get me inside, and I'll make us a dinner. Let me make a drink and calm down. Then you can leave, and that will be the last of me for you. I promise."

She was offering yet another chance for a final, peaceful solution. I didn't believe it. But it sounded like the best exit strategy for the moment. I thought to myself: *Go over and tuck her in. Do her this favor and then see what happens. You have to get out of the building anyway, and it's probably safer to leave with her at your side rather than somewhere back behind in a dark hallway.*

So I drove over to her place. I went inside. She fixed a couple of hamburgers. We ate them and had a drink. I wished her goodnight. And, I'm sure she was more surprised than me when I declined her invitation for one last night in her bed. I walked out the door hoping we had finally placed a peaceful seal on our story as a couple.

Sure. And those monkeys were just then taking wing from heaven to deliver bags of gold for everyone on earth.

FORTY-SIX

January 10, 1980

How had I forgotten Barbara?

I still ask myself that question decades after my entanglement with Mehaffey. Things likely would have been quite different had I only remembered Barbara sooner. She was a smoldering blonde a couple years younger than me. She worked in the advertising sales department of the rival *Houston Chronicle* and ranked as one of the paper's top producers. That did not surprise me. I had a hard time imagining any local businessman refusing her solicitations for a sale. We had met by chance in late 1978, about a year before my break-up with Cindy and my introduction to Catherine. At that time, I had been mired in coverage of that marathon trial of the Fort Worth billionaire, T. Cullen Davis. One night after a lengthy session in court, I had wandered into a downtown bar where Barbara was shooting pool. Unlike a lot of the newspaper sales staffers, she enjoyed the company of the reporters and liked to hang out with us. Someone introduced us, and I experienced another moment similar to what I would experience later with Catherine. I felt that natural magnetic connection that happens only so often in a person's life. I knew that Barbara and I were destined somehow to get together. Since then I had filed her away in my mind as someone more important than a one-night stand. I had seen her as an option for a serious relationship. Still married to Cindy and too busy at work to want more than a detached romp, I let our night in 1978 over beers and a pool game slide with only a little flirting and a promise to give her a call.

Somehow then, a year had passed. Distracted by the turmoil of my break-up with Cindy and its link to Catherine, I had forgotten about Barbara being at the top of my list of options. Then I had just happened to bump into her at another downtown bar during December on one of those rare nights when Catherine was elsewhere for a couple of hours. I was walking in as she was headed out. I was surprised when she recognized me and stopped to chat.

"Barbara, right?" I asked, playing coy as if I had forgotten the name of option number one. I almost slapped myself in the head as my mind screamed: *You dumb fuck! What are you doing with that crazy Catherine when you had this chick in the card file from a year ago? You should have called this Barbara the day after Uncle Al ran you off!*

"Gary? You never called," Barbara said with a wink and a grin. She didn't strike me as the type to sit by the phone, and I wouldn't have been interested if she were. With a hint of sarcasm, she said, "Been busy, I guess, huh?"

"You wouldn't believe it. I've been wrestling with a divorce."

Eager to gauge her response to revelation of my newfound availability, I was rewarded immediately with a quick smile she could not hide, a wonderful green light that indicated full speed ahead. Just then I realized we had blocked the doorway to this bar. I recalled my holiday obligation to Catherine and the importance of shedding her from my life before I invited anyone new into it. I pulled Barbara out on the sidewalk and held her hands.

"We should get together," I said. "You interested?"

"I'd ask you to give me a call, but we both know how that works with you," she said with a giggle.

"I will call you this time, you can count on it," I promised. "I'm really glad I ran into you. First of the year. January. I'll call you at the *Chron*, we'll have some drinks and get acquainted."

"I expect it to happen this time," she said and turned to walk away.

So, after I had achieved what I considered a final split from Catherine on Sunday and with my Wednesday divorce hearing on the front burner, I had called Barb that Monday and made a date to meet her after work on Thursday, January 10, at a bar called Corky's. I hoped this would be the first step toward a new beginning. And I was thinking about the possibilities that afternoon in the courthouse press room, finishing up a story, when Catherine stormed in unannounced. Our experiment with locking that door had been a dismal failure as soon as we had tried it back around Thanksgiving, when Strong played the *Exorcist Tape* for our press room colleagues. It had just proved too much of a hassle to go unlock it repeatedly for all the traffic coming through that room. Of course, every lawyer or reporter had demanded an explanation for the heightened level of security, and I had realized quickly it was more embarrassing to explain than to just take my chances with an unlocked door. Catherine hadn't even visited the press room during our Christmas reconciliation. But now, just a few hours before my date with Barbara, she suddenly felt the urge. When she demanded we leave for a private talk, I refused and then asked her to leave the room.

"It's important," she pleaded. I realized her demeanor had changed from the night before, when we had parted company at her place after her invasion of my divorce hearing. Her tone had grown desperate. I had become so immersed in her moods, I believed we had reached a crossroads. I thought her dangerous and considered it my responsibility to evict her from our work area. So I picked up the telephone and started to dial.

"I'm calling the sheriff's department, Catherine, and I'm going to tell them to send deputies up here to remove an unwanted guest from the press room," I said, wondering if anything like this had ever happened before. She glared and slammed her fist down on the phone, breaking the connection. I ignored her and started dialing again, but she leaned across my desk and killed the phone again. When I tried dialing a third time, Catherine reached down and jerked the phone cord from the wall.

"OK," I said, trying to stay calm. I had decided after our physical confrontation at Thanksgiving that I could never again touch her in anger, recalling her regret over failing to tell those cops about "the beating." She would exaggerate any touch as a "beating" and, as the male, I knew I always would appear the aggressor. So I pulled on my jacket and scooted around my desk, where she blocked my path. "Since I can't use the phone, I'm leaving here and going to the sheriff's department to tell them in person to come here and get you out."

She responded by grabbing me around the waist as I walked toward the door. She dug her toes into the floor, forcing me to drag her across it. The other reporters did not know whether to react with anger, laughter, or assistance so they all just sat there watching the show. Realizing I had to loosen her grip somehow, I stopped just short of the door as if I had given up. Catherine took that as a sign of surrender and relaxed for a second while coming to her feet. I seized that opportunity and broke for the door, leaving her in my wake. I opened it and raced through, heading down a hallway toward a staircase. Relentless as always, Catherine came crashing behind, and I heard her on the steps above as I reached the third floor on my way down. So I stopped.

"Please, Gary, if you will just listen to me I will stop chasing you. It is important."

"OK," I said, turning as she came down the steps. "What is it?"

"I know what you are getting ready to do, and I don't want you to do it."

"Huh?"

"I know who you are taking out tonight. You can't do that. We have to be celibate for a while until we get things straightened out."

Celibate? I thought. *Did she just say celibate? She's lost her mind.*

I did not know any way Catherine could know about my pending rendezvous with Barbara unless Catherine truly had supernatural powers. In that case, I concluded, I would just surrender and let her keep me in her apartment for the rest of my life. So, I figured she had just made a wild guess that I would be flexing my independence. She had let her paranoia bubble to the top and was testing me out. I decided against saying anything that might confirm my plans. Instead, I wanted to be as forceful as possible at this moment because I saw it as the true breaking point of no return. If the mere thought of a rival for my affections makes her anxious enough to babble about celibacy, I thought, a peaceful split would be out of the question.

"Catherine," I said firmly, "you have to accept the fact that I am going to be seeing other women. There will be no celibacy. I'm tired of letting you bully me around. The holidays are over and so is our relationship. Didn't we talk about this on Sunday?"

She looked stunned and bit her lip, so I continued my lecture.

"I am going to live my life from now on the way I want to live it."

"I am begging you," she said. "Don't do this. There will be trouble if you cheat on me."

"Cheat on you?" I asked, dumbfounded. "I don't know what you are talking about. But I do know whatever I'm doing is no longer your business. I have a right to live my life without you in it, if that's what I want. I did not cheat on you during Christmas. I kept my word. And now we are separate individuals. I don't want this to be ugly, but if you make it that way, then that's how it will be."

Then I turned and went down the stairs. I left the courthouse early and headed to Corky's where Barbara arrived right on time after I had loosened up with a couple of drinks while waiting for her. She smiled when she spotted me, then came over to my table and sat down. She ordered a drink, and we made small talk for a few minutes. Then she placed her drink on the table and looked into my eyes.

"Do you know someone named Catherine Mehaffey?"

I couldn't believe my ears. I leaned my head back and twisted the muscles in my neck to keep them from getting stiff with stress. I wondered if she had heard about my relationship with Catherine and just wanted to know more. I nodded, took a sip of my drink, and asked, "Why?"

Barbara took a deep breath and said, "She came to see me today."

"You're kidding me."

"She came to my office at the *Chronicle* and introduced herself as your girlfriend."

I started shaking my head and groaning. Trying to contain my anger, I just said, "She's not. Don't listen to her."

Barbara looked a little sad. She sipped her drink and said, "She scares me. I'm worried for you. I just don't know how she knew we were going out tonight."

Wondering the same thing, I reached instinctively into my inside jacket pocket for my appointments book only to find that pocket empty.

"Oh, shit," I mumbled. "My appointment book is gone."

"You wrote our date down in your appointment book?"

"I only wrote initials and the number for the Chronicle. She must have done some serious detective work to find you. I'm really sorry about this."

Barbara finished her drink before she spoke again. Then she said, "Damn. I think you are really a neat guy, and I would really like to get to know you better. But you should know you really have a serious problem with her. She is frightening. She said she wanted me to understand that you are taken. And even if you say that isn't true, and I believe you, I can't take the risk. I'm sorry, for both of us."

I nodded and ordered another drink for me.

"I understand," I told her. "I really do, and I think you are smart to back away from me right now. I see I still have some work to do with her."

"Good luck," she said, rising to leave. She walked out as my fresh drink arrived, and I sipped it trying to devise a new strategy. Clearly, I realized, I had been naïve about my ability to break away without trouble. I had never heard of anything like this, much less suffered it myself. It was an alien dilemma. In my experience with lovers, girlfriends, and wives, we always had just walked away. If one partner wanted out, the other one accepted it and went on with their life. I recalled how spooked Barbara had looked as she revealed Catherine's visit that day. Just as I rehashed her words and expression from moments before, Barbara returned unexpectedly and approached me at the table with an added reminder of how scary Catherine must have been.

"Can I ask you one other thing?" Barbara said. I just squinted my eyes, wondering what that possibly could be.

"I have two dogs," she continued. "You don't think Catherine will hurt them, do you, to get at me?"

"Two dogs?" I mumbled. Despite the fear in Barbara's eyes, I started to laugh a little at the kind of impression Catherine obviously had made. I moved quickly to reassure her.

"No," I said. "I can't see her hurting your dogs. You've done the right thing here. I'm the only dog she wants to hurt."

"Good luck," she said again, then turned to leave for good—or, at least for *that* night.

FORTY-SEVEN

January 13, 1980

I finally realized that, for the first time in my life, I had engaged with true insanity. And the recognition had an enlightening impact on me, an epiphany of tremendous proportions. Catherine's behavior had become so foolishly cross-twisted that, despite the dangers, it made me laugh. I knew I never would suffer from jealousy or obsession myself again just from watching her deterioration. I was like the kid who became a cautious driver after a weekend viewing those gory old Highway Patrol car wreck films or the guy who quit smoking after a counselor forced him to eat cigarette butts. Watching Catherine disintegrate had become my version of a scared-straight, tough-love antidote for jealousy and obsession.

As for her sanity, I wondered if it reflects the outlook of a sane mind to fight the humiliation of rejection with the greater humiliation of desperation. Was it less embarrassing to make a public spectacle of obsession by begging for my attention in front of other people instead of suffering in silence? Although I had experienced jealous feelings in the past, particularly at the end of my marriages, I never had fallen so low as to beg in public for reconciliation, much less launch a campaign of threats against potential rivals. I concluded no relationship could ever be worth that investment of time and dignity. From that day on, I have stifled laughs when observing the smallest outbursts in public—the loud voice of a woman after noticing her date ogle a stranger or the interrogation of a woman late to a party by her husband. But I have winced at the annual news stories about men so consumed with jealousy they slaughter their wives and children before killing themselves in one final dramatic display of depression. All those incidents remind me of Catherine and the lesson I learned that week.

And it is all about control, I whispered to myself, recognizing that Catherine's behavior had nothing to do with love or even physical attraction. *She's terrified about the loss of control and is struggling any way she can to recover it.*

As foolish as her behavior had become, however, I still had to appreciate the threat it posed. Because, after all, I realized the ultimate expression of control could potentially be murder. So, I also began to appreciate the dangers I posed to my friends, with Barbara's chilling visit from Catherine just one example of the responsibility I had to assume for others in my life. I could chuckle at Barbara's concern for her dogs, but then I stopped to wonder how far Catherine really might go. What if Strong's house caught fire, and we both died? What if a car ran over me and my daughter while walking across a street? I weighed those fears in my mind while Don Stricklin's words from my November visit to Special Crimes kept ringing in my ears: *We think she stalked Tedesco.* And after my experience with Barbara, I had evidence Catherine had begun stalking me. But anti-stalking laws remained at least a decade away in 1980. I realized I would have to face this all by myself. "Grow some balls," the cops had advised Tedesco when he sought help about her. They wouldn't have to tell me. I thought I already had a pretty large pair, anyhow.

While I had failed to adequately conceal plans for my date with Barbara on Thursday, I had managed to keep everyone in the dark about a trip I took to Austin the next day. I had been approached by someone at the *Austin American-Statesman* about a job in the newspaper's capitol bureau. The paper planned expansion for coverage of Texas state government, and I had always seen that kind of assignment as my ultimate goal. So I flew up for an interview, hung around town all weekend, and came back on Sunday. Besides fulfilling my professional ambitions, I felt that a new job in another town also would place a crucial geographic hurdle between me and all the problems in Houston.

I also had made plans for another date for Sunday night, January 13, in an effort to test my post-Catherine options. This time I had turned to Denise, the young girl from my ill-fated canoeing class the week before I had connected with Catherine. I wasn't very excited about that evening, but I also was eager to flex my independence. By coincidence, Denise actually had called me during the week wanting to get together, completely out of the blue. So I called her when I returned from Austin and invited her to a movie. She picked me up in her car at Strong's. After the movie, we had a meal at a Mexican restaurant, and she wanted to go swinging in the dark on a playground in a nearby park. I felt secure from Catherine, believing she had no way to know about this outing. As I talked with Denise at the park, however, both of us realized our age differences left us little in common. We agreed to go our separate ways, and I was in bed by eleven after she dropped me at the house of Strong.

I had been asleep about an hour, however, when a nightmare began unfolding in real life around me in the bedroom. The lights went on, and I popped up, rubbing my eyes, to see Strong standing in the doorway and Catherine beside my bed. I bolted up in the bed and stared at them both.

"You let her in?" I asked Jim, ignoring her.

"She insisted," he said. "She pushed open the door. I couldn't stop her. What's going on?"

"Get out," I barked at her, still fighting to come fully awake.

"I watched you tonight, and I'm not putting up with this!" she shouted. "I'm going to stay here tonight. You're my whore!"

So, I thought, she followed me tonight. I began weighing the danger she posed with my need for more information about her deteriorating state of mind. I also feared the result of any physical confrontation required to remove her from the house, once Strong had let her in. But more than that, I felt weary and burned out. I was half asleep. I didn't think she would do anything with Strong in the house as a witness. And I wanted to give her a message as bizarre as the one she'd just delivered to me.

"Fuck you," I said. Without seriously considering it further I acted on instinct. I scrunched back down in the small single bed where I slept and rolled over, speaking without looking at her face. "I'm going back to sleep. You can do whatever you want. As far as I'm concerned, you are not here."

Then I drifted back to my dreams wondering if I would wake up in the morning.

FORTY-EIGHT

January 14, 1980

I awoke unharmed with Catherine still there, sleeping in that small bed beside me. I yawned, rubbed my eyes, and climbed around her to get a shower, thinking all the way to the bathroom about how I must be going crazy, too. After all that concern about her potential for violence, I had just gone back to sleep instead of running her out of the house and locking the doors. Then I realized a more vigorous response might have gotten us firebombed. But I concluded our dance of disengagement could not continue. All debts, whatever those might be, would have to be paid with the devil faced like a man might take his wife: for better or worse. As I scrubbed myself clean and prepared for a new week at the courthouse, I couldn't help wondering what could possibly come next.

I returned to the bedroom to find Catherine wide awake, standing up, and going through the top drawer of a dresser I used for my underwear. I looked around this room I rented from Strong and took stock. Besides the underwear in the dresser and a collection of outer clothes hanging in the closet, I couldn't think of much else in there worth stealing. I had a cheap stereo with a built-in turntable sitting on a nightstand. And I decided she could have that if she wanted it. I ignored her and pulled clothes from the closet with a plan to just get dressed and leave her standing there. Strong was about to leave and when he did, his belongings in the other bedroom might be vulnerable. But, I rationalized, he had let her come into the house, so he

205

would have to accept the consequences. And I was determined to avoid any physical contact with her at all costs. I wondered: *Won't she sooner or later just grow tired of being invisible and go away?*

When I was dressed and ready to leave, however, I reached on the top of the dresser for my keys and found them gone.

"Not the keys again," I muttered. She had taken a seat on the bed to watch, so I turned and said, "I need my keys, Catherine."

"Tomorrow is our anniversary," she said. Catherine considered the 15th of each month to be our anniversary date, commemorating that first outing on October 15 to collect the rent on my beach house. She said, "Something special might happen."

"Catherine, I don't come to your house any more. Why did you come to mine? Please leave."

Just then, we heard Strong exit the front door, and I realized I was alone with her in the house.

"No," she said. "We are going to get some things settled this morning. And you can't leave until we do because I have your keys."

"What do you want?"

"Someone told me that you did something else to me, something so horrible that if I found out what it was, I would lose control. What do you think that could be?"

"And you think you are under control now? I don't know what the fuck you are talking about."

"I want you to go into the courthouse this morning and tell Special Crimes you were crazy when you made that tape and that you want to take it all back."

"If I do that, I can have my keys back?"

"Yes."

I acted as if I were thinking about it, and then I said, "Ah, I can get another set of keys somewhere. It's not important, and I really don't have anything you can take that is important enough to make me do that."

"You don't?"

Before I could confirm my position, however, I had another thought: *This is about the silliest negotiation I could imagine. My statement about her can never go back into my mouth, even if I tell Don Stricklin I'm crazy. If I turn up dead, they're still looking at her.*

So instead of resisting her demand, I changed course and relented with a sigh.

"OK, Catherine, why don't you get one of them on the phone, and I'll tell them all that. But then I get my keys, right?"

"Right," she said, already picking up a phone and dialing the district attorney's office number from memory. I heard her get through to Henry Oncken, who served at that time as the first assistant, a position above Stricklin. She identified herself and then handed the phone to me, after telling Oncken I needed to speak with him. I knew he had been briefed on my situation, so I took the phone and said hello.

"Henry, I just wanted to call and tell you I am crazy, and I take it all back."

"Gary, are you are in danger?" he asked.

"No," I said, realizing this all had started sounding even more bizarre than I had imagined. "I'm just trying to get my keys so I can drive in to work. Catherine wanted me to tell you I'm crazy first."

"OK," he said. "I got it. You are crazy and you take it all back. And you are with her now."

"That's correct. I'll stop by your office when I get to the courthouse."

"Make sure you do. Thanks for the call."

I hung up the phone, looked at Catherine, extended an arm with palm up, and demanded with one word: "Keys."

When she started shaking her head and saying, "No," I realized I had reached my limit and decided to drop my non-contact pledge. I snatched her purse from the bed and pushed her down on the mattress. I looked through the purse but couldn't find the keys. So I offered it in exchange for the keys, and she agreed. When I told her to leave, however, she refused. I grabbed her by the hair and dragged her out of the house until she agreed to leave the house as well.

But, I had no sooner settled in behind my desk at the courthouse when she made an encore appearance there. I tried to ignore her again as I watched from the corner of my eye her efforts to conduct private meetings with my colleagues in the room. When one of them returned from a trip with her down the hall, I leaned over and asked, "What does she want?"

"She's asking about that *Exorcist Tape* and whether it was played for us in the press room," said Tom Moran, the courthouse reporter for the *Chronicle* who would later become a Houston attorney. "She thinks she has a case for slander or something."

"You do remember that it was Strong who actually played a small part of it, don't you? That's his voice on that tape with her, not me."

Tom waved me away and said, "Sure, sure, she's grabbing straws."

Just then she re-entered the room, approached my desk, and crossed her arms on her chest. She checked to make sure she had an audience among the other reporters, and I checked to make sure they were enjoying the show.

"You are in serious trouble, now, Mr. Taylor," she began. "I'll be filing a suit against you and *The Houston Post* for $2.5 million for holding me up to public ridicule. And another thing. I have someone else ready to testify you have been running around town distributing naked pictures of your wife. When her attorney finds out about that, your divorce will get real nasty, won't it?"

Tom and Strong started to laugh, and I was barely holding it back.

"Catherine," I said, "you are making an absolute fool of yourself. You are the one holding yourself up to public ridicule. I don't have to do a thing. Now it is time for you to leave so we can get back to work."

"No," she said, standing her ground. So, I took a sheet of typing paper from my desk and started to write on it. When I finished, I showed it to her: "Catherine Mehaffey is barred from this Press Room by unanimous vote." I got up with a tape dispenser, walked around her to the door, and taped it to the outside. Before I could come back inside, however, her hand snaked around the door and ripped it off. As I re-entered the room, she backed into a corner and grabbed a ballpoint pen from my desk, extending it like a knife.

"Catherine," I said, "you are going to leave."

"No," she said. So I grabbed one of her arms and started pulling her across the floor. Halfway there, she snatched the back of a small desk chair with rollers and used it to propel herself faster out of my hand. Then she dove onto the floor while I stood there watching her.

"You saw him," she screamed at the other reporters. "You saw him beating on me."

Tom looked at her without rising from his chair and asked, "Catherine, can we call you an ambulance?"

I started laughing at that remark as she sat up on the floor and then climbed into the chair while Tom continued to offer aid, asking, "Can I get you a doctor? Do you need a doctor?"

"No, I'll just sit here," she said. The rest of the press corps decided then would be a good time to check the courts for news, and they scattered faster than normal while she sat there looking at me and Tom. Without a pause, I picked up the phone, dialed the sheriff's office, and said, "We have someone in the press room who is not welcome, and she won't leave. Can you arrest her for trespassing?"

Before I heard an answer, she jerked the phone off my desk and slammed it onto the floor. Then she yanked the connection from the wall.

"OK," I said. "I guess I will have to file my complaint in person."

As I got up to walk across the floor, Catherine sprang, grabbing my necktie and trying to slide the knot against my throat. Recognizing the danger of this confrontation, Tom rose to action and tried to step between us.

"Catherine, Catherine, calm down," he said. "Don't be this way."

When she turned to face him, Catherine relaxed her grip, and I spun away heading out the door. A couple of minutes later, I returned with two deputies to find Tom and Catherine sitting there chatting.

"I want to tell you he beat me," she screamed, pointing at me.

"Is this a family disturbance?" one of the deputies asked me. I shook my head and said, "No way. We are not related, and she is disturbing our work."

The deputies looked at Tom for support, and he nodded.

"Tell them what happened to me," she barked at Tom.

"Catherine fell over the chair trying to attack Taylor," he said.

The deputies had heard enough. One of them looked at her and said simply, "Miss, you will have to leave."

"I think I'm going to vomit," said Catherine. She grabbed her purse, stood up, and left the room with the deputies in her wake.

"Thanks for sticking around," I said to Tom, after Catherine had left the room.

"Wouldn't miss it for the world," he said with a grin. "I'm sure I'll be writing a story about you pretty soon anyway and may need these observations for background. I was having coffee with a couple of lawyers last week, and one of them said he expects the next time he sees you, you will be wearing a toe tag."

"Schaffer bet me a hundred dollars I won't live to attend Ramsey's Christmas party this year. I took the bet because I don't see any way he can collect on it if he wins."

Tom chuckled and offered another observation: "I just don't see any heroes in this story."

I hadn't thought about that aspect until then, but it sounded right. I just looked at him, grinned, and said, "What about you? You're my hero. Why don't you follow me around for a while and be my witness?"

"No, thanks."

Turning back to my desk, I hoped that maybe I had finished my business with Catherine for this day.

Sure. And those monkeys from heaven finally had reached the mountaintops, carrying bags of gold for everyone on earth.

FORTY-NINE

January 14, 1980

"Your psycho girlfriend is over here in the newsroom right now."

"Ahh, shit," I mumbled after answering the phone and receiving that whispered message from Ed Jahn, a colleague on the city desk at *The Post* building, about fifteen minutes from downtown. I told him: "But she just left this place."

Ed had called me about two hours after deputies had evicted Catherine from the courthouse press room. I speculated she must have collected her thoughts and launched a Plan B in an attempt to trample me at work.

"Catherine certainly is having a very busy day," I said. "She seems to be popping up everywhere. What's she doing over there?"

I enlisted Ed to serve as my eyes at headquarters.

"She's in Logan's office pacing around and telling him all about something, probably you," Ed said. "Oh, man, now she's waving her arms around and pointing in his face."

Logan was our managing editor, and he worked in one of those offices with glass walls that allowed him to monitor the staff at all times. Of course, on this occasion, they also allowed my scout to monitor Logan and provide a play-by-play of Catherine's surprise visit.

"What's he doing?" I asked.

"He's just sitting there watching her without much of an expression at all. He looks like a virgin who wandered into a porn movie and is seeing a real pussy for the first time in his life. He knows what they are supposed to look like, but he wants to make sure this is real."

I figured Logan had never experienced anything like Mehaffey, even in his long career with newspapers. I still had to laugh as I imagined him sitting there listening to a tirade similar to what had just occurred in the press room. I wondered if she had gotten to the part about the naked pictures of my wife. I still didn't know what she had meant with that allegation, beyond just throwing out anything that might embarrass me even if it were imaginary. So, I had just let that slide. But I realized her visit to my boss had just dismantled any effort to separate my private life with her from my professional life at *The Post*. And I had a good idea what might be coming next. Two of my three separate lives were about to merge.

"It looks like she's leaving now," said Ed. "Logan's still just watching her, and it doesn't seem like he said much. She's going through his door. Now she's stopped and answering a question. Now she's turned and left, and he looks pretty confused."

"Thanks for the warning, Ed. I owe you."

About fifteen minutes later, Logan called me at the courthouse and issued a succinct command: "Gary, I need you to just stop whatever you might be doing and come into the office. I don't want you to even take time to put anything away. Just get up, get in your car, and come over here."

It marked the only time in my career that Logan had ever called me on the job. I routinely worked under the direction of his city editor, Johnny B. It was highly unusual to receive a call directly from the managing editor, but, given my experiences of the past few weeks, I was not surprised. I reached his office from downtown in about twenty minutes. Then it was my turn to sit there with everybody watching through the glass.

"What's up?" I asked politely, feigning ignorance as I took a seat in a chair across the desk from my boss.

"I'll get right to the point," he said. "I had an interesting visit a little while ago from a Miss Catherine Mehaffey, and she had some disturbing things to say about you."

I just furrowed my brows in a way to encourage him onward.

"She believes you are working secretly for the district attorney's office as an investigator in a case against her."

"That's not true," I said, eager to make a definitive denial as quickly and forcefully as possible—without laughing. "She has some gripes with me of a personal nature. None of it involves my job here. You are the only one paying me a salary."

"She says you've made tape recordings of conversations with her and shared them with outsiders."

"I recorded her telephone conversations threatening me, but I never played them for anyone else. A friend of mine did play part of a conversation he taped with her because he wanted the other reporters in the press room to let him lock the door."

Logan grunted and stroked his chin while locking eyes with me.

"OK," he said, "Here's what I have to do. Mary Flood is on her way over to the courthouse to relieve you there—"

"Aw, c'mon," I raised my voice interrupting him. "Don't let Mehaffey get away with this. Can anybody just come in here with any sort of story and ruin me? I like that job."

Mary Flood was a younger reporter destined to attend law school and build a national reputation for legal reporting in the next twenty years—a period in which I often would boast that she owed her start on that career path to me and Catherine Mehaffey. While I argued my case, Logan just sat patiently and allowed me to vent. Then he laid down the law.

"Nope, it is already done," he said. "I talked to Johnny, and he said you've been over on the courthouse beat a couple of years anyway. It's time to rotate on some of these beats. He has a desk ready for you back in the office. Now, I don't even want you going back there to get anything you might have left. Make a list of anything you need, and Mary will bring it in."

"Don't punish me for this," I pleaded.

He looked stunned and said, "Punish you? I'm not punishing you. I'm concerned for your safety. I just want to put as much distance as possible between you and that woman. It's obvious she's interfering with your work at that location, and it's my responsibility to make sure everyone at this paper has a chance to succeed in their job. You'll have plenty of good stories to work on general assignment. Now, go see Johnny, and he'll show you to your desk."

"OK," I sighed and got up to leave.

"Gary," he said, "I don't meddle in reporters' personal lives, and you certainly don't have to tell me this if you feel uncomfortable. But, after talking with her, I'm really curious about something. What did you do to her?"

There it was: Always the man's fault. In his mind it had to be me who did something to her. Or, I thought, maybe he was kidding. The question made me laugh as I imagined him sitting through her tirade wondering if aliens had invaded from Mars. Realizing any accurate explanation would be much too complicated, I searched my mind for a shorter version and finally just said, "Oh, I forgot to put her picture in my wallet."

Logan stared a moment trying to figure that out until he saw me grinning and then laughed himself.

"OK, OK, I think I understand," he said. "But you should know something she told me right before she left. I asked her what she wanted me to do about any of this, and she just got this strange, faraway look in her eyes and said, 'I just want him to disappear.'"

We stood there a moment considering that until I shrugged my shoulders and moved to the door.

"So, go on, get your new desk, and welcome back to the newsroom," Logan said as I left. Then he added, "And, Gary, under no circumstance do I ever want you to initiate contact with that woman again."

So I walked out, went to my new desk, picked up the phone, and immediately dialed Catherine at her office.

"Hope you're happy now," I said when she answered.

"You went to my bosses at Special Crimes so I thought I should go to your boss to teach you a lesson. Where are you now?"

"I'm at my new desk in the newsroom. They took me off the courthouse beat."

"Wait a minute. You mean you haven't been fired?"

Instantly I realized I had an edge, as she revealed her primary mission had been to get me fired. She had failed. And, as I thought about it, I realized Logan had been right in my reassignment. Digesting a universal truth about stalkers, I concluded I was lucky to still have a job. *Wouldn't it be easiest for any employer to just eliminate the whole problem by cutting the worker?* I thought. In this case, however, Logan and my paper had backed me. Suddenly, I felt grateful and decided to twist the knife with her.

"Fired? No way. He said he wanted me in here for my safety. You know, we have a lot of important elections to cover this year, and *The Post* will need its best people available on the desk for those stories. I'm really kind of excited about this promotion."

"Promotion?" I thought I heard her choke a bit as she repeated my mischaracterization of what essentially represented a lateral move.

"And, I will have plenty of time for a little sideline project in this new job," I said. "I want to do a little research on the lawyer ethics requirements of the State Bar of Texas and see if maybe you've slipped up on something I might know about."

"Uh, OK, OK," she said calmly, as if distracted. "I have to go."

That night at home I picked up a ringing phone to hear her voice and hung up before she could finish a sentence. For the next two hours the phone rang repeatedly, but I did not answer. When Strong arrived back at the house, I told him not to answer either. I had decided to end all communication with her. She would be easy to ignore now that I no longer needed to visit the courthouse daily. I believed I might never see her again.

Later, after studying the psychology of the narcissist personality, however, I would learn that my new strategy that night had merely set the stage for an escalation of tensions in our relationship because I had denied her the one thing she actually needed the most: an opportunity for confrontation. And, I would learn on our anniversary the next day, that confrontation was the one thing she really could not live without.

FIFTY

January 15, 1980

I started the first full day of my new assignment in the office with an attitude adjustment. Reviewing my conversation with Logan, I became convinced he had been right to move me out of the courthouse. Catherine definitely would have a harder time stalking me, particularly since I had decided I wouldn't even take her calls. My hours as a general assignment reporter would be less attractive, with occasional night and weekend shifts replacing the Monday-through-Friday, daytime rhythm of the courthouse beat. But I could live with that. In exchange, I'd have more opportunity to work on the so-called big picture stories designed to change the course of Western Civilization. I planned to immediately develop a list of hot-shot ideas for Johnny B to consider. As the political season intensified, too, I expected to assist on any number of intriguing local election coverage issues. I even wondered if my long tenure at the courthouse had been partially to blame for my attraction to Catherine.

Maybe I've been hanging around lawyers and judges for so long I've gone native, I mused. *I was drawn to her like some rogue undercover operative who has fallen too deeply into a culture he only wanted to observe.*

Despite Catherine's threat regarding big plans for our anniversary on the 15th, I had a smile on my face as the evening approached because a special gal had signed my dance card for that night. I had arranged to attend the political barbecue fund raiser for Harris County District Attorney John B.

215

Holmes, Jr., as he kicked off his first campaign for the office he'd held since his appointment a couple of years before. And I was taking my four-year-old daughter, Little E, as a date. I hoped that maybe with a new year and decade I had turned a corner on all that domestic turmoil of 1979. I had allowed Catherine to short-circuit what should have been the most important relationship in my life. As an agent once told me while pitching a life insurance policy, "You may divorce your wife, but you don't divorce your kid." I bought the policy as well as the philosophy and always thought it a shame that so many angry divorced men fail to focus on their kids. Determined to put Catherine and her volatile behavior behind me, I had arranged for Little E to spend the night at the house of Strong after the Holmes event. Both of us were excited about the prospect of the sleepover and, more importantly, the prospect for retying what had been an unusually close but fragile bond.

At four-and-a-half, Little E had reached a wonderful age where her body and mind seemed at peace with themselves. She hungered for new experiences and insights to feed a developing intellect and rubbing shoulders with the power brokers at the Holmes barbecue overwhelmed her desire to expand the potential boundaries of her world. As we toured the room and I introduced her to an endless parade of attorneys and judges, I felt an awesome sense of pride. Not only had Little E blossomed into a bright, precocious little girl, but she was a cutie, too—lithe and athletic with her reddish-blonde straight hair cut short in a wedge and freckles dotting her cheeks. I had a feeling the future truly belonged to her, and the realization filled me with shame about the way I had lived the last few months. Cindy had said she landed a contract to sell our house and that bolstered my spirits, too. I planned to use my share first to buy a car and then settle into an apartment where I could spend more time with Little E and her sister, who was too young that night to attend the Holmes barbecue. Thoughts of the future finally had me grinning as I drove home from the event with Little E in the passenger seat.

But that mood changed abruptly when I pulled up to the house of Strong and saw Jim patrolling the sidewalk outside with a shotgun in his arms.

"Get down on the floor," I told Little E, as I swung into the driveway and Strong came to my window.

"We've been hit," he said. "Burglars have been here. I just got home, and they may still be inside. I grabbed the shotgun in the garage and waited for you when I saw you turning up the street."

I got out of my car, and we walked cautiously toward his front door, which was standing open. I looked around over my shoulder and motioned for Little E to stay down on the floor when I saw her peeking over the dashboard. We entered the house and looked around. Once we concluded the invaders had left, I went back to the car for Little E and brought her inside. Then we took a mental inventory of the damage.

I saw immediately they had snatched the cheap stereo in my room, along with the Eagles' *Desperado* album which had been on the turntable. In addition, I noticed they had been through my dresser drawers. I tried to remember what might be missing. The list included some inconsequential items such as my copy of Catherine's *Exorcist Tape* and a couple of photos of her. If it had just been the stolen property, I could have laughed this off. As I thought about this invasion, however, I realized it meant much more than the loot. I doubted that the primary mission had been theft and concluded Catherine had sent over some boys to teach me one of her lessons. My anger started to rise when I imagined what might have happened had I stumbled across them with Little E in tow.

Strong, of course, suffered greater material losses than me. Atop his list was one of the original Sony BetaMax video recording units, a prized electronic possession at that time. In addition, the burglars had known to crawl under his mattress for the .357 Magnum revolver he kept hidden there. They also had snatched a police officer's heavy duty black flashlight that Strong once had sarcastically offered to Catherine as a weapon for defense in ridiculing her complaints about beatings from me.

We didn't need a Mensa card to focus quickly on a chief suspect. And although Don Stricklin did not normally take burglary calls as head of Special Crimes, he took ours at his home and dispatched a police unit to get fingerprints. After the cops left, we decided to assist the investigation ourselves. We hooked a recorder up to a phone and each made a call to Catherine at her apartment. She reacted to both of us in a similar fashion, assuming a recorder was running and firmly denying our allegations. But she laced her denials with giggles and laughter I took as a subliminal acknowledgement she had triggered an intended reaction.

In his conversation, Strong appealed to any sense of fair play she might have had, telling her he wanted a return of his stolen belongings and separating himself from me by emphasizing he had done nothing to hurt her.

I took a different tack, insisting I did not care about my stolen property and laughing about this latest attempt to get my attention. With this plan I hoped to trick her into an angry rebuttal on tape that would allow me to provide Stricklin with more evidence that could at least prompt questioning about this burglary. We knew it was a long shot, but Strong and I had decided to do everything possible to use this burglary as the mistake that would take her down.

"Celebrating tonight?" I asked, when she picked up the phone.

"Gary, I don't know what you are talking about. Jim just called me, too. I'm sorry to hear about your problem over there."

"Yeah, yeah," I said. "I just wanted to let you know that stereo isn't worth a shit, and I can't even find anything else of mine that's missing. Your goons may want you to pay them to make up the difference for loot that's fit only for a homeless shelter."

"I don't know what you mean."

"Yeah, yeah. I just wanted to let you know this kind of work is really beneath you. It's about like the Mafia rolling a wino for pocket change, really a joke, you know—"

"I have to stop you, Gary. I have a young man here with me tonight, and I have to say, he's giving me a look like he thinks you must be crazy. I certainly don't want him thinking I consort with lunatics."

"Yeah, your alibi is solid, huh? That's good because—"

Then she hung up. I looked around my bedroom where Little E had fallen asleep on my bed. Strong was wandering around the house making a list for his insurance carrier and shaking his head.

"This is Tedesco all over again," he said. "Interesting to note your initials are GT, too. I wonder if this is the end of it."

Reality then smacked me square in the face. I recalled Catherine's response when I had asked her how our relationship would end. She had said, *One of us has to die!* Then, I flashed on Logan's comment from his meeting with her: *I just want him to disappear!* I dredged the old news stories about Tedesco's mangled body into my consciousness. Then I looked again at Little E sleeping there. I couldn't join her. I sat up all night in the dark, almost hoping that Catherine's team would return to finish the job they had failed to do. Maybe then, I thought, I could die fighting, and at least it would be over for innocent bystanders like Strong and my daughters. I decided the time had really come to force a final confrontation—hopefully in a place where I would be the only possible target.

We can't surrender to people like her, I told myself. *We don't have to leave town and live in fear of obsessive psychos. We turn that fear around and make them run.*

I knew that is what I would have to do.

FIFTY-ONE

January 16, 1980

As soon as I sat down at my desk the morning after the burglary, my telephone extension started to ring. When I answered, I recognized the voice of another reporter in the newsroom. It was Mark—the guy I had introduced to Catherine at the Ramsey Christmas party in hopes he would sweep her off her feet and deliver me from her vengeance. I could also see that he, too, was in the newsroom, sitting at his desk about fifty feet away. I wondered why he had called instead of just walking over to chat. I also wondered why he was whispering his message that he wanted to huddle with me in one of our private conference rooms.

"I need to tell you something," he said sheepishly when he sat down in the room, which was about the size of a large closet with no windows. Each of these rooms held a small table and a couple of chairs. The staff used them for interviewing sources and private conversations when managers discussed a reporter's work. In deference to our current city editor, Johnny B, this room had been named the "Boo-Boo room." About five years younger than me, Mark was a handsome specimen—a tall, bearded, athletic guy who had been a star football player in high school. But now his face looked racked with a combination of guilt, fear, and suspicion. He looked broken. I knew he was going through a divorce and figured he probably wanted advice.

"It was me last night," he said, and at first I wasn't sure what he meant.

"You?" I asked and he nodded. "You what?"

"Me with Mehaffey."

I didn't know whether to laugh or yell as the pieces of my conversation with her melded together.

"You're the young man who thinks I'm crazy?" I said, as I started to laugh.

"No, I don't think you're crazy, but I was there. Taylor, what did you get me into?"

"You know what this makes you in this case, don't you? You are Mr. Alibi," and I laughed again as he nodded, then buried his face in his hands. "How did you get mixed up with her?"

"She called me about four yesterday and asked me out. We had dinner, then went back to her place for drinks."

"Did you fuck her?"

Once again he nodded and buried that face in his hands.

"Once you fuck her, Mark, you have to continue until she says you can stop."

His head shot back to attention with that observation, and he appeared terrified until I laughed to let him see I'd been joking.

"In your case, however, she might grant immunity," I said. "No offense, but it sounds like you were being used for a larger mission. Of course, I'm sure you gave her pleasure."

"Really, she was pretty much of a bum fuck."

"Huh?" I was taken a bit by surprise that, in the midst of this turmoil, he would stop to give her performance a critical review. But then, I knew as well as anyone that boys must be boys, and I couldn't miss the chance to gig him a bit about it. "Don't worry about that. I bet she was distracted thinking about what was going on at my place. A bum fuck, eh? That's pretty harsh."

"Don't tell her I said that, man."

"Hell, I'm not telling anybody about that one. People would think I am crazy for going through all of this other bullshit with her, and she just turns out to be your bum fuck. That's embarrassing for me. People have to think I at least got some dynamite ass from her. So I won't let you destroy my image."

I smiled, but he didn't return the pleasantry. I could see he was suffering, so I got serious.

"You know what you have to do, now, don't you?" I asked. When he answered with a look of confusion, I continued, "You need to call Don Stricklin at the DA's office and tell him you were there. Did she have any other phone calls you heard? Maybe you have some evidence and that would change you from Mr. Alibi into Mr. Star Witness."

That comment seemed to worry him more. He shook his head and said, "I just want this to go away. That woman is poison. I never want to see her again."

"I don't see any way around calling Stricklin," I said. "Or you may eventually end up as Mr. Co-Conspirator doing five-to-ten in state prison. And, I think for your job security, we need to include Johnny B in this conversation."

Mark reluctantly agreed and said he would contact Stricklin after meeting with our boss, who came into the Boo-Boo Room with a curious look on his face. Mark's confession failed to improve Johnny's disposition on this day. The look of curiosity transitioned to shell shock and then I sensed a bit of rage, as Johnny lifted a finger and indicated for us to sit there while he stood and opened the closet door.

"I want everyone's attention," he yelled across the newsroom, where a couple dozen reporters sat working at their desks or chatting in the early hours of the news day. The place grew quiet as a church while everyone turned to Johnny, who would have looked strange, indeed, from that perspective—hanging in the open doorway of the Boo-Boo Room about to make some serious announcement. Good reporters all, they obviously wanted to learn why.

"If any one of you has had any personal dealings with Catherine Mehaffey—anything at all—I need you in this room right now."

I traded glances with Mark, and we both suppressed a giggle. I peeked around Johnny's back for a look into the newsroom and noticed several faces looking dumbfounded at his instruction. I couldn't remember anyone else out there who had encountered her, but, then again, I knew she was full of surprises.

"Last chance," he warned when no one moved. "I only want to go through this once."

Satisfied that Mark and I were her only *Post* connections, Johnny re-entered the room and issued a quick set of instructions. He told us he didn't want the Mehaffey cancer spreading any further into his newsroom. He ordered us to do what we already had vowed: "Leave that woman alone."

Throughout the day I heard twice again from Mark, after he had called Stricklin with his piece of the burglary story. One time, he said Catherine had called him for another date, but he had refused, telling her he did not want to get involved because the burglary had been too coincidental. The second time, Mark said he'd been contacted by another woman, one of Catherine's friends, asking him out on a blind date. He had rejected her as well.

"You're a real popular guy with the Mehaffey gang today, aren't you?" I joked as he scowled and mumbled again, "Taylor, what did you get me into?"

I tried to console him by adding, "I think you're OK. She won't want to alienate you as her alibi." As far as I know, he never heard from her again.

Blended into this mélange of work, Mark, and Johnny B, however, I spent part of the day fielding calls from Strong, as well. He had been doing a bit of work on Catherine, trying to convince her that the burglary had separated him and left me isolated. They had met for lunch, and she had insisted on frisking him before they talked. He demanded a return of his Beta Max and other property in exchange for a promise to disavow my existence. Although Catherine continued to deny involvement in the burglary, Strong said, she also indicated she might know someone who could help.

"I think we're making progress," he told me in a phone call. "If we can catch her returning any of that property, she goes straight to fucking jail."

FIFTY-TWO

January 17, 1980

It took only a day for Strong's prediction to come true, or, at least part of it. Whenever he called me at the office to update, his messages were cryptic but optimistic. He finally told me to stay away from the house that night. He said I should just call later to see what had happened. He assured me he was continuing to share his maneuvers with Stricklin at Special Crimes. I thought he was enjoying this role as an undercover go-between a bit too much, but I had to play along and trust him. The more I thought about that night after the burglary and the danger to my daughter, the more I realized I had to bring this standoff with Catherine to a conclusion, regardless of the consequences for me.

Mark had invited me to drop by his lonely condo for dinner that night and swap some stories over a few beers. After grilling steaks, we recounted our impressions through the unique bonding experience available only to men who have shared the same psycho-babe. He even had grown receptive to my constant teasing of his use as an alibi.

"You know, Mark, you must be careful not to violate the 11th commandment," I advised with all the wisdom gleaned in my nearly thirty-three years.

"I'm not familiar with that one," he laughed, anticipating sarcasm.

"That's the one that instructs: 'Thou shalt not take thyself too seriously.' In five years you will look back on all this and be really disappointed if you failed to have fun with the experiences."

"Heh, heh, and the wind cries *Mooohaaaafeee,*" he chuckled, doing a weak imitation of Jimi Hendrix on *The Wind Cries Mary.*

"Hey," I said, "we should each get a T-shirt that identifies each of us as a 'Mehaffey Surivivor.' From what I hear around the courthouse, there might even be a market for those."

"That's assuming we do survive. But promise me again you won't let her know we were talking like this," he said in a tone that still sounded about half serious.

"Lips are sealed," I vowed with a laugh. "And I've even already forgotten you called her a bum fuck."

When he responded with a laugh instead of a grimace, I slapped him on the arm and said, "That's the spirit."

As I drove from his condo I couldn't help but grin at our locker room bravado. I knew even then that she had given both of us a new perspective on the sexual revolution. Looking back, I realize that cultural watershed was entering a new phase in 1980, as the first period of unlimited experimentation and sexual muscle-flexing was drawing to a close for the Boomers. Experiences like those with Catherine had reshaped the outlook of many more than me and Mark. I recognized for the first time that no one can predict the individual demons to be unleashed when two strangers have sex. I wouldn't stop answering the call, of course, whenever opportunity knocked. At the same time, however, I knew I would always recognize the reality of the unexpected emotional element more than ever before and strive to understand my partners a little better than I had in the past. I believed Catherine's demons were extreme, but it took that to make me understand there is more to getting laid than just getting laid. I wondered if maybe I had failed to give due credit to the prudes who always warned us to go slow. Maybe they actually had a good reason to incorporate such precautions into their moral code. I believed Mark had experienced a similar awakening. Maybe in the future he would foreswear sex until at least the second date. I wasn't prepared to go that far. But I certainly would be watching my potential partners a lot more closely than I had in the past.

"Buzz on back, I've got a surprise for you," said Strong, when I called him from a bar on the way back from Mark's. I thought perhaps he had somehow resolved all of our problems. But I was unprepared for his "surprise" when I walked through the door into a darkened entryway and spotted him sitting in a rocking chair in the living room talking to someone on the couch a few feet away. He looked at me, stopped talking, and grinned as Catherine peeked around the side of the couch with a scowl on her face. She said nothing.

"C'mon in," said Strong. "I think we may have a deal working that will allow all of us to live in peace."

"Sounds like some serious talk is under way," I said, taking a seat on the edge of the couch opposite from Catherine, who eyed me warily.

"Yeah," said Strong. "We've made our peace. If my shit comes back, I've agreed to tell you to move out and tell everybody else that I think you are crazy. And I'm going to Special Crimes and get her copies of all the tapes we made."

I just looked at him and then at her. She still said nothing, so I just shrugged my shoulders.

"Catherine," said Strong, continuing in the tone of a labor negotiator, "what can Gary do to end this, so that you don't have to kill each other?"

"He has to apologize, go to Special Crimes, and tell them he is crazy," she said, repeating what had been her list of demands for the last two months.

"Hey," I said, looking to the ceiling. "Do you hear that?"

"I don't hear anything," said Catherine.

"Exactly," I said. "And that's the sound of me ignoring you."

"I guess there's nothing else to discuss," she said, looking to Strong for guidance. When he said nothing, she asked to use the phone to call a cab. Strong explained that she had ridden to his house with him after a meeting a Rudyard's Pub, where she had left her car. He started insisting on taking her back there. As he talked, I had second thoughts about the abrupt way I had handled her. Unaware of exactly what Strong had been trying to do by injecting me into these negotiations, I suddenly felt I should reopen them.

"If Strong is getting his shit back, I want mine," I said. "I know it's paltry, but what about it?"

Catherine turned and, for the first time, showed an interest in a reasonable discussion with me. She motioned for Strong to leave the room.

"Do you really want it back?" she asked, once Strong had moved to a bedroom around the corner. "It's not far away. I can make a call and get it if you'll go with me to do that."

As soon as she said that, I suspected she wanted to get me somewhere alone and kill me, or at least to try. I also saw her invitation as my chance to force that showdown in a place where I would be the only one involved. I didn't hesitate. I just looked at her and said, "Sure."

"Let me make a call," she said, picking up the phone again. She pecked out a number and spoke into the receiver, saying, "I need my stuff. Take it to the U-Tote-Em near my house, and then call me there." Then, she looked at me and said, "Take me to my place. Some Mexicans will bring it to us."

Still unsure about this decision, I told her I wanted to change clothes first and then moved to my bedroom where Strong was waiting.

"Great," he whispered. "If you can go with her, go ahead and go. Get a transfer of stolen property. I'll call Stricklin and tell him what's going on. And I'll come over there with my shotgun and wait outside in case something goes wrong."

If I hadn't spent the last four months listening to Catherine's preposterous, melodramatic outbursts, I probably would have laughed in Strong's face and asked him what 1930s gangster flick had produced that dialogue. But constant exposure to Catherine's film-noir world had numbed our senses to the façade of tough talk. More importantly, it didn't matter how silly all of this sounded. After she showed her potential with that burglary, I knew what had to be done. I had to give her a final chance to do to me whatever she might be capable of doing. And Strong was right about something. A trap was being set for someone. I just hoped I could become the trapper as well as the bait.

FIFTY-THREE

January 17, 1980

"Isn't this the time when you are supposed to confess everything to me?" I asked, almost as soon as we climbed into my car and started the drive to her place. Out of context, it sure sounded silly. But, in my car that night, the question meshed perfectly with the mood.

"You need to explain it all," I said.

She stared ahead into the windshield for a few moments, then turned, and said forcefully: "I will tell you one thing. If you fuck me on this, if I give you this stuff and you end up back at Special Crimes, Gary, I will kill you."

"Oh, hell, Catherine," I said. "You're going to kill me anyway, aren't you?"

Fight or flight? Stress management experts remind us our distant ancestors faced that question several times a day when confronting life and death challenges from wild animals or enemy tribes. Despite the elimination of true life-and-death threats on a daily basis, they say modern humans still demonstrate similar physical responses to lesser challenges, such as a broken television set or rude drivers on the freeway. I knew researchers had measured typical responses that included everything from accelerated heartbeat to pooping your pants. Most visible, however, is the release of adrenalin and endorphins to dull pain and impair judgment so you can function on instinct for the quickest reaction when attacked. Except for soldiers and cops, rarely do humans have the chance to experience the full effect of the fight-or-

227

flight response. But I was feeling the full effects already as I drove into the night beside a woman I feared wanted me dead. I already had committed to fight, rather than flight. I had a rough plan for action, and my body went on autopilot as the adrenalin took control. I couldn't shut up, but I also felt strangely detached, as if I were watching the two of us from the back seat instead of driving the car. I had never felt anything like it before and never would experience it again.

"You know," I said, trying to goad her while using language to bolster my courage, "Mark called you a bum fuck."

That grabbed her attention.

"He told you that?"

"Why did you bring him into this? Surely you could have found some other stooge to fuck you for an alibi."

"He really called me a bum fuck?"

Pleased to see I had at last found a raw nerve, I decided to pinch it.

"Oh yeah, he was pissed. He expected big things from you, and you treated him like your mind was on another planet. And then what about me? Now I have to explain why I spent the last three months taking nothing but shit from a bum fuck. Do me a favor. Next time you fuck one of my friends, please, give him the time of his life. I have a reputation to maintain."

Catherine hesitated before speaking again, obviously amused by my excited state. Then she said, "Gary, you need to get control of your mouth. When these men come to bring your property, they aren't going to listen to it. They will just take you outside and shut you up."

"Ha, huh, just like you planned for them to do on Tuesday night anyway, right?"

"Are you wearing a wire?"

"A wire? No. Be my guest. Check me out."

She leaned over while I drove and patted me down, checking for recording devices while I continued to blather.

"You know, I had Little E with me that night. Did you know that? What would have happened with her there?"

Apparently satisfied with the frisk of my body, she moved back onto her seat and said, "These were honorable men. They would have seen her and taken her somewhere to be safe."

"That would have been over my dead body."

"Then, it might well have been."

Her admission shut me up as I mulled her words. In my mind, not only had she conceded a role in the burglary but also exposed it for what I actually suspected she wanted: a serious beating, or something much worse, for me.

"So you admit somebody came over there to get me."

"Teach you a lesson."

"And what's happening tonight?"

"I told you. I've had enough. This isn't worth my time any more. Take your stuff and Strong's, too, and be out of my life for good."

"If that's what you truly have in mind, it sounds like we finally have a deal."

"Did Mark really call me a bum fuck?"

"Yes, Catherine, that's exactly what he said."

About eleven-thirty we pulled up to the curb in front of the duplex I had helped her rent just a couple of months before. I realized it had been just about a year to the day since the brutal slaying of George Tedesco. And now, I was about to meet in private with the woman suspected in that case.

C'mon, bitch! I said to myself. *Let's see if you are a real killer or just a little woman with a big mouth. Show me something. Fuck Strong's hope for a penny-ante burglary conspiracy charge. If I leave here, I expect to see you facing life for attempted murder.*

FIFTY-FOUR

January 17, 1980

Catherine's duplex apartment was a simple structure with the layout of a one-bedroom mobile home. Some would call it a shotgun-style arrangement—but I've always hesitated using that term where she is concerned. It was just typical of a duplex made from a one-story house divided into two equal-size single-bedroom apartments. A front door opened into a living room and a hallway ran along a side wall to empty into a bedroom at the rear. Off the hallway to the right, as you headed toward the rear, was a kitchen and then a bathroom. Besides the door on the front wall of the living room, Catherine's apartment also had a large window.

She had furnished the living room with a couch, a wicker chair, some sparse bookcases, and a table that held her prized Sony color television set and a stereo. She had decorated a table with a framed, black-and-white, eight-by-ten studio photo of Humphrey Bogart striking a 1930s gangster movie pose. In the kitchen, Catherine had a small, mobile dishwasher with a butcher block top. Her cabinets held a variety of liquors. In her bedroom, an average size closet sat in the wall immediately to the left beyond the hall, with a wooden door that opened outward. Catherine's double bed sat across the floor from the closet. Beside the closet doorway, farther into the room, still sat that chair I had helped bring down from the attic for her Christmas party. The front door in the living room was the only way in or out of the place.

When we came inside, I took a seat in the wicker chair while she went straight to the phone and made a call. She said she wanted to make sure "the Mexicans" were still on schedule. I took her comment in stride, wondering if she really had any "Mexicans" working this mission at all. I knew she was physically incapable of handling me without a weapon, so I felt comfortable as long as I could keep her in sight. I did have concerns, of course, about the arrival of reinforcements that might include anyone like my bounty-hunting associate Kenneth. But I had faith in the vision of Jim Strong parked somewhere out on the street, ever vigilant with shotgun primed—ready to spring if Catherine's "gang" were to approach. I believed I had reinforcements of my own. So I kept a careful eye on Catherine as she made her call and prepped me for what would be a much longer night than I had expected.

"We have to wait a while," she said, taking a seat on the couch. "I don't know when they will be here."

I was prepared to wait until Catherine attempted an assault, or, at least, until she reassured me with her hesitance that she lacked the courage to try. I wanted to offer myself to her as a target and give her every opportunity to strike. I resolved to just go along with just about anything she wanted. I kept an eye on her as she went to the kitchen and mixed a couple of drinks. At that time, Campari and soda had become her cocktail of choice. I stayed with scotch and water.

"We've got some time," she said. "Maybe we should talk."

"Sure. What's on your mind?"

"I want to know if you ever really loved me. Did you?"

"Of course. But I've told you that doesn't mean two people can be together. And in our case, that's particularly true."

She nodded and started to adopt what I perceived as an air of detachment. As it turned out, Catherine had plenty to discuss before getting down to the real business of the night—deciding what to do with me. I sensed an internal agony in her demeanor, as if two conflicting personalities were debating some action inside her skull.

"I want to read something to you," she whispered. Catherine was a voracious reader, but she had only a small shelf of books with her in this place. She went to the shelf and extracted a copy of one her favorites: Mario Puzo's *The Godfather*. During our time together, she had quoted it often. And now, sitting there waiting for her "soldiers" to return my stolen property, she selected a section from Book One outlining the fate of mob enforcer Luca Brasi when dispatched by Don Vito Corleone to infiltrate the camp of a rival family. At a meeting in a bar, the rivals surprise Luca and strangle him from behind with thin silken cord. After an anxious day wondering what had happened, the Corleone brothers are startled to receive a package that holds a fish wrapped in Luca's bulletproof vest. They look to their consigliore, Tom Hagen, for an explanation.

Catherine read the final passage with emphasis: " 'The fish means that Luca Brasi is sleeping on the bottom of the ocean,' he said. 'It's an old Sicilian message.'"

I wondered if I should take that as a message for me, as well. In her version, I suspected, Special Crimes became the mob with Stricklin as the Godfather. Of course, I was Luca Brasi, exposed while trying to infiltrate her bush league criminal camp and soon to be sleeping with the fishes.

"Eloquent," I said. "What's next? *The Adventures of Huckleberry Finn?*"

"Dance with me one last time," she said, laying the book on the table and ignoring my sarcasm as a slow song came onto her stereo. I agreed, although I couldn't remember when we had ever danced before in the first place. It came as no surprise when she tried to lead.

When we stopped dancing, she made another call and frowned when she couldn't get an answer. Then she looked at the phone and asked me for a favor.

"Anything you want," I said.

"I need you to call Denise and tell her something. Tell her you made a mistake when you took her out. Tell her you meant to take out Catherine."

"I don't think she'll take my call, and besides, it's getting pretty late," I said, more perplexed than ever by this request. I suspected Catherine wanted me to establish contact with another person outside her house who might later testify, "Yeah, he called me late and sounded creepy."

"Also," I said, "I don't recall her number, and it is in my address book— you know, the one that's been missing since that last day you visited me at Strong's house but before the burglary."

"If I can find it, will you call her?"

"Sure," I said, confident Denise would decline to talk. Catherine immediately reached beneath the couch and produced my address book. She handed it to me along with the telephone. I dialed my one-time canoeing partner and, after about seven rings, she picked up the phone.

"Denise," I began, but she hung up as soon as she heard my voice. Aware that Catherine had no way to know I only had a dial tone on the other end of the line, I continued as if Denise were still there. "I'm calling because I want you to know I should not have gone out with you. I wanted to go out with Catherine, but she rejected me—"

Just then Catherine ripped the phone from my hand, put it to her ear, and recognized the dial tone. She grabbed my address book and redialed the number, only to receive the same rude treatment by Denise.

"Imagine that," I said. "The girl won't even take our calls. Anybody else I can dial? Mario Puzo maybe. How about Humphrey Bogart? You know, listening to your shit is enough to make my blue eyes brown."

She said nothing and returned to the couch, where she sat with an obvious aura of detachment. I wasn't sure about the time, but I did know I had been in there long enough. Obviously, I thought, her gang had let her down. I had given her every opportunity to attack, but it looked like she only wanted to dance, read from *The Godfather,* and make ridiculous phone calls. It was time for me to go.

"That's it," I said, rising from my spot in the wicker chair. "Nobody's coming, are they? No Mexicans? I'm going to leave, and I guess we'll all just have to handle this another way."

As I made for the door, Catherine rose from the couch and spoke very slowly. She said, "Wait, Gary. I do have something for you. It's back in my bedroom closet. You can go and get it now."

I turned and looked down the short, dark hallway between the rooms. A slight grin slid across my face as I realized our moment had arrived. Something or someone awaited me back in her bedroom.

"You want me to walk back there and look in your closet?" I asked, considering if I really wanted to honor her request. I flashed on an image again of Little E hiding on the floorboard of my two-hundred-dollar car and remembered the promise I'd made to finish this business with Catherine that night.

"OK," I said. "I'm going to do that—exactly what you ask. I'm going to go back there and look in your closet. Then I'm going to leave and go home."

FIFTY-FIVE

January 18, 1980

A chill ran up my spine. It's one of the oldest clichés around. I had used it myself a number of times before that morning. I'd heard many others toss it around casually over the years and still hear it said quite often with a laugh. But the truth was, I never really had felt a chill run up my spine until then—as I stood in that closet at the rear of her apartment and stared at nothing through the shadowy light from the lamp in Catherine's living room some fifty feet away. Up my spine? It did not stop there. It covered my shoulders like a shawl, spread down my arms, and under my fingernails. In the other direction it ran down the back of my legs and into the crack of my butt. I closed my eyes and took a deep breath.

I barely had had time to realize the closet sat empty before that living room light went out and threw everything into an eerie twilight, the inside illuminated only by stray beams sifting through the windows from lampposts in the street beyond the house. I stood just inside the closet holding the knob on the light wooden door that opened outward toward the hallway as I searched the empty shelf above the rod for a sign of anything she might have had for me. I froze there for a second until I heard her soft footsteps padding slowly down the hall. When she cocked the revolver, however, that chill covered me like majesty on the queen, and, before the sound stopped echoing like thunder around the dark apartment, I had pivoted, stepped inside the closet, and pulled the door behind me, hoping it would form some kind of a shield as I faced the bedroom beyond the door.

I peeked through the crack between the door and jam, a space that offered a thin, narrow view of her silent movement into the bedroom. I watched her holding the pistol pointing down with both hands as she turned away from the closet and took a position on the opposite side of the room facing me from beside the head of her bed.

Moron was the first thought that leaped into my head. Then, I thought— *No, not strong enough. Imbecile? Idiot? One of those, whichever is dumbest. That's what I am, unless there is something even dumber!*

Trapped inside her closet like that, my mind began scrambling for options as my eyes raced around the small space searching for anything I might use to escape. But nothing was there. So, I watched carefully through the crack, hoping I might find something to give me an edge.

"I am going to kill you now," Catherine began, after lifting the pistol to shoulder level and pointing it at the hollow wooden closet door that stood between us. I knew the bullets could rip the wood before hitting me if she had started shooting right away. Instead, of course, she wanted to talk a little first. Recalling the *Exorcist Tape,* I thought: *I guess this is the place where she wants me to beg for her mercy.*

"You know there is nothing more after this life, so it won't help to pray," she continued in a tone of voice I had never heard from her before. She seemed completely detached, devoid of feeling, speaking like a robot on autopilot. Her eyes looked blank in the dim light and I couldn't even be sure they focused on me. As she spoke, strange thoughts crossed my mind.

Maybe, I thought, *I should just step out and take it. Maybe I've had enough of this life. There would be insurance for Cindy and the girls.*

I remembered suddenly we had passed the midnight hour into January 18. It was my youngest daughter's second birthday. *What a present this would be! Would they be better off without me? Would I be better off without this life? Did I really want to continue this fight?*

As if on cue, Catherine offered a suggestion in the midst of her lecture: "Don't worry about your wife and kids, I won't do anything to them. But, you—you have done things to me that nobody has."

Suddenly, I wanted to cry. During the last three months I had seen several different Catherines. At times she had been witty and charming. Other times I'd seen her uncontrollable anger. I had seen her trying to con me or play on my sympathy. As I watched through the crack in the closet, I realized I was seeing yet another Catherine, the most dangerous of all. This Catherine with the cold, lifeless eyes was the killer. I wondered if this Catherine was the last one Tedesco had seen as well—before his brains were bashed on the floor of his garage.

Maybe this is what I deserve, I wondered. Then I recalled something Catherine had said once while philosophizing on the question of just deserts. She had said, "Here's how you tell if they got what they deserve. You look at what they have. And that is exactly what they deserve."

As all these thoughts and emotions raced around my brain, I also realized that Catherine actually was giving me a unique opportunity most people never have. She was forcing me to decide the meaning of life under intense pressure that would help me focus finally on an answer. *Do you really want to live?* she was asking. And suddenly I realized my answer was, *Yes*. There would be no more hesitation, no further thoughts of surrender. No tears. A searing new heat started melting the icy chill that had paralyzed my mind. It was the heat of anger. My temperature was rising. And I realized I could harness this anger for deliverance.

We don't allow people like Catherine to run our lives and paralyze us with fear, I thought to myself, as my mind began to clear. *We face them and make them break us, if they can, or we break them instead.*

Rejuvenated by my new resolve and driven by a seething but disciplined rage, I searched the closet again, this time with more attention to detail. My eyes moved slowly from right to left, from the crack between the hinges of the door to the little opening beyond the knob. And suddenly I spied my salvation. I had a plan. It might not work. But at least I wouldn't go down begging her for mercy.

I knew I needed patience to strike at the right time. Outlining the steps in my mind, I returned to stare out the crack, keep quiet, and watch her for any sign of opportunity.

"You should just come out now," she said, her voice droning listlessly as she held the pistol aloft in the policeman's position pointed at the closet. "I know how to use this. Officer Joe taught me."

Then, it appeared she had run out of things to say. As if searching for some other words to coax me out or force herself forward, her arms wavered a bit, and I watched her eyes. Their focus dropped to the floor. Confident she had relaxed, I sprung into action.

Kicking open the door, I reached in a single motion for the wooden chair I had parked beside that closet so long ago. I grabbed the chair by the back and swung it around pointing the legs directly at Catherine while advancing straight toward her.

"Motherfucker!" I screamed my battle cry as adrenalin bubbled to a boil.

With the chair blocking my view, I couldn't see her startled reaction, but I could sense a frenzy of movement from her direction as I advanced with the chair, like a lion tamer in the circus. Suddenly, the seat of the chair splintered as a .32-calibre slug came sailing through a hole in the bottom and smacked into the left side of my head, just above the ear, grazing my skull and ricocheting to the side. I remained oblivious, drugged by the action. I felt nothing and continued my advance, focused only on the blueprint I had plotted moments before.

Following that plan, I flung the chair in her direction hoping to knock her back against the wall and create a distraction for me to pivot empty-handed and rush headlong down the hall toward the front door. Fight or flight? I guess my ultimate plan had become a combination of the two basic options. But I noticed the adrenalin was working on either one.

Looking back, I also recall my impression of entering what professional athletes often call "the zone." That's an ill-defined, adrenalin-induced state of mind in which physical senses heighten to their ultimate powers. Baseball Hall of Famer Tony Gwynn has described it as a place where the baseball appears to move slower than it really does. I have experienced the zone myself sometimes in amateur sports. Playing basketball in high school, for example, I enjoyed some times when every other player seemed to be moving in slow motion. Playing shortstop on a softball team when in the zone, the ground balls seemed to take extraordinarily slow, looping bounces that made fielding them a snap. If I could live permanently in the zone, I certainly would. But you only enter the zone at special times when your adrenalin is pumping perfectly to control your reactions—and, in particular, it now seemed, when someone is trying to murder you. That night in Catherine's apartment I felt the zone take hold as I grabbed the chair. Running down Catherine's hallway pushed my adrenalin to full throttle. The sequence of events transpired in a matter of minutes. But in my mind, it seemed like hours. Everything in that apartment stood in a time warp except for me.

As I entered the living room, I focused on the deadbolt above the doorknob and noted the next obstacle in my path. Catherine, of course, had taken the time to lock the door.

You will only have one chance to unlock it, that little voice in my head instructed as I sped across the room. *Stop and do it right. Then get the hell out of here.*

Fortunately the dead bolt had an inside handle of its own so I didn't need a key. I knew I could not use any precious time to look over my shoulder for her. So I stopped at the door. I reached down and twisted the dead bolt handle to unlock it. I opened the inside door and pushed the handle of the outer glass storm door standing between me and her front porch. It opened, and I started to run again, toward the yard and the street beyond.

But I suddenly felt myself propelled faster than I knew I could run. I was moving out above her concrete front porch, flying headlong into the yard, almost parallel with the ground. I also felt a pounding sensation, as if someone had popped me in the back with a bath towel. But I knew I was moving much too fast for that. I landed face down in the grass about ten feet beyond the front door and clutched the turf with the fingers on the end of my outstretched arms.

That bitch shot me! My thoughts screamed inside my head. I was finally growing angry. *She really shot me!*

FIFTY-SIX

January 18, 1980

Although I knew she had shot me in the back, I also was aware that I felt no pain. It had to have been the adrenalin. Somehow, I had escaped the house, and I pondered my next move. I lay spread-eagled on the turf and looked around the street. I had thought maybe Strong would be coming with his shotgun, but the only car I could see was mine, parked in front of Catherine's duplex. I noticed porch lights coming to life at a couple of houses across the street, but I lay as still as possible. I glanced over my shoulder and caught a view of Catherine in the corner of an eye—standing on the porch and admiring her pistol-work. She probably would have enjoyed firing a few more rounds into my prone body, but she couldn't do that with me down in her front yard where neighbors might see.

Since I felt no pain, I wondered if the shot had hit my spine and paralyzed me. I wiggled my toes and felt them move. Then I grabbed some grass with both hands and noticed my hands could squeeze the blades with no problem. Satisfied with my continued mobility, I didn't hesitate launching the second phase of my plan. I jumped up and ran to my right along the south side of Kipling, toward Dunlavy—a little busier street that crossed Kipling about four houses to the east. I thought I heard another gun shot in the background, but I was so focused on my escape I could not be sure.

"Murder," I yelped, without much imagination but determined to make an impression on anyone who might be listening. "Help."

Then I thought, *Shit, is she going to chase me down the street?*

I moved into the shadow of a line of trees just in case and ran hard, finally feeling like I might survive this showdown after all. I must have put on a pretty good show because Catherine later described the scene from her view to a writer for *The Dallas Times-Herald* newspaper, saying: "I never saw a man run so fast or jump so high. He was jumpin' like a rabbit."

I had planned to run another couple of blocks down Dunlavy to where it crossed the much busier Alabama Street. There was a traffic light at that intersection and a large twenty-four-hour grocery store. But I foolishly tried to flag down a car going past on Dunlavy. It carried two teenage girls who had snuck out for an early morning joy ride, and, of course, they weren't going to stop for some guy in a panic claiming to have been shot. But I learned later that they did stop for Catherine, much to her regret. I looked back to see her standing on the corner with what appeared to be a pistol in her hand, hanging down at her side while she watched my flight. I relaxed with the realization I could probably make it to the grocery store. I just wondered if the bullet in my back would prove fatal.

"Can you call an ambulance?" I asked a startled clerk in the store who had just sat down to a meal of Church's Fried Chicken. Eager to leave an evidentiary trail in case I expired there in the store, I added: "I've been shot by Catherine Mehaffey."

The guy just looked at me dumbfounded at first, and I had to give him the fire department's phone number in those days before the advent of the 911 emergency dial. From my years covering police and fire, the department's telephone number was engrained on my brain. After he made that call, I gave him Strong's number and asked him to call that one, too.

"Hey man," I told a sleepy Strong when he answered after six or seven rings, "that bitch shot me."

"Bullshit," he replied, snapping quickly alert.

"Not bullshit! I'm at that Weingarten's grocery at Alabama and Dunlavy waiting on an ambulance. Next stop is probably Ben Taub. What the fuck happened to you?"

"I waited outside for a long time. Finally I figured you two had made up again. Are you OK?"

Given the history of my relationship with Catherine, I couldn't blame him for leaving. I had lost track of how long I had been in her house and figured it must have been longer than it seemed. Things probably would have been worse if he had been there, anyway, and started blasting with a shotgun after I burst through the door.

"I don't know how I am," I said. "I know I took something in the back and side of my head. You need to get over to Taub and find me. Call Cindy for me, too, if you can, and George."

Ben Taub was Houston's primary emergency hospital and boasted one of the nation's top trauma rooms. I figured Cindy needed to know what had happened in case I died. And I thought my old roommate George should know since he also was my boss. As soon as I hung up, I noticed a fire truck had pulled into the parking lot, and I scowled at the guy eating chicken. He just shrugged his shoulders, so I walked out and told the fire fighters I'd been shot and actually needed an ambulance. It arrived about the time a Houston police patrol car pulled in, as well as a nighttime news photographer from the CBS-network affiliate, Channel 11.

"Who shot you?" asked the TV newshound as I lay inside the ambulance with the paramedics checking me out.

"The lawyer Catherine Mehaffey," I said. "That's M-E-H-A-F-F-E-Y. She's a lawyer."

The patrol officer shooed him away and asked me where it happened.

"It was at her place at 1723 Kipling, right up Dunlavy a couple of blocks. She's got a gun and could still be trouble."

They wrote down my name, then left to go find her. Just as I smiled while envisioning the scene of a potential SWAT standoff, I looked up to see one of the paramedics with a catheter line in his hand.

"C'mon," I whined. "I don't need that yet, do I? Fuck."

"It's procedure."

"Fuck that bitch," I grumbled while he threaded the line into my penis. "This feels worse than the gunshots."

Both paramedics started laughing, so I asked, "How does the gunshot wound look?"

"We'll take good care of you, and they'll look at the hospital," said one of them. "Are you in any pain?"

"Just in my cock, motherfucker," I said, and they laughed again. "Fuck her to hell for this."

Of course, I had no way of knowing what was happening back at Catherine's duplex. But I later would learn that she had asked the teenage girls for help. They at first considered Catherine a possible rape victim who had successfully vanquished me as her attacker. They would later testify they saw her drop two pistols in the grass beside the sidewalk before accompanying them back to her apartment where she broke down.

"I'm ruined," Catherine was telling them about the same time I was talking to Strong. "I have to call the police, and I'm asking you to please not tell them about those guns."

We had a big reunion at Ben Taub—Strong, George, Cindy, and me—while the doctor tried to keep things somber.

"I don't know why you aren't dead," he said, shaking his head and unfurling an X-ray that showed a slug sitting right up against my heart. "It must be trapped in some muscle tissue there. Were you bent over or something when she shot you?"

"I was opening a dead bolt lock. I guess I would have been hunched over."

"Man," he said, "if you are a poker player you had better give it up because you have used a lifetime's supply of luck tonight. She really nailed you. A fraction of an inch one way and you're paralyzed, another fraction forward and you are D.O.A."

I looked at Cindy and said, "Don't start spending that life insurance money yet."

She frowned as the doctor continued his prognosis.

"We cannot go in there tonight and get that bullet. It's just too close to the heart. We'll have to leave it in. Hopefully it won't move. You may need a note to go through metal detectors and get on airplanes. But you are going to have some terrific pain the next few days. I will get you started on Demerol and an antibiotic. You need to stick around here a couple of hours, and, if you aren't running a fever, I don't see why you can't leave."

"So, can you get that catheter out, now?" I asked.

He nodded with a grin and pointed to a nurse who ended that misery.

"Fucking bitch," I mumbled. The nurse turned to stare, and I apologized, "Not you. I'm sorry. I was thinking of somebody else."

By then they also had stitched up the gash in my head. All I could do was sit there and wait to be released. For the first time in my relationship with Catherine I was truly angry.

"That fucker is going to jail, now," I said. "That fucking bitch."

Strong started giggling and shaking his head. "I'm sorry," he said. "But I have to tell you, when you are sitting there with that bandage on your head and your eyes popped out, you look just like Wile E. Coyote after the dynamite goes off."

"Thanks," I said, then I started to chuckle a bit, too, euphoric, I guess, that I apparently would survive, and this moment of confrontation had ended. I also felt some pride in my escape, having employed a wooden chair to defeat a woman with a pistol. But I also felt fear, wondering what was happening at her apartment and thinking she might have fled with a plan of her own to wipe out anyone associated with me. I told Cindy to make sure her door was locked and said I would stop by later in the day for Shannon's birthday.

"I'll probably need a sick day today," I told George, with a little grin.

George and Cindy left, but Strong hung around. We had decided to get a hotel room for the night rather than go back to his house, exaggerating Catherine's ability to stage another attack. Just as we were celebrating what appeared to be a victory over her, however, a hospital aide handed me a telephone with detective John Donovan on the line ready to spoil the fun.

"How are you?" he asked.

"Shot in the back and the head, but it looks like I'll live. What's up?"

I had known Donovan for years, considered him an ace investigator, and was pleased he had landed the case. He couldn't resist a little jibe.

"Taylor, I have to tell you, I'm over at Mehaffey's, and this place looks like something out of a Roadrunner cartoon. I can see where you ran by looking at the bullet holes in the walls."

"Yeah, John, ha, I, uh…"

"But I do need to ask you a question. Which gun was yours?"

I was stunned. I had never even held a gun in my entire life, much less that night. I did not even know two guns were in play. Suddenly, I realized Catherine had an escape plan of her own.

"I didn't have a gun," I said.

"She says you did."

I flashed on a scene from the first *Halloween* movie that had been popular recently and recalled the image of that psycho killer Michael Myers rising up in the background to attack again while everyone was celebrating his death.

"It's a lie, John. I had no gun. I don't know what she is talking about. Does this mean there's no arrest?"

"Oh, no, we're arresting her, taking her in right now. You're shot in the back, and she'll have to show it was self-defense. But I had to call as soon as possible and get your reaction. I also wanted to let you know this probably isn't the end."

FIFTY-SEVEN

March 1980

"Hey, I know you, don't I? You're the guy who…"

I didn't let him finish. I was sitting alone one night a few weeks after the shooting at the bar in Houston's Hofbrau Steak House, sipping on a scotch and water. This guy in a suit sat down and stared at me before he started speaking. I took him immediately for a local lawyer somehow familiar with Catherine's latest escapade of trying to murder me two months earlier. I wondered if he were friend or foe, but I didn't really care. In those three months between my shooting and her trial, a great deal had changed in my emotional attitude and my life in general. I was a tough guy taking on all comers. So I nodded.

"That's what I thought," he said, ordering a beer, and then telling the bartender to fetch me another scotch on his tab. He turned and said with a grin, "I don't know anything about you. But I once knew her. And whatever you say she did, I believe it."

Hmmm, I thought, *maybe I should take your order for one of those 'Mehaffey Survivor' T-shirts Mark and I might start producing.*

Instead of verbalizing that thought, however, I just winked and thanked him for the drink, acting much like a soldier sharing a war story with no need for the details. Besides, I thought he could just as easily be an investigator for Catherine's impending trial, trying to get some sort of wedge against me through an innocent barroom conversation. I drank up and left, looking over my shoulder all the way to my car, which at this time had become a brand new, dark blue 1980 Ford Bronco purchased with my share of proceeds from the sale of my house.

My sex life had perked up as well and diversified. I learned that a man wounded by a notorious femme fatale ranks only behind one in a uniform for appeal. Although I was a little surprised at the response, I figured I should milk that advantage as long as I could. A couple of days after the shooting, for example, I got a call at the office from Barbara. No longer fearful about the fate of her dogs, she wanted to get reacquainted and apologized for brushing me off just because Catherine had visited her before our date. She told me she had once had a similar, but less violent, experience with a rejected boyfriend and knew how I must feel.

After Cindy and I closed on sale of the house, we closed on another reconciliation that resulted in a regular gig as her secret lover when Uncle Al was working nights. About that time she also had officially become my second ex-wife, and I began to realize how seriously conflicted she must have been. But I enjoyed being the other man *with* her for a change, and the thought of cuckolding Uncle Al just added more spice to the meal. I had an easier time visiting our daughters, too, because I didn't have to leave after they went to bed.

And then, there was the woman I met in a bar who just walked up and said, "Let's see if it's worth killing for."

"It's not," I replied. "It was a lot more complicated than that. But you strike me as someone who would demand evidence anyway, so I'm not going to try and convince you otherwise."

Once I had them aligned on a convenient, rotating schedule, I had a greater appreciation for what life must have been like for Warren Beatty. I tried to understand the attraction and decided I must have been reflecting a greater air of confidence—the kind that comes from squaring off against a gun with a wooden chair and living to testify in court. I certainly felt stronger then and acted the part. Some might have thought such a close call with death would have shown me the light of religion, but I just hadn't had the time to think about it.

The night after the shooting, ramped up on Demerol, I started a new hobby, too, when Strong took me to a bar to play British steel tip darts. It seemed like I had a natural talent for the sport. I did well enough to immediately join a league team and start playing tournaments for money around town. One night at a bar called Sherlock's Pub, we had prevailed in a tournament, and I couldn't resist taunting the losers.

"Dig you an early grave, did we?" I asked. "Kick you while you were down?"

Fists started flying, and, before we were able to back out of the bar, an entire wall collapsed—the one displaying a framed collectible of Queen Victoria's pantaloons and much beloved by the proprietor. Once we got outside, the mob retreated back into the pub, but I was shaking as I got in Strong's car to ride home.

"What is going on with me?" I asked him. "I'm thirty-three years old and getting into barroom brawls now? In just six months I've seen my marriage collapse, dated a psycho, and gotten shot. Now I'm fighting in bars? What the fuck is next?"

He just shrugged his shoulders and laughed at me.

We had decided to live under the assumption that Catherine probably would have enjoyed nothing more than to successfully finish the job she started January 18. Just to feel safer, I bought a .357 Magnum. I recruited our police reporter, Fred King, to take me to a pistol range and teach me how to shoot it. I carried it everywhere in a canvas knapsack. On our nightly forays, Strong would bring his shotgun, too. We must have looked like cartoon characters, coming home drunk after a darts tournament, stopping in the driveway, and then grabbing weapons from the trunk. One time a tree limb made a noise brushing against the garage door in the wind as we walked toward the house, and Strong defended us by blowing a hole in the garage wall. Our friends felt the need for arms as well. One night playing poker in Strong's kitchen with a group of lawyers and reporters, we heard tires squeal in the cul de sac outside his house.

"Whoaa," I shouted, as our guests produced at least four large pistols from under the table, ready for action.

"And the wind cried MOOOOOHAFFFEEE," laughed Mark, mimicking Jimi Hendrix again as the other players holstered their weapons. The he begged me to never tell that he'd made fun of her that way.

"You know I told her you called her a bum fuck, don't you?" I said.

"Can't trust you worth a shit. Now I'm on her list."

"But we know who's still on top, don't we?" laughed Kent Schaffer, the private investigator who had bet me a hundred dollars I'd never live to attend Mike Ramsey's 1980 Christmas party, still more than nine months away.

"Want to cancel that bet?" I asked.

"Nope," he said. "I still think it's good."

"I think that as long as I can find a chair, I could handle her again."

Of course, there was work as well, and I found I enjoyed the change back into the office for the variety of general assignment duties, covering whatever story might arise on any given day. Both newspapers appeared so confused about what to do with me as a story that they relegated the shooting to the back pages. My management likely was embarrassed about the news of their reporter getting shot in a domestic squabble. But they didn't punish me or try to make me quit by assigning an unpleasant work schedule. I saw the situation as placing *The Post* in a bind because the paper needed me to prove myself before a jury as a truthful man. An acquittal for Catherine might have painted me as a liar and diminished the paper's credibility. But I also thought everyone at the paper believed my version of the events. Familiar as they were with the vagaries of the criminal court system, however, I also was sure they were holding their breath to make sure I could prove it.

But it wasn't all fun and work during the weeks between my shooting and Catherine's trial. I also had preparations to attend with the district attorney's office for that big event. And I was about to learn that the pleasant months of early 1980 were just the eye of a hurricane, with the second wall of rain and winds gathering just then to dump all over my head.

FIFTY-EIGHT

March 1980

Frustrated for more than a year by their failure to touch Catherine on the Tedesco murder, the brass at the Harris County District Attorney's office saw me as the vehicle for their second shot at her. And they liked their odds of success. Not only was she the suspect in both cases, but the facts of her relationship with both me and Tedesco boasted many similarities, with one crucial exception. I would be able to testify about mine.

So it had come as no surprise to find a who's who of local law enforcement gathered in a large conference room in the DA's building about eight hours after the shooting to take my official victim's statement, a document that normally would have been prepared by a homicide detective like Donovan. Instead of just me and a cop in his cubicle, we had a court stenographer taking my testimony under oath in a room filled to capacity with DA assistants and special investigators. Donovan was among them. Also in the crowd were Stricklin, Rosenthal, Oncken, and Carpenter, plus some others that had not surfaced in the early days of my case. Further emphasizing the importance the law enforcement community placed on my case, the man interrogating me for two hours in front of this audience was none other than Harris County District Attorney John B. Holmes, Jr., himself.

Everybody wants a piece of her ass, now, I thought, taking a mental roll call around that room. *And they believe I can pimp her out.*

That was fine with me. I hoped I had done just that. Later I grinned when I learned that Catherine had spent two nights in jail, unable to post bond while facing a possible life sentence on a charge of attempted murder. I also enjoyed seeing Don Stricklin himself visit Strong's house unannounced two nights after the shooting to warn us personally that she had finally made bail. Stricklin also said the office had decided to assign a prosecution team from the regular assistant ranks to avoid any hint of conflict that might arise if he or another Special Crimes Bureau lawyer took the case. Stricklin had a good chance of being called as a witness based on my statement to him in November.

But I was pleased a few days later to learn that a veteran prosecutor named Bert Graham would lead the team with the help of another veteran, Ira Jones. Bert was about my age, and I had watched him handle a number of trials during my time covering courts. In fact, he had been the lead prosecutor in the trial of the two Houston police officers accused in 1977 of killing the Hispanic laborer, Joe Torres, by throwing him into Buffalo Bayou. During that month-long trial moved to Huntsville, we had become close acquaintances while living in the dormitory on the campus of Sam Houston State University. Consulting frequently with Bert on plans for the Mehaffey trial, I learned a lot more about what actually had occurred the night she shot me and two days before with the burglary at Strong's house.

"It's a good news, bad news situation," Bert warned as he began outlining the case strategy for me. I knew Bert to be an extremely fastidious attorney. Although he had never lost a case as a prosecutor, he always worried that he would. He was destined to remain a career prosecutor in the office and rise in the next twenty years to the position of chief assistant. But his tone discussing the Mehaffey case in early 1980 left me wondering if it would actually be the cakewalk to conviction I anticipated. After all, I thought, hadn't I been shot in the back?

"You were inside her house," Bert explained. "And there were two pistols involved. She told the officers on the scene you had used one of them to threaten her, so she has established a claim of self-defense."

Catherine had tried to tell the first officers that all the action had occurred in the living room. But one of them was skeptical, noting bullet holes along the walls and through the picture window in the front of the apartment beside the door where I had run. He walked into the bedroom where he discovered a bullet hole in there and the chair with a bullet hole through the seat.

The investigation convinced detectives she had fired a total of seven times at me that night. One slug landed in my back. I laughed when I heard they found another slug just laying on her bed where it had fallen after sailing through the chair and bouncing off my head. In addition, they marked holes in the hallway wall and another in the picture window beside the front door. They believed she fired two more times outside the house as I ran down the street.

"Blasting away," I muttered, musing on the image of those holes in the wall.

Bert said the officers believed Catherine had kept a .32-calibre pistol stashed on the floor beneath the couch in the living room, waiting for the best moment and working up the courage to actually use it.

"She could have pulled it out and shot you in the face any time she wanted while you were in the living room with her earlier," said Bert. "For some reason, she waited until she could entice you to the bedroom. Maybe she wanted to make sure it looked like you had been in the bedroom so she could call it attempted rape. Or, maybe she was waiting for someone else who decided not to come. At any rate, when you got loose back there, she had to change her plans. She shot up the walls trying to kill you as you fled but couldn't hit the moving target. She even threw one slug into that picture window at the front of the house, probably just before she shot you in the doorway."

After using the last bullet in the .32 to put me on the ground outside her apartment, Catherine apparently withdrew to the bedroom where she retrieved a .22-caliber pistol from the top drawer of her dresser, Bert theorized. The first cop on the scene found that drawer still open when he checked the bedroom. Bert said they believed she had used the .22 for any shots outside the apartment, as I fled down the street.

"But the physical evidence verifies your version of the incident," Bert continued, offering his view of the good news for his trial strategy. "In fact, it's hard to explain it any other way. That bullet hole in the seat of the chair, for example, is crucial. She will have to explain that somehow. We all feel if she testifies she will lose control and show jurors that temper."

"Or, at least the Medusa stare."

"Yeah," he chuckled, "that, too. Anyhow, we also have the other stuff leading up to that night, testimony from Strong and the burglary. There are the tape recordings with the threats against you she made to Jim Strong. And we hope to find some way to at least mention the unsolved death of George Tedesco. Could you testify that you knew about her reputation and the suspicions in that murder?"

"Better than that," I said. "She talked about it constantly. She told me what I had done was worse than anything George had ever done."

"Did you take that as a threat?"

"You bet your sweet ass."

"We'll need you to say that in court, without the sweet ass part, of course."

I nodded. Bert also said he needed to get that slug from my back to prove she had been shooting the .32. So I arranged day surgery and went to a hospital with John Donovan. He stood beside the surgeon with a tin pan to preserve the chain of evidence as the doctor deposited the .32-calibre bullet into his custody. They just deadened my back with local anesthetic, and the doctor dug around in there until he could grab the slug with a forceps, much like a scene from an old western movie. I felt quite a bit of pressure when he grabbed the slug, but nothing went wrong. Of course, I needed another round of Demerol.

Just a few days after my shooting, the family of George Tedesco filed a civil, wrongful-death lawsuit seeking damages from Catherine and alleging she had conspired with a man the family identified as Tommy Bell to murder Tedesco. Although the criminal investigation into Tedesco had stalled, the family's attorneys felt strongly enough about their private investigation to make those allegations in a suit. I hadn't heard much about Tommy Bell to that point. But I was destined to hear much more in the weeks ahead.

My first Bell connection arrived in the mail, when I received a receipt for a late January gasoline purchase in New Jersey on a credit card of mine stolen in the burglary at Strong's. I took it to Bert, and his investigator, John Ray Harrison, tried to chase it down. The license plate number on the receipt was partially blurred, but Bert and John Ray tried a combination of digits until they found one that made sense. They traced one of the combinations back to the mother of Tommy Bell. He was known to have been a client of Catherine's. They thought they might finally have hit the jackpot, gaining leverage against an insider who could deliver Catherine on a number of crimes—maybe even Tedesco.

So, just before the March 24 trial date, they interrogated Bell for three hours. They persuaded him to admit Catherine had dispatched him to Strong's house the night of the burglary. He told them she wanted him to "rough Taylor up." But Bell denied stealing anything. Since Bell had missed me at the house, Bert decided against trying to squeeze him on a flimsy charge like unlawful use of a credit card. He wanted more. But, with the trial fast approaching, he had to keep Bell in the wings. Bert knew he couldn't trust Bell enough to force him to testify. And Bert thought he had a strong case without Bell. Bert just saw Bell as a potential ace in the hole, should something go wrong.

Should something go wrong? Bert didn't' know the circus was headed for town with plans to set up tents at the trial of Catherine Mehaffey and turn all his assumptions about jury psychology and presentation of evidence inside out.

FIFTY-NINE

March 24, 1980

"Gary, are you all right? I am such a bad shot. But I still don't know how you got out of there."

Catherine was sitting alone with me beside the desk in the chambers of State District Judge Jon Hughes. Just before jury selection in her attempted murder trial, she had made another of her bizarre requests—one that had led directly to this strange conversation. I had not even seen her since that night in her apartment, when I peeked around that chair I held as a shield in her bedroom before she fired the first shot. Back then, she resembled a zombie. With the trial set to begin this day, however, she was cleaned up, now perky and composed, ready to crack a few jokes and charm the world. She asked Bert for a private audience with me so we could sort some things out. Bert, of course, was skeptical, called it "highly unusual," and recommended I ignore her. But, of course, I couldn't resist. And the judge, eager to facilitate any meeting that could eliminate a trial, offered his chambers for our chat.

"No, I thought you made a pretty good attempt," I replied with a compliment, rubbing my back for affect.

Catherine tilted her head, batted her eyes, and cackled. Then she stared into my eyes and said, "You're not wearing a wire, are you? With you, I can never tell."

"I'm not. But I'm also not going to let you search me this time. You'll just have to take my word."

"Of course, I believe you. We have to talk."

"What's on your mind?"

She sat in a high back chair with her legs crossed. Her blonde hair was curled and bouncy, a lot like her demeanor. She was vivacious and smiling. Catherine had something to sell, and she wanted me to buy.

"Gary, we are making fools of ourselves. Don't you realize it?"

"I don't understand."

"This trial. You know, every lawyer in town thinks it's a big joke. I can't work."

I already knew that. The State Bar of Texas had suspended her license pending the outcome of this case. That organization will ignore a lot of misbehavior from its members, but an attempted murder charge tested its limits.

"And you," she said. "Look at you. You're ruined."

"I'm ruined? How so?"

"Oh, c'mon. They've got you back in the office running errands, hiding you, and hoping nobody knows you're there anymore."

"So, what's the solution?" I asked, unwilling to engage in debate over her deliberate mischaracterization of my job status and eager to get the trial under way.

"Call it off. Tell them you withdraw the charges. Forget about it. You know, I have two great lawyers handling this for me. And they are going to make you look very foolish."

I knew both of them. I had great respect for Catherine's trial lead, a lawyer named Jim Skelton. I had interviewed him numerous times and even shared a few drinks on occasion. But I had to chuckle as I thought of his associate on this case. He was an older, bearded man named Will Gray who already had a legendary reputation as an appellate wizard. I respected him, too, and knew him better. I knew him so well that I had asked him a few weeks back to serve as a character witness on my behalf if we needed anyone to testify about my stalwart reputation for the truth. He had quickly agreed. Then he called back a week later and withdrew. Sounding a bit sheepishly, he explained Catherine had hired him for her team. As a result, of course, he could not testify for me. Then he said something else that made me laugh: "Don't tell her I agreed to testify for you, will you?" I didn't mind losing Will as a character witness because I recognized that her retention of a crack appellate counsel for the trial itself spoke volumes about her concerns. She wanted Will Gray at the defense table raising every objection and finding any technical misstep that might eventually overturn an inevitable conviction.

"They are good," I agreed.

"Skelton is the Last Cowboy, you know. He is a real man who wouldn't betray his lover no matter what happened. He knows there are lover spats, and you just work around those things. I wish I had met him before I met you."

"The Last Cowboy," I said with a grin, stroking my beard. It sounded like they had kindled more than an attorney-client relationship. Maybe that's how she is paying for the high-priced legal counsel, I mused. I had heard rumors that she and Skelton had hooked up, and, with her gushing praise of his manhood, I couldn't help but suspect Catherine viewed him as something more than her lawyer. I also saw her glowing comments about the Last Cowboy as a feeble attempt to trigger a jealous rage. But she hadn't even been able to make me jealous when I liked her. So I ignored her discourse on the Code of the West and pressed for a quick end to our private session.

"So, what can I do for you?" I asked.

"I told you. Drop the charges. Tell Bert Graham you changed your mind, and you don't want a trial. It will only destroy both of us."

"I can't do that. It's really not my case, is it? It is styled 'The People of the State of Texas versus Catherine Mehaffey.' I'm just a witness in that case."

She frowned and snarled, "Don't give me that technical crap! You know in a case like this you could smash it with a single word, maybe even leave town."

"Leave town?" I asked, looking shocked. She had suggested this alternative a couple of times and friends had recommended it, too. She considered herself more of a Houstonian than me, having lived here since childhood, and had boasted to me once that Houston belonged to her. So I used this opportunity to challenge her territorial imperative.

"Houston has become my home," I said. "If anyone is leaving town, it's going to be you."

Then, before she could close her wide open mouth and respond, I delivered my final decision on her request.

"Catherine, we are going into that courtroom now and pull a jury. Then I am going to tell them everything I know. Then they are going to deliberate for about ten minutes and send you straight to fucking jail."

She sat back in her chair and delivered another Medusa stare. After a half-minute of that, I rose to leave. But before I could walk off, she offered her conclusion on the question of how I escaped that night.

"Now I know how you got away," she said. "Billy Joel is right. Only the good die young."

SIXTY

March 31, 1980

By the time my testimony had ended on the second day of trial, Catherine's reputation should have been in shreds. Jurors had learned as much about the unsolved murder of George Tedesco as they had about the attempt on my life. I believed I had been an effective witness. In my career, I had covered at least a hundred trials from start to finish, plus bits and pieces of hundreds more. I didn't require much coaching from Bert. I knew to look at the jury and answer the questions succinctly. When Skelton took his turn on cross-examination, he didn't ask many questions at all. I thought he was being cautious. But he did say he expected to recall me to the stand at a later time.

Since court rules prohibit witnesses in a case from hearing the testimony of other witnesses, I couldn't stay in the courtroom for the rest of the trial. As the defendant, of course, Catherine was allowed to face her accusers and assist her lawyers at the defense counsel table. So, I didn't hear the first part of the testimony from Jim Strong. But I did return to the courtroom at Catherine's request while Strong sat on the witness stand to present the *Exorcist Tape*. And during that second visit I had a strange premonition: "The state's case is falling apart."

Catherine and her attorneys wanted jurors to watch me while Bert played the *Exorcist Tape* and introduced it as evidence through testimony from Strong. So they asked the judge to have me return and sit in the front row behind the bar. I felt a strange transformation occurring in the courtroom. Every time we had listened to that tape in the confines at home, she had sounded spooky and chilling as her raspy voice threatened: "He has to beg for my mercy." In the sterile environment of that courtroom, however, she sounded more like a pitiful trapped animal. She sounded like a small, defenseless woman victimized by two large men who had recorded her weakest moment and ridiculed her with it for their own amusement. I wanted to puke.

Listening to that tape in open court, I felt embarrassed and ashamed. And I'm sure my face betrayed it. In contrast, Catherine sat weeping tenderly at the counsel table, looking every part an innocent forced to withstand this greatest of public humiliations by yet a third bully in her story, prosecutor Bert Graham. I could see the Last Cowboy had succeeded in making every defense attorney's dream come true for Catherine. He had turned his client into the victim.

I grew even more nervous as I watched the jurors and reviewed my testimony, imagining the questions they undoubtedly would be asking: "Is she on trial for Tedesco or Taylor? Why would Taylor continue to see her if she had such a dangerous reputation? Why would he even date her at all? What kind of person records his lover's most vulnerable conversations? Could that small woman really be as vicious as they say? What is this trial *really* all about, anyway?"

Indeed, I decided, my shooting had become just a footnote to something larger, more confusing, and possibly sinister.

Despite the boatload of incriminating evidence against Catherine, suddenly I felt like the villain with Jim Strong and Bert Graham as accomplices. Skelton and Gray just sat there shaking their heads in disgust while Catherine wept. Even Strong looked like he wanted to be anywhere but the witness stand. Then Skelton rose and delivered the final blow.

"Your honor," he said, "the defense demands that the state surrender all the tapes these men made of my client without her knowledge."

Above the twelve jurors I saw a single dialogue balloon disclosing their collective reaction: *More tapes? These guys made even more of these secret tapes?*

When the judge agreed, Bert's assistant, Ira Jones, opened his briefcase and dumped the contents on the defense table with a loud crash that echoed around the room. At least a dozen cassettes tumbled onto the wood. I had no idea we had taped her that many times in the week after Thanksgiving, and I didn't know whether to laugh or cry.

Skelton had no intention of playing any of those tapes, but he had made his point in dramatic style. From that moment on, he controlled the case. He didn't even present witnesses. Catherine did not testify. She just sat there crying. In final arguments Skelton described Strong and me as "fat worms" used by the district attorney's office in its single-minded and unfair pursuit of Catherine Mehaffey for the murder of George Tedesco. The jurors deliberated ten hours before declaring themselves hopelessly deadlocked. Judge Hughes declared a mistrial and scheduled a new trial for late May.

"Five? Five of them voted to acquit?" Bert was flabbergasted, and he looked a bit like Wile E. Coyote himself as he dissected the jury's reaction to this case. He sat on the couch in his office shaking his head and mumbled, "I thought maybe one would be fooled, but I can't believe five voted to acquit her."

"We're trying this again, aren't we?" I asked.

"One more time," he said. "That's all we can do. Who would have ever thought we would have all that stuff, and they still don't understand?"

"Bert," I said, "I have a suggestion. You have to force her to the stand. Let's not confuse them with all this Tedesco background and the tapes and everything. Just give the next jury a plain old, garden variety lovers' quarrel. No frills. Show them we dated. No details. I don't kiss and tell. I tried to break up. She shot me. Keep it simple as that. Then she'll have to take the stand."

But Bert was way ahead of me. He already had decided on a simpler strategy like that for the second trial and quickly agreed with my observation of the obvious. But he had plans to cut even more fat from his presentation. Next time, he said, he didn't even want Strong to testify, unless needed for rebuttal. And, as an evidentiary sword, the *Exorcist Tape* had shown a double edge. He believed neither side could introduce it and win. He would place the case totally on my back.

But we also were about to recruit an important ally in a strange turn of events that would slice one more notch in Catherine's reputation.

SIXTY-ONE

June 10, 1980

The evening after day two of Catherine's second trial found me back at Corky's, buying drinks for yet another dangerous woman. Actually, there were two dangerous women at the table along with Jim Strong. But I had focused on one of them. She was the sister of the *late* Tommy Bell, acknowledged that day in court as a professional burglar and alleged in a recent civil suit as the hit man for the murder of George Tedesco. While our conversation that night at Corky's would have its share of dark overtones, the mood nevertheless was decidedly celebratory, even though both ladies were still in mourning over Tommy's unexpected and violent death just a few weeks before.

"I know that bitch was responsible for killing him," Bell's sister said, after lighting a cigarette and taking a sip of her beer. She was about ten years my junior and I found her exceptionally attractive in an earthy sort of way. She had been in court that day to lend support to the other young woman sharing drinks with us at Corky's—a woman who had identified herself during testimony as the former girlfriend of the late Tommy Bell.

Her appearance had followed my testimony, much abbreviated from that first trial. As Bert and I had decided after that March debacle, I told a simple story of love gone wrong with Catherine. There had been no mention of Tedesco or the tapes. Jurors heard only my abbreviated account of the relationship that had ended with a burglary and my shooting. Then Bell's girlfriend took the stand to rock the courtroom and drive Catherine's legal team into the corner for a standing ten-count.

Although Tommy Bell had never agreed to testify against Catherine, the pressure had grown intense in the weeks between the trials, with Bert seeking any sort of wedge that might force him to turn. The climax occurred on May 5 when police responded to an ambulance call at Bell's apartment and found he'd been shot to death while watching television. His roommate reported Bell had been playing Russian roulette with a pistol and had accidentally killed himself with a shot to the head. While they could find no evidence indicating anything different, the police did discover something that would prove crucial in the second Mehaffey trial. Right there at the death scene, connected to Bell's television, they found Jim Strong's Beta Max, which had been stolen in the January 15 burglary. Finally Bert had secured physical evidence linking Bell to the burglary. He just needed to link Catherine with Bell

And Bell's girlfriend was quick to oblige. She testified only briefly to make two points. She told jurors that her boyfriend had not acquired the Beta Max until after the middle of January. And she also told them that Bell had been a client of Catherine Mehaffey.

"What was Tommy Bell's profession?" asked Bert.

"Lots of things," she replied. "But he did rob and do a lot of burglaries."

In his turn with her, Skelton drilled a little deeper into Bell's death and saw it backfire when he raised a question about the cause. His questions allowed her to challenge the assertion Bell had died in an accident, leaving jurors to question the mystery themselves and demonstrating Bell's girlfriend possessed a Medusa stare of her own, directing it at Catherine.

"He had a shot to the head, but he wasn't playing Russian roulette," she testified in a steady voice that made clear these two women hated each other. "I have no way of saying for definite. The case hasn't closed."

All that remained was for me to return to the stand and positively identify the Beta Max as the one stolen from Strong in the January 15 burglary. As quickly as that, Bert had shown jurors that Catherine was not the type to walk quietly away from a simple domestic dispute. He had linked Catherine to a professional burglar who had died violently in possession of something stolen from my home. Further investigation of Bell's death had produced no evidence to bring charges against anyone. The name of Tommy Bell would, however, fill another space on the list of Mehaffey associates and lovers to meet an untimely death. He no longer was eligible to receive one of our "Mehaffey Survivor" T-shirts since he had failed to survive. And his sister was convinced Catherine had orchestrated his death somehow.

I had been sitting beside Bell's sister on a bench in the hall outside the courtroom and would not learn until later from reading a transcript exactly what Bell's girlfriend had said in court. Bell's sister had been subpoenaed to testify, too, but Bert had been reluctant to call her for fear she might say something to trigger a mistrial. Neither of us was allowed to sit in the courtroom and hear the testimony of other witnesses. So we had a little chat ourselves that led to the drinking session that night at Corky's.

"You're Gary Taylor," she said, introducing herself. "We have a lot in common."

"We should get a drink," I offered and made plans for Corky's.

The rest of the trial that day had gone well. Bert called a parade of police officers, forensics experts and other witnesses who assembled the jigsaw puzzle of my shooting for the jury. One detective told of finding both pistols outside near the street. A forensics expert testified that the bullet hole in the seat of the chair had entered from the bottom in a manner consistent with someone holding the chair out as a shield. The two teenaged girls told about my race from the apartment and Catherine's pursuit. And my surgeon testified about removing a .32-caliber slug from my back where it had been lodged about half-an-inch from my chest cavity. Still, Will Gray tried to get the doctor to say I had not been in mortal danger from the wound because the bullet had stopped before killing me. It seemed like a strategy that jurors might find deceptive.

"I saw him after the injury and at that time he was up, walking around," the doctor said when Gray asked if the wound posed the possibility of permanent injury or death.

"Wasn't any thanks of Catherine Mehaffey that bullet didn't go into the heart?" asked Bert sarcastically, with his question interrupted by the expected shouting of objections by both of Catherine's attorneys. But he had made his point.

Then, at Corky's that night, Bell's sister was making her point about Catherine, vowing the vengeance of a feud that would continue until one of them was dead. Admitting her role as a fence for selling the property her brother had stolen, she said she also had worked with Catherine from time to time. She said she knew Catherine owed her brother a large sum of money for a secretive job he had done for her, but Catherine had never paid. Although Bell had never confided the nature of that job to his sister, she just assumed it had been the murder of George Tedesco.

"Taylor, you know, I don't want to offend you, but your stuff was really shit," she said, changing the subject with a giggle. "I knew right away I couldn't sell that stereo, so I just threw it into a dumper behind a convenience store."

"I'm not offended. My luggage by Kroger days are over now, and I bought a nicer stereo already. That stuff was junk, wasn't it?"

"But Jim Strong," she said, nodding at him, "that man had some quality equipment. Tommy wanted the Beta Max for himself. But the pistol and the other things I turned into cash."

Jeez, I thought, looking right into her eyes, *I would really like to fuck you tonight.*

Then I wondered if I hadn't slipped and mumbled that out loud because she grinned and winked at me. I looked at Strong and realized he must have been eavesdropping on our subliminal conversation because he started shaking his head in the negative, reminding me how dangerous a fling with Bell's sister would be. Bert Graham had become something of a probation officer for me, ordering me to avoid controversial situations that could disrupt the trial. I knew he would have had a palsy attack to learn I had taken Tommy Bell's sister out for drinks in the middle of the trial. And his eyes would have popped right out of his head if he were to learn from some defense witness later in the week I had started a sexual affair with that girl. Jurors would likely find some way to convict me of something if they heard about that. So I sighed and made a mental note to myself: *Some day figure out why I find bad girls so irresistible.*

"Say," I said, changing the subject, "what do you think would have happened if I had been in the house the night your brother came by? Think I could have taken him?"

She tilted her head and ran her eyes down the front of my body, humming as she did. Then she said, "You are bigger than he was. But he was quick and wiry with street smarts. It might have been a pretty good match."

I doubted that I would have given Tommy Bell much trouble at all. But I would have tried, and I was glad there hadn't been a chance to find an answer.

"You know," Bell's sister said, "after today we're all on Catherine's list now. When she gets around to settling all of her debts, she'll want payment from us."

"I don't know what we can do about that," I said.

"I do," she said. "I want us to make a pact. If any one of us turns up dead, the other three will go after her."

I looked at Strong, who blinked long and hard. We'd been invited to join a death pact.

Well, I thought, *why not? We've had just about every other silly thing in this adventure, why not this, too?*

I could predict with some certainty I'd never see these girls again, anyway, so I didn't see the harm in a drunken promise of this sort.

"All for one?" I said, with more than a twinge of sarcasm, and raised my beer bottle to the center of the table.

"One for all," said Strong, snickering and clanging his bottle against mine. Then the molls of the depleted Bell gang joined our salute. We all drank up and went our separate ways, our paths never to cross again.

SIXTY-TWO

June 11, 1980

"I went to the movies last night, Gary, and you'll never guess what I saw."

Catherine had returned from the lunch recess really full of herself and startled everyone in the hall outside the courtroom by walking straight to me with her chatter about the movies. It marked the first time we had spoken since the start of her first trial—when she had explained my survival as evidence that only the good die young. Now she wanted to talk movies. Sitting beside me on the bench outside the courtroom, Strong's head snapped around to look, and his mouth flew open.

"I could never guess in a thousand years," I told Catherine, chuckling a bit and inviting what I anticipated as a well-rehearsed explanation.

"I saw *The Long Riders*—you know, that movie about Jesse James."

"Like it?"

"It was great. You know what happened to Jesse James in the end, don't you?"

With that she whirled and entered the courtroom with attorneys Skelton and Gray in tow.

"What the fuck was that?" asked Strong breaking into laughter.

"Jesse James was shot in the back, just like me," I said, "She's getting ready to testify. She was pumping herself up so she could take the stand."

We both leaped to our feet from the benches where we had sat in boredom all morning after our night out with the molls of the Bell gang. As witnesses, we could not enter the courtroom. But the rules could not stop us from peeping through the small rectangular windows on the double doors, and we smacked our shoulders together vying for a look at Catherine taking the oath before climbing into the witness box. I saw Bert sitting at his table—perched like a tomcat outside a rat hole. All he would have to do is wait for the Last Cowboy to guide Catherine gingerly through that minefield of physical evidence, where she would try to explain everything from the bullet hole in the seat of the chair to the placement of the two pistols, without anything blowing up in her face. Then Bert would have a chance for what might be the prosecutor's dream cross-examination of a lifetime. Catherine was considered a defendant who might even erupt in a violent outburst if forced to trip over her own lies. Word spread quickly around the building, and within minutes Judge Jon Hughes had standing room only left in his court. I expected Skelton would soon need to adjust his nickname and be looking more like the Lost Cowboy once she started to speak.

Catherine really had no choice but to take the stand in her own defense, despite the dangers of offending the jury with obvious lies. Bert had executed his simplified strategy without a hitch, leaving jurors to decide between my testimony verified by the physical evidence and her explanation, if she chose to provide one. Besides Bert's successful streamlining of the case, the quality of the evidence against her had improved thanks to my courtroom performance. Courthouse insiders are constantly critiquing the appearances of each other whenever called to the stand, and I had won high marks from several observers for a polite but firm presentation to the jury. Although standing my ground during cross-examination, I had not argued with Skelton and projected honesty, according to more than one reviewer.

But I also knew as Catherine strode to the witness stand, the jury would have my final words from the day before still ringing in their ears. Those words had followed an exchange with Skelton when he challenged my veracity about going back to Catherine's apartment despite concerns about my safety.

"You sat there for two hours in fear of your life, I suppose?" Skelton had asked with disdain. When I volunteered to explain, he hastily ended his turn. But he left an opening for Bert, who jumped to his feet and asked, "Why did you go over to that house even though you were afraid she would explode?"

"I wanted to get this thing over with without my kids being involved," I replied. "She had proven she was capable of sending people over to burglarize my house. I had my child with me, and it was time I either faced what she was going to have for me or not. So, I thought I should just go over there and see what would happen."

"Did she, as a matter of fact, explode?" Bert asked.

"She, in fact, exploded and justified every fear I had."

I had seen the jurors watching intently as I explained my decisions that night. I could feel how the sympathy toward her from the tapes in the first trial had shifted to me in this second event. We had forced her to a point where she would have to neutralize the state's case with her version of the events. And it wouldn't be easy. Besides trying to contradict the physical evidence, Catherine had her own domineering attitude to overcome. Before her testimony would end, I knew, she would be objecting to questions from her own lawyer and overruling the judge.

I learned later from reading the transcript that she wasted no time mentioning the tape recordings that everyone had been working so hard to ignore. Neither side wanted to hear that *Exorcist Tape* again. But there she was, telling jurors how desperate she had been to recover some tapes that I had made. She denied orchestrating the burglary but said she played along with my accusations in hopes of retrieving these tapes, even though she did not know for certain what was on them. She said she had just heard from someone that I had some tapes.

"It sounded like this was my chance to get the tapes back," she told the jury. "I was sorry they had been burglarized. I played along."

Then she started laying on the drama, describing why she began negotiating with Strong for return of the stolen property: "I said, 'Yes, yes. Whatever you say. I am sure I can help you.'"

Catherine admitted taking my address book and also said she had taken a letter I had written to Cindy on an earlier occasion. She said she thought she could use those to negotiate for the tapes once she had taken me to her apartment on the pretext of returning items stolen in the burglary.

"He had a bunch of private numbers for assistant district attorneys in the book—" she volunteered in an obvious attempt to hint that I might be somehow connected to a law enforcement conspiracy against her. But even Skelton cut her off on that charge and moved directly to the shooting. In her version, she decided I should leave. When she told me to go, however, she said I went to the kitchen instead. That was where I must have found her smaller .22-calibre pistol. To explain why the police did not find my fingerprints on that gun, she testified I emerged from the kitchen with it wrapped in a white paper towel and called her a "rotten bitch."

According to her I said, "Cindy and you are both bitches."

Seeing me with the gun, she said she replied, "Gary, I am sorry. I have been all wrong. I will do anything." Then she told jurors with a sigh, "And you always think you will be brave if somebody points a gun at you, but you're not. You will say anything."

To buy time, she said she told me I could find the missing address book and letter back in the bedroom. Instead of walking back there to look, however, she said I forced her up from the couch and made her walk backwards into the bedroom.

"He was trying to keep his eye on me and the gun and he was still really wanting to go for the closet," Catherine testified. "I'm not a very good housekeeper, which the pictures show, and my shoes were all over the floor of the closet. He couldn't reach the top shelf."

In her version, I held the pistol with one hand and tried to maneuver that chair with the other so I could use it as a footstool to see the shelves in the closet. But I couldn't get past all those shoes in the floor. As I struggled with the chair, Catherine said she dropped to the floor.

"Everything I have read about this," she testified, "you make yourself humble to the person shooting at you, and you make them back down."

In her version, Catherine had stashed the larger .32-caliber pistol on the floor beneath her bed, where her kneeling position allowed her the chance to grab it.

"I know this is going to look silly," she said, twisting in the chair to demonstrate for the jury. "I saw this in a movie. You hold yourself sideways, and the bullets don't hit you. I went like that, and I just shot. Then I fell on the bed rolling. I was just trying to get out the door."

In her version, she said I then started backing down the hall in retreat.

"He wouldn't drop the gun," she said. She apologized for confusion in describing the scene to the jury and said, "I was still shooting."

She said she saw me exit through the front door. Then, she claimed that she was the one yelling, "Murder!" She said she followed me out the door.

"I thought maybe he might have been shot, and he might fall down somewhere in the street and die, and I knew he was crazy and repentant for everything he did probably, and he was stoned. If he died, I didn't want it on my conscience. I was going to throw him down on the ground and call an ambulance or something."

But I ran on to the grocery store, she said. So, she said, she returned to the house with the teenaged girls to await the police.

Then Skelton sat down, surrendering Catherine to Bert, who wasted no time lighting her fuse.

SIXTY-THREE

June 11, 1980

"Ms. Mehaffey, you know how to shoot a gun, right?"

"Obviously I don't."

Three jurors raised their eyebrows in surprise, Skelton banged his forehead against the wooden table, and Bert paused, wondering if he had heard that answer correctly.

With her first response on cross-examination, Catherine set the tone for what would be a defensive disaster. Did she really think she had forged such a bond with the jurors that they could quickly share an inside joke? She was grinning all by herself.

"Why did you say, 'Obviously I don't know how?'" Bert asked, hoping she would dig a deeper hole.

"I don't know why I said that."

Catherine's sassy response had given Bert a quick opening to delve into one of the darker events of her past. He questioned her further about her use of firearms over the years and then asked about the time she had shot a pistol at her first husband, Matt Quinlan, while living in Japan where Matt had served in the military.

Possibly still enthralled by her viewing of *The Long Riders* the night before, Catherine finally snorted, "If you are making me Jesse James, Bert, I am not."

Unable to resist, Bert just said, "Right. Maybe Jessica James."

"I would object to your sidebar remarks, Jessica James," Catherine said before her own attorneys could rise to admonish him.

"You don't like that?" Bert asked.

"I don't think you would like it, either."

Before Bert could respond, the judge intervened and ordered: "Both of you keep your remarks to yourselves."

Catherine finally admitted firing a pistol while sitting in a living room with Quinlan but argued it had been accidental while he was teaching her to use it. Then Bert asked her about firing at an attorney named John Grant on another occasion, but she denied that one.

"Why don't you subpoena John Grant and ask him," she said.

Unknown to Catherine, Bert and his investigator had located Grant, who had moved to another city. But when the investigator flew there to deliver the subpoena, Grant had packed up and moved again, apparently unwilling to come testify against her. Unable to impeach her denial of the shooting with testimony from the target himself, Bert changed the subject and started asking about the tapes. Although he had no intention of introducing the *Exorcist Tape* again, Bert wanted to force her to repeat her threats from it. If she denied any of it, she knew he could play it then in an effort to show her as a liar, forfeiting any sympathy the tape itself might generate.

Bert asked if she had ordered Tommy Bell to burglarize Strong's house so he could get those tapes, and she denied it. So, he started asking about Bell.

"He was a burglar and a robber, just as his girlfriend testified," she conceded.

"So," asked Bert, "it was just a big coincidence that Tommy Bell happened to have burglarized Taylor's house?"

Before she could reply, Will Gray objected to the question, telling the judge it was "invading the province of the jury." The judge agreed, leaving jurors to determine the degree of coincidence, and Bert was satisfied they would understand his point. So, he asked her about threats she had made on my life.

"I never said, 'Gary, I am going to kill you.' I told him I was going to sue him," she said.

When Catherine charged that the tapes had contained "intimate conversations" between us, Bert challenged her, saying the tapes actually contained her threats.

"You never told anybody, 'He has to beg for my mercy?'"

"I certainly made that statement," she admitted, aware that any denial would bring the tape into the trial in a way that would show her as a liar rather than a victim. Then she added, "He should have begged for an apology."

"Did you make the statement, 'I never killed anyone before, but he has done so much'?" Bert asked, running down the list of threats from the *Exorcist Tape*. And Bert forced Catherine to continue admitting her threats.

"And I am starting to hate him now," said Bert. "You're saying that?"

"I dislike him intensely."

"And you are sorry you weren't successful in your attempts to kill him?"

"I am not sorry I was not successful in my attempt to kill him. I am very glad he's not dead. I wouldn't like to have any human being's death on my conscience, no matter what they had done first."

"Are you saying you had tremendous hostility, and you cannot forget it?"

"I do have and have had tremendous hostility, and it's been very hard for me to put out of my mind the events of that night and what he did."

Bert challenged her further about the tapes, charging that she actually had wanted a tape that had exposed her "activities" to the district attorney's office. And Catherine countered with unrelated comments designed to generate as much sympathy as possible from the jury.

"Any lawyer in Houston does not like to have Special Crimes have their wife or husband or girlfriend go and whine and moan—"she began, but Bert cut her off.

"So anybody could go to Special Crimes and tell them about their activities, and they would be very concerned?"

"Any lawyer would be. It's just making a fool out of you, going with somebody like that who is going to Special Crimes and making tapes about you."

"If they didn't have anything to say about you that would cause you harm, anything not illegal, there wouldn't be any concern, would there?"

"Your intimate relationships with another person do embarrass you."

"You mean Mr. Taylor told the DA's office about your intimate relationships?"

"I believe he did in the last trial. He sat here and talked about our intimate relationship, and I had to listen to it."

"That gave you great concern, didn't it?"

"It humiliated me. It caused me great grief. I was ashamed to face people that I had taken him around. I was sickened with myself that I had ever gone out with him. I thought he was a despicable person to do something like that."

Although Gray and Skelton demanded Bert play the tape for the jury, they never asked the judge to order it played again. Neither side wanted the *Exorcist Tape* as evidence. So Bert just continued questioning Catherine about the things she had told Strong on the tape, forcing her to enter her threats as evidence without using the tape itself.

"Isn't it true that the tape recording you talked about contained no intimate relationship or evidence of an intimate relationship with you and Mr. Taylor, but rather the kind of words on that tape that would cause some person great fear and concern if they were directed toward them? Isn't it true they played the tapes in the press room to show the other working members of the press why they were trying to keep you out? Wasn't there a time when a deputy was called to the press room when you were there?"

Although Skelton had successfully objected to all those questions, Catherine intervened and said, "That's a question you asked that I didn't get to answer."

Skelton stared at his client and asked the judge, "Instruct the witness to answer questions that are asked."

Bert led her through our confrontation in the press room when she grabbed my necktie. At one point, he asked her about her law practice and triggered this exchange:

"It's none of your business who my clients are."

"You made it our business when you shot Mr. Taylor."

Guiding her to the night of the shooting, Bert asked if Strong had been present when she told me, "There is only one way this can end. One of us must die."

Catherine snarled, "That is an incredible statement. One of us does not have to die."

Bert led her back through her version of that night and asked her about my demeanor.

"He was very upset. He was wigged out," she blabbered, unable to stop. "He had been continuously talking that night about the breakup of his marriage. He could be divorced in the morning. His wife is a bitch. I said, 'I don't want to hear any more of it. Whenever you run to her, you call me one. Whenever you run to me, you call her one. I don't want your problems.' I guess I didn't do right that night. I should have listened to Mr. Taylor because he was a soul in torment."

Well into her version of the shooting, Bert started asking about discrepancies. He reminded her that one of the teenaged girls testified she told them she had hidden her gun in the living room under a table.

"That may have been her misunderstanding. I might have been hysterical."

Then he asked about discrepancies when she answered questions on the scene from the police.

"When the six policemen and the two girls were there, they were all talking to me at once. It's like the children's game where everyone whispers, and, at the end of the game when the last person gets up and tells what he heard, it's not what the first person started with. Nobody was asking me. People would say, 'Would that be right?' And I would say, 'Yes.'"

Bert recalled testimony from a detective who said she told him that night she had gotten her pistol from under the couch.

"Yes, I remember that," she said. "But you just can't jump up and say, 'No, that's not what really happened.' Nobody would listen."

She tried to belittle my injuries with another feeble attempt at humor. When Bert cited the wound to my scalp and asked, "That's pretty close to your brain, isn't it?" she replied sarcastically: "In his case?" But no one laughed.

"You want this jury to believe that is not a serious act, shooting somebody in the skull?" asked Bert.

"I am not the murderer, either, who goes over and tries to shoot an unarmed woman or whatever he was trying to do."

"You wouldn't be here now if you hadn't have shot him in the back," Bert said.

"Why didn't he drop the gun? What was he doing in the house?" she demanded.

Asked about the number of shots she fired, Catherine said, "You start, you can't stop."

When she finally admitted that my wounds could have been more serious, Catherine spoiled the humility by adding, "I don't think Mr. Taylor will ever again walk into somebody's house and pull a gun on them like that."

And Bert invited her to share some philosophy with jurors, asking if she had ever told anyone, "Don't make a threat you don't intend to back up."

"I have heard that statement and made it a truism," she replied. "Don't make threats to people. You don't know how they are going to react."

"You shot him in the back somehow when he was backing away from you?" Bert asked, emphasizing the confusion in her story.

"I must have been the one," she sighed, apparently worn down. "There was no one else there but he and I."

SIXTY-FOUR

June 12, 1980

The jury had been deliberating barely an hour when Judge Hughes summoned them back to the courtroom at the end of the day. It had been a long one, too, and the judge knew the jurors had a mountain of evidence and testimony to analyze. He figured they had had time enough to elect a foreman. The judge wanted them to go home, rest, and return fresh on Friday morning to sort it all out, so we could have a decision before the weekend.

"I don't know how close you are to a verdict, and I don't want to know," the judge began. "Unless you want to deliberate longer, I am going to recess for the night and let you come back in the morning."

"We have arrived at a verdict," one of the jurors replied. His announcement stunned the small audience that had gathered for what they expected to be a routine adjournment. Catherine and her lawyers snapped to attention at the defense table while Bert whirled his head to find me in the crowd. Another assistant DA caught my eye and shot me a thumbs-down gesture. He believed they could not have reached a guilty verdict in so short a time with so much physical evidence and testimony to discuss. He was predicting an acquittal.

"You hadn't buzzed," said the judge.

"We were getting ready to buzz," replied the juror who apparently had been elected foreman.

As Judge Hughes ordered him to surrender the written verdict, I held my breath. I couldn't tolerate an acquittal. In my mind I began rehashing this last day of testimony in my mind, working to pinpoint what might have gone wrong…

I remembered how the defense had called only one other evidentiary witness besides Catherine. And that, too, had backfired. Skelton had demanded that the state produce Ralph Byle, who was Catherine's landlord and next door neighbor. Bert had given Byle permission for a fishing trip because the landlord-neighbor had not seen anything relevant the night of the shooting. When Catherine and her attorneys realized this witness had left Houston, however, they decided to demand his presence in what Bert considered a ploy to accuse the prosecution of hiding a crucial witness. In her own testimony, Catherine had even set the stage for an accusation about the missing witness, mumbling to Bert mysteriously in a non-responsive answer to one question, "We wanted to call him, but you sent him away," She did not identify him, leaving jurors to ponder the mystery.

So, Bert responded to Skelton's request for Byle and sent a helicopter at taxpayer's expense to fetch him from the Gulf of Mexico. Byle walked into court none too pleased, still dressed in his fishing gear just so he could tell the jury he had not noticed whether Catherine had a pistol in her hand or not. Then Bert had him flown back to his trip.

After him had come a parade of non-evidentiary character witnesses for both sides, each called to answer just one question about Catherine or me: Did we have a good or bad reputation for truth in the community? My witnesses had included lawyers, judges, neighbors, and media professionals who all agreed my reputation was good. The list included Marvin Zindler, a flamboyant reporter for the local ABC affiliate, Channel 13. A tremendously popular local character, he had served as the model for the broadcaster lampooned in the stage play and movie about *The Best Little Whorehouse in Texas*. I had known Marvin for years, and he easily ranked as the perfect character witness. Thousands of Channel 13 viewers trusted him to tell them about all kinds of consumer information. And there he sat in the witness stand at Catherine's trial, telling her jury to believe me.

Skelton and Gray had screamed foul, complaining that prosecutors had no right to bolster my testimony. But Hughes allowed it after Bert's assistant, Ira Jones, charged that Catherine had called me a "fool" and a "liar" during her testimony.

Besides calling witnesses for me, they also had found a string of witnesses willing to describe as "bad" Catherine's reputation for telling the truth. Those included her former brother-in-law, working then as an assistant district attorney in San Antonio.

These veracity witnesses moved quickly through the proceeding since they were not allowed to elaborate on their opinions unless prompted by an errant question from Skelton, who did not make the mistake of asking any. But he did stumble again when he offered testimony from a judge designed to attack my credibility.

"What is Jimmy James doing on their list?" Bert had asked me outside the courtroom. I started laughing. Jimmy James was a state district court judge who had received some unwanted publicity in a story I had written about his frequent appearances as a character witness for criminal defense attorneys charged with drunken driving. I enjoyed teasing Jimmy and often would step inside his courtroom early in the morning to shout, "What's happening today in the court of King James?"

"I guess he's been more offended than I thought and is here to have a shot at me," I said, explaining the relationship. "I consider it a badge of honor that he thinks I'm a liar."

Bert grinned and, during cross-examination, reminded Jimmy about my article after Jimmy had throttled my reputation for honesty.

"Nope," said the judge, "never read those papers."

Two of the jurors started laughing, and Bert felt he had successfully neutralized the only character witness to testify against me.

In final arguments, Skelton had ridiculed my version of the events by calling it irrational for anyone to walk into a dark bedroom closet while fearing for their life.

"I don't know what he's waiting for. A piñata to hit him in the head? Or maybe it's like the bird that used to be on Groucho Marx that comes down with the little card," Skelton said.

He urged jurors not to fault Catherine for trying to protect "what little dignity she had left" and described the case as an effort to ruin a criminal defense attorney. He addressed the tapes and told jurors he hadn't played them because Catherine had not contradicted anything on them. And he also played the gender card.

"Now this is Catherine Mehaffey's big sin, and this is what infuriates me about this trial. For years in our society, and I don't know why, we have some attitude it's feminine to get beat up, or it's not feminine to defend yourself. What an outrageous crime, not to sit there and defend your life when some fool is holding a gun on you."

Bert and Ira had been forceful and articulate in summarizing their case against Catherine for the jury. They both urged jurors to follow the physical evidence, telling them it could not lie and had no reason to deceive them. They called my version the only one that reflected the facts and made sense.

"Physical evidence doesn't lie," said Ira. "It has no motive, no bias. It just exists. How in heaven's name do we get bullet holes into this chair? She has no explanation for that."

Ira also urged jurors to consider Catherine herself and said: "You are going to have to hitch your wagon to one woman who will not look you in the eye and give you a straight answer."

He reminded them of Tommy Bell and her apparent relationship with him. He also ridiculed her attempt to characterize my wounds as superficial. He told jurors to take the pistol into the jury room and hold it. He asked them to consider: "Could you actually fire this thing with the intent to cause a superficial wound?"

Bert focused on the unanswered question of motive. He reminded the panel that he hadn't been required to demonstrate a motive, noting that could only be done with the power to look inside Catherine's brain. But he speculated on a couple of options. Maybe she feared my knowledge of her activities, whatever those might have been. Maybe she worried about my pursuit of the burglary complaint. Or, he suggested, maybe she had just felt like a woman scorned, unable to contain her rage. Whatever the reason, he argued, jurors could consider only one thing. The evidence showed she had tried to kill me.

Motive remains a question that has haunted everyone familiar with my case. I can't count the times I've been asked the pivotal question: "Why did she shoot you?" I have usually laughed it off with a buzz line, such as: "She didn't thrive on rejection." But I did have my own explanation, one I needed to confront as I asked: *Why did she shoot me?* My answer has not been one easily understood by anyone who has never peeked inside her brain, as Bert had suggested. Why did she shoot me? I've always believed she did it simply because she thought she could. I had become just another potential notch on her narcissistic belt, a skeleton to hang in her closet, and another statement to the world, notifying it that she was smarter than everyone else.

Shifting gears back to the jury's surprise announcement of a verdict, I tried to figure what might have gone wrong as I watched that written verdict form pass from the jury to the bailiff and on to the clerk in what seemed to take an eternity. I listed the possibilities. Maybe Catherine had generated pity from the panel. Maybe they couldn't understand my plan to run an attempted murder sting on her, using myself as the bait. Maybe they didn't like Bert. Maybe they feared a government conspiracy. Or, maybe they just didn't like me and decided I deserved to get shot.

That thought made me laugh. I recalled Catherine's oft-stated philosophy: "How do you tell what a person deserves? You look at what they get. And that's usually exactly what they deserve."

Her words floated ironically through my head as the verdict form finally arrived in the clerk's hands, and she began to read the jury's decision:

"We, the jury, find the defendant, Catherine Mehaffey, guilty as charged in the indictment."

While the judge polled the jury to ensure a unanimous verdict, Bert turned in my direction and smiled. I grinned and watched Catherine, seated stoically between Will Gray and the Last Cowboy. She looked as if she had used the Medusa stare in a mirror and turned herself to stone.

SIXTY-FIVE

Friday the 13th, June 1980

Catherine and her legal team knew she faced a real dilemma. Now would come her turn to beg for mercy in sentencing from the same group of people who had rejected her story the day before by taking only an hour to convict her of attempted murder. Obviously they had concluded her version lacked some significantly persuasive element—perhaps even the truth?

They have to be pretty pissed, I thought, arriving in the courtroom that morning for this punishment phase of her trial. *They obviously think she lied. Even worse, though, she offered a whopper. She insulted their intelligence like she does with everybody. She just told them, "Fuck you, fools. Eat this load of crap." But they threw it back in her face, and now they'll want to feed her some more.*

I tried to imagine what must have transpired for the jury to reach such a quick decision. They likely had used fifteen or twenty minutes alone to elect a foreman. Then they probably had taken a straw vote, just to see how best to proceed. Even if everyone voted guilty on that first poll, I knew from my years covering courts that they normally would have reviewed some of the evidence, at least for appearances. I had seen juries delay their verdicts on slam dunk convictions just to demonstrate their respect for the system. But it looked like this jury just wanted to race back to the courtroom and share their decision as fast as possible.

In most states, the trial judges handle the sentencing of defendants convicted in their courtrooms, following extensive investigations by the local probation authorities. Those investigations probe the defendants' backgrounds and potential for rehabilitation in an effort to determine the best punishments for their crimes. The process can delay sentencings for months while shifting the focus from the emotion of the trial itself. In contrast, the Texas system requires the convicting jury to reconvene and determine the punishment after another court hearing in which prosecutors and the defense can present additional evidence to sway jurors on the proper sentence.

Of course, a defendant can opt out of that system and request a sentence from the judge. In Catherine's case, however, that would have presented more risk. Texas law limits prosecutors in their punishment phase presentations to jurors. Bert would not have been allowed to present allegations about Tedesco, for example, unless Skelton and Gray inadvertently opened that door during their questioning of new witnesses. But Catherine's team also had to assume that any in-depth pre-sentence investigation would uncover more details about her troubled past for the judge to consider in his decision. They would have expected him to deliver a harsher sentence than the jury, which might still be swayed by pity for her. So, they wanted to take their chances with the panel of twelve citizens who had only just met her.

Bert's witnesses could answer only general questions on their opinion about Catherine's reputation as a peaceful and law-abiding citizen. That morning, he offered three who took an oath and called her reputation "bad." One was a judge and another was a homicide detective. The third was a former FBI agent named Kent Ferguson, who had served as the lead private investigator for the Tedesco family's investigation of the doctor's death and Catherine's claim on the estate. When offered his turn to question those witnesses, Skelton quickly declined, knowing that any misstep might unleash a torrent of really damning condemnation as they explained the reasons behind their opinions.

In her second turn on the witness stand, Catherine sat in a black dress and wept softly, asking for probation on this first conviction and promising to abide by the terms. She also presented a couple of lawyers who vowed to help her stay out of trouble. Bert pressed her for an apology on my shooting and she grudgingly agreed. The punishment hearing had ended on schedule without any of the characteristic high drama and the court broke for lunch. Just as soon as jurors had left the building, however, I learned from Bert that our lunch break would last a little longer than expected.

"Catherine may have just attempted suicide," said Bert, shaking his head and whistling a bit as he approached me on the bench outside the courtroom. He had tossed out this comment so randomly it caught me off guard. He, too, had been hypnotized by the unpredictability of life with Catherine. He'd made it sound as if a suicide attempt were just another normal episode of the day, following a break for the bathroom and a sandwich for lunch.

"Say what?" I asked, uncertain whether to be more confused by the first news of an attempt or his inability to report whether it actually had happened.

"I don't believe it," Bert said. "She said she went into the judge's chambers and took twenty-seven Valiums. So, we sent her to Ben Taub to have her stomach pumped. The trial will probably be delayed a little."

"Pumping her stomach on the lunch break? She will not like that."

If she had designed her claim of a suicide attempt to delay the final judgment, Catherine not only failed but then had to endure more indignity as the judge withdrew her bond and ordered her handcuffed during the hospital exam. Then Bert insisted on testimony from the emergency room doctor outside the jury's presence to make sure the court record showed she still maintained the mental faculties to assist with her defense. After watching Catherine vomit the contents of her stomach, the doctor told the judge he concluded she had taken nothing. Jurors, of course, heard none of this and didn't even realize they had missed a rich luncheon performance from the star of this matinee. By early afternoon they were all back in their seats, waiting for the lawyers to again summarize their views on punishment that could range anywhere from probation to life in prison.

Skelton did not try to insult them further by criticizing their decision. Instead, he told them his job was to "cauterize that wound, try to stop the hurt at this point." He employed a standard argument from his repertoire, citing the American literary classic *Catcher in the Rye*. He noted the section where the hero, Holden Caulfield, laments the tendency for pranksters to write "Fuck you" on clean white walls as soon as someone has painted them. Of course, Skelton didn't use the phrase itself. In his rendition, Holden lamented the writing of "dirty words" across clean walls. Then Skelton told them that, as Catherine's lawyer, it was his job to try and erase those "dirty words."

Bert countered that he considered Catherine the author of her own "dirty words" written across my back with a pistol and told them "She is crying because she got caught."

While the jury deliberated on punishment, I sat in the courtroom trying to digest the impact of all I had heard and reconcile that with an unusual phone call I'd received the day before. It had come from a lawyer in Washington D.C. who identified himself as a kindred spirit in the Mehaffey chronicles.

"Congratulations," whispered Ferris Bond, identifying himself as a former boyfriend from her law school days. Things had not worked out well for them, either, after he'd decided they should split up. Before he graduated, he said, she had stalked him, assaulted his landlady, stolen and wrecked his car, and set his apartment on fire. Once he received his law degree, he had joined the military primarily to get away from her. He said he had waited many years for someone to bring her down.

"Do you want a T-shirt?" I had asked. When he stammered in confusion, I just cut him off with a laugh and thanked him for the call of support. You can count on everyone to have a few skeletons in their closets, I thought, but here's a woman who needs a separate closet just to hold all of her skeletons. I couldn't feel guilty about my role in her demise. Had I unfairly exploited her for sex? I wondered. I just didn't buy that charge. She was a woman who used her demure femininity like a bully. Sooner or later, some poor schlub had been bound to trip her up. The timing just turned out right for me.

The jury only needed another hour. They marched out before quitting time and ordered a sentence of ten years in prison. As a reporter, I had seen juries award probation to first-time offenders who actually had successfully murdered someone. Yet, here was Catherine as a first-offender female, headed for hard time on an attempt. I considered it a strong sentence.

I realized the cops likely would never nail her on Tedesco. But any conviction is better than nothing. It's hard for an existentialist to consider concepts such as universal justice or destiny. But this turn of events made me wonder.

What the hell, I rationalized with a chuckle. *Maybe it's enough to say universal justice does exist as a law of nature. Then all an existentialist needs to do is acknowledge it.*

And, I reasoned, if the scales of justice do indeed occasionally perform some sort of cosmic balancing act, it probably had been my destiny to square things for Tedesco and lesser victims like Ferris Bond. Give people like Catherine enough rope, and they eventually will make a noose. Some would always say she got away with murder, but who was I to know? I only knew for certain what she tried to do to me.

Others would ask if I considered her pure evil, but I've never been able to confirm that one, either. I have a hard time grasping what philosopher Roy Baumeister likes to call the "myth of pure evil." He views that concept as a way for folks to blame their problems on unknown outside powers. In a book called *Evil: Inside Human Violence and Cruelty*, Baumeister offered this explanation: "In simplest terms, violence is a tool for taking power. The violent person in a relationship gains power over the other."

I'm sure he never met Catherine. But, Baumeister did describe a familiar stereotype he dubbed the "badass" and identified that type as someone who "gains considerable power over other people by getting them to perceive him as irrationally violent."

In addition, Baumeister said, the badass employs another crucial tactic associated with evil—the stimulation of chaos. He wrote: "By refusing to be rational, he forces other people to think irrationally and adjust themselves to him. The fear of unreasoning chaos is almost as deeply rooted in human nature as the fear of harm, and the badass plays on both fears."

Baumeister also cites the flaw of egotism as another factor, calling it "an overlooked motivation for evil and violence." He wrote: "Villains, bullies, criminals, killers, and other evildoers have high self-esteem, contrary to the comfortable fiction that has recently spread through American culture. Violence results when a person's favorable image of self is questioned or impugned by someone else."

So that would be the academic response to what might loom as the crucial quandary in the story of my ill-fated relationship with Catherine. I preferred to boil down my response to something more basic.

No such thing as pure evil, I usually say. *She just had her own agenda.*

Nevertheless, it would have been interesting to know more about her background and the factors that had created her psyche. But I realized all I could ever learn would have to come from her lips. And anything she said would have been suspect. Psychological literature likely would speculate that, at some point in her early childhood, a parent had demanded perfection, and she had responded by forging a value system in which the ends would always justify the means. In her view, the motto "Never quit" actually translated into "Never get caught." Without an accurate dossier, however, no one could ever know for sure. All we would know is what she had become that week in the courtroom when a jury of twelve Houston citizens dubbed her guilty of attempted murder and ordered her to spend the next decade in a cage.

Bert and I just walked quietly from the courtroom, possibly musing on all these deep metaphysical insights but keeping our mental ramblings on karma and universal justice strictly to ourselves. We planned a few celebratory beers and had war stories to share.

"She really pissed them off," I just said, shaking my head.

"Yes," Bert agreed. "She certainly did."

SIXTY-SIX

July 31, 1980

"Come and get these kids. They're yours."

I usually preferred my wake-up calls limited to "Good Morning, the time is seven forty-five." But Cindy's simple message at about the same time that morning had a much more profound effect, launching the most pivotal day of my life. In the past year, Catherine had tried to change my life with a pistol. But Cindy would accomplish the same goal with that phone call. I really wasn't surprised to pick up the ringing phone and hear her voice after the events of the night before. But it was hard to take her seriously.

The night before had been a slow one for news. I had been counting the minutes until my evening shift on the city desk would end at ten. Cindy had interrupted the boredom about nine-thirty with a call to me there.

"Help us," she said when I answered the call. "Al is going crazy, and we are stuck at his place. My car is in the shop. Can you come and get us?"

I got the directions and told the night editor I needed to check out a little early for yet another personal emergency. In the months since Catherine's conviction, Cindy and I had barely spoken. Around the time of Catherine's second trial, Uncle Al had wooed Cindy back from our brief reconciliation at the start of the year. She had announced she was going to try fidelity for a change and told me to stay away. By then, I had settled into a semi-serious relationship with Barbara anyway, so I obeyed. Visitation with the girls grew difficult, but I hadn't decided on any strategy to do something about it. In those weeks after Catherine's conviction, the days just seemed to drift along. Then Barbara and I fought over something unmemorable, and we just quit talking. I was considering the options for the rest of my life, even thinking about traveling the world or joining the Houston Police Department for a new adventure. I had hoped that Uncle Al was behaving—that his telephone-shooting days of rage were behind him—but I didn't know for sure. I figured that, sooner or later, I'd find out, one way or the other, and, sure enough, I received my update that night.

When I arrived in Uncle Al's condo complex, I spotted my three girls walking like refugees in the street. Little E strode barefoot, dragging a blanket and toting a little bag. Cindy had Shannon in one arm with another bag in the other hand. A wave of despair swept across my brain. Then, as it retreated, a second wave of anger came crashing down.

"Uncle Al hit mommy," Little E told me as they climbed into my Bronco. I gave Cindy a look of disgust.

"This is what you wanted for our daughters?" I asked.

"Just take us home, please. I don't want to talk about it."

"You don't want to talk about it? Just call me to pick up the pieces, collect our children from the street, and get on with your life? I'm the one who needs to talk about it."

But she didn't respond, sitting stoically on the fifteen-minute drive to her rent house. Little E started crying. I'm sure Shannon didn't know what she was supposed to do, so she said nothing. I realized they didn't need any more displays of anger or rabid shouting, but it was hard to control. When we reached the house, I helped them carry their things to the door, and Cindy offered to give me a can of beer. But she wouldn't let me inside the house. I stood on the porch while the girls vanished into their bedrooms.

"What are you going to do about this?" I asked. "Is this finally it for this guy?"

She just stared at me, looking as if this had been none of my business. Before I had time to think about my response, I had done it—throwing beer from that can straight into her face. She wiped the suds from her eyes and looked into the distance.

"Maybe we'd all be better off if I wasn't around anymore."

And then, again, before I had taken time to think about my response, I blurted out the first thing that flashed through my brain: "Maybe we would." I returned to my car and drove back to Strong's where I received that wake-up call from her the next morning. I showered, dressed, and drove back to her house, where she let me inside. The girls were watching television in the living room, and Cindy had their bags packed with enough clothes for a few nights.

"You can get the rest of their stuff later," she said in a frightening, disconnected tone of voice that sounded almost as if she were reading a script that left her bored. I noted a blank look in her eyes and realized she had reached a new low. I had thought maybe she'd decided to run and would be leaving town. But suddenly I knew that flight would have been a best-case scenario. I had never known anyone who attempted suicide, but I had given the concept a lot of thought over the years just as a subject of curiosity. I had even read a book about suicide and recognized her display of the classic signs. She had been cleaning the house. She was taking care of all the last minute details and tying up loose ends, like making sure I could take the girls. I began to wonder about my own role in this ultimate decision, worried that my rough response the night before had pushed her past the edge.

"What are you planning to do?" I asked.

"Don't worry about it."

"I didn't mean what I said last night. I'm sorry. I was angry."

"It doesn't matter."

I knew I needed to proceed with caution, but I also realized I didn't know what events had pushed her this far. I concluded my thoughtless reaction of the night before could not have been anything more than an excuse, if that. I would never blame myself if she actually did attempt a suicide, but I also did not want her to succeed. My daughters needed their mother, even if she seemed troubled. Perhaps that could be fixed, I thought. But I knew I would do whatever I could to derail her plan, if that was what she had in mind. Then she gave me a tool to help.

"Here's your child support check," she said, endorsing the $465 document back to me. "It came in the mail yesterday. I won't be needing it."

"Please let me help you."

"Nobody can help me anymore."

I recognized debate as a lost cause. I always believed that people often must sink all the way to the bottom of the pool before they can bounce back to the top. Maybe it was Cindy's time for that. But I wanted to make sure she had a bottom from which to bounce. I took the check, grabbed the bags, and drove the girls to their Montessori school. Little E had just been accepted for a gifted students program in the Houston Independent School District and would be starting an advanced kindergarten class in just a few weeks. Until then, however, they both still attended the same pre-school.

After dropping them off, I drove quickly to *The Post*, where I was scheduled to report for a day shift by ten. I had no intention of working. Arriving a bit early, I went to my desk and tried to recall the name of a psychiatrist who had been treating Cindy. She had mentioned the female doctor in a couple of conversations, and I managed to locate the name on a list in the phone book. So I called, identified myself to the receptionist, and said I needed to talk about Cindy.

"The doctor won't talk with you about a patient," the receptionist said.

"I think Cindy needs help. She's done some things that worry me."

"Like what?"

"She told me to come get our kids. She packed their bags. She cleaned her house. And—" I paused, inviting the receptionist to demand my clinching piece of evidence.

"And what?"

"And, she endorsed her last child support check back to me."

"I'm getting the doctor."

The line went dead for only about a minute until I heard the doctor herself.

"You're not making this up, are you?"

"Nope. I'm really worried and will do whatever you want to help."

"She gave you the check?"

"Yes. I haven't been in close contact with her for a while so I'm making assumptions in the dark. Am I jumping to the wrong conclusion?"

"No. I can't go into the details, but here's what you have to do. Go to the sheriff's department immediately and sign a commitment affidavit. You'll have to write down some of things you just told my secretary. I'll call and sign the order. Then they will arrest her and put her in a hospital."

Jeez, I wanted to say, *if I had known it was this easy to arrange a commitment, I would have called you months ago about somebody else.*

Instead, I just said, "Thanks" and headed for my car.

SIXTY-SEVEN

July 31, 1980

As I drove toward the sheriff's office determined to have my ex-wife locked in the nuthouse, I really had only a foggy idea about the twisted chain of events that had left her so vulnerable. Despite the torment she had caused for me in the last year with her on-and-off-again attention, I wasn't angry. I considered myself a big boy, and, frankly, I admitted, the sexual reconciliations had always been worth the splits. I realized I did still love her, but in a way very different from the volatile concoction of lust and respect that first had brought us together. We had made beautiful children. We had a future of some kind built on that foundation. I never would do anything to hurt her. I wanted to help her live. But, I also wondered: *What the hell has been going on?*

Later I would learn more about that chain of events, where I fit in the chain, and even how to technically identify the affliction that apparently had pushed her to the edge of suicide. The headshrinkers would call it "adult situation reaction."

Wow, I grinned, upon first hearing the diagnosis later. *That sounds like a phrase some doctor invented to make a bad day sound like something that needs a prescription. I'd swear I could have argued I suffer adult situation reactions all the time.*

But I did find some literature on the subject. Therapists used it to describe situations of potentially unbearable but short-lived anxiety. The reaction occurs when someone has piled on so many varying stress factors that she

286

can't carry any of the load. I imagined a woman gathering firewood for a campsite and carrying it up a hill. Each stick by itself might not matter. But, at some point, she could load up one stick too many and then go tumbling back down the hill, scattering all the wood, and busting her head. An adult situation reaction patient would have a list of stress sticks that, when added together, created the image of a life too burdensome to continue.

Cindy had a list, and my name was on it. I had created one of her stress sticks because I hadn't been involved in her life enough to help with the girls, she would say. But I was just one of many stress factors. Once I learned about her list, I was able to divide it into factors I considered serious or negligible. I placed my transgression in the negligible section after I reviewed her diary of activities for the previous few weeks. Clearly, there would have been no time for me anyway—unless I had quit work to serve as a full-time babysitter while she and Uncle Al juggled scuba lessons with a variety of other equally high-brow outings. So I placed myself on Cindy's list of lesser woes alongside other temporary, but repairable, irritants such as "car trouble."

More serious on Cindy's list, however, were fundamental complaints like "crazy boyfriend" and "feelings of worthlessness." I imagined that life with her "crazy boyfriend" could be every bit as stressful as my time with Catherine Mehaffey, and I knew Uncle Al boasted similar potential after seeing his bullet hole in Cindy's telephone. There was no way, however, that Cindy should ever have felt worthless. She had always just impatiently crowded too many personal goals together, positioning herself for failure. She was a walking confrontation of classic clichés: Reach for the stars but don't bite off more than you can chew.

I respected and loved her for her personal ambition, a characteristic that can't be acquired. But she still punished herself for dropping out of law school, destroying her self-esteem eight months later. She refused to face the reality that she would have been unable to blend that course work with a stressful full-time job, child-rearing, and the hectic recreational life demanded by Uncle Al. As a result, she was suffering a traumatic overload of unfulfilled desire mired in a bog of guilt from the damage she feared she might have caused every one in her life, particularly the girls.

If asked about me, Cindy would credit me for always encouraging her to reach for the stars and pursue her dreams. But she also would blame me for being the one to say when she had bitten more than she could chew. She would describe me both as a lover and a father figure, a man who helped her get a start in life but then restrained her by warning of the hurdles. Instead of serving as a necessary counterweight to her impulsive behavior, she would insist I tried to dominate her by denying her the impossible. As a result, I could never win. She needed my discipline to help organize her plans but resented it when confronted with the reality she did not have the time to do all that she wanted.

Asked about Uncle Al, Cindy would have admitted she had fallen star-struck with the idea of becoming a doctor's wife and adding the material trappings of that life. She would rationalize that eventually this change would pay off for her daughters by giving them access to things they would never have in our financially-strapped, middle class home. I could see where the attraction likely began. Uncle Al probably loomed as some sort of emergency room hero at Ben Taub Hospital, where Cindy also worked long, serious hours helping abused and neglected children. He had been married when they met and promised to divorce that wife to offer Cindy something she would say she had never had in her life: "fidelity."

I would have to chuckle upon hearing that complaint a few months later. This desire for fidelity was coming from a woman who had ended two marriages with her own adultery. What's more, the promise of fidelity she so suddenly cherished also had come from a married man. On top of that, she had cheated on him multiple times with me, her ex-husband? I detected several personality quirks in that track record but an obsessive search for fidelity did not seem like one of them. Cindy would say she so desperately wanted this marriage to a doctor that she was determined to cure his alcoholic-induced anger management issues. But then, what is new about that scenario: Woman finds ideal man and immediately starts working to improve him?

At the same time, however, she knew she had to keep him separated from our daughters until he could become a more model step-parent. Just as I had worked to keep the kids isolated from Catherine, Cindy was working to keep them away from Uncle Al. In her case, I understood, the challenge had been dramatically more difficult since the girls lived with her. Later on, I would hear chilling tales about how Shannon could never get to sleep because she feared if she did, her mom would bring in a babysitter and sneak out with Uncle Al. While Cindy worked hard to keep things together, she had to have known in the back of her head it was never going to work. Had Uncle Al been more of a psychopath, Cindy might have dumped him as quickly as I had decided with Catherine. But it took her longer with him to face it. And it was her final recognition of that reality the night they fled his condo that prompted her decision to end her own life.

In the weeks before that night, they had even been attending couples therapy to help Uncle Al behave. And they had been planning a trip to the mountains that would require leaving the girls with a babysitter for ten days. Cindy had reluctantly agreed to the trip but also was growing exhausted with the hyper activity level of her prospective mate. He simply was beginning to wear her out. And his drinking didn't help. When she nagged him about it again, he lashed back and pushed her around. She called me for help and fled with the girls into the street.

After I took them home and threw beer in her face, Cindy put the girls to bed and then climbed into the shower. The water felt so refreshing and her life outside so hopeless, she did not want to return. So, she decided she would take pills in the morning, after arranging for the girls by calling me. A feeling of resolution arrived with a rush and calmed her nerves. Yes, she decided, we'd all be better off without her and her selfish, rationalizing ways. She had awakened in the morning even more convinced it had to be done.

I didn't know all these details at the time. All I knew was that she had fallen under the spell of something dangerous for all of us. And that's why I had come to the sheriff's office, where I watched a deputy process Cindy's paperwork as if it were another delivery of junk mail—just another part of his day.

"We can't get anyone over there until later this afternoon," said the sergeant, handing a copy of the commitment order to me. "Can you go sit with her a while and make sure she's all right?"

SIXTY-EIGHT

July 31, 1980

Although I hadn't used it in weeks, the extra key I kept for Cindy's house came in handy. She had given me a copy earlier in the year during one of our reconciliations and then never retrieved it when she and Uncle Al took their vows of fidelity.

But the key alone did not get me through the door when I returned to the house in the early afternoon. Besides locking the door, Cindy had jammed a kitchen fork into the woodwork at the base, perhaps anticipating someone might try to interfere. But the fork sprung quickly when I kicked on the wood, and the door flew open without much of a fight.

I strode quickly through the living room and back to the main bedroom, where I figured I would find her.

"Cindy," I yelled, more than a little concerned that Uncle Al had arrived before me and was waiting inside with his gun. But no one answered, and I reached the bedroom doorway without trouble. I saw Cindy lying on the bed and tried to wake her, but she was genuinely unconscious. I could barely hear her breathing, and I noted an open bottle of pills on the table beside the bed. I picked up the phone and called for an ambulance that arrived in a matter of minutes with a West University Place police car right on its tail. The paramedics confirmed her weak life signs and carried her outside where they said they would take her straight to Ben Taub. What a rendezvous point that place had been in the last year! It was where Cindy worked with Uncle

Al, where I had gone after Catherine shot me, and where Catherine had gone from court after faking her suicide attempt. It might be embarrassing for Cindy to show up there on a death-watch, but the "Tub," as reporters lovingly called it, still ranked as one of the nation's most effective trauma centers. I wasn't going to tell them to take her anywhere else.

"Sorry, Cin," I whispered as they slid her gurney through the doors. "But I think you need the Tub."

I ignored the handful of neighbors who had gathered in the street and walked back inside the house, where two cops from this jurisdiction were looking around.

"Look at this medicine cabinet," I heard one of them say. "She has a pharmacy in here."

Intrigued, I wandered into the bathroom and took a peek for myself. I noticed a couple of shelves of pill bottles, many of them identifying Uncle Al as the prescribing physician. It looked like the doctor had used more than his natural charm to weave his spell. While the cop in the bathroom was dumping the bottles into an evidence bag, I heard the other cop shout, "What the hell is this?" back in the bedroom. I rounded the corner to see him holding Cindy's telephone in the air and pointing at the bullet hole left from Uncle Al's November temper tantrum.

"That's a bullet wound," I said. "Her boyfriend shot at it last year."

The cop raised his eyebrows and placed the phone back on the table. I showed him the paperwork I had brought from the sheriff's office and answered questions for his report. I showed him my key and told him I would need access to the house to help gather the rest of my daughters' clothes, and he accepted that explanation. Both cops offered apologies for the situation and wished me well. After they left, I looked around a bit to see if I could find anything else to help me understand. I thumbed through a date book that had become a diary for Cindy's activities of the last few months but found nothing more shocking than the sheer volume of different events. It was clear that Uncle Al was the kind of guy who had to be doing something all the time and likely suffered from adult attention deficit disorder or had cultivated an extensive speed habit. I'd heard those ER docs needed that stuff to stay awake for long periods of time, and, from Cindy's party and hobby schedule alone, it looked like he fit the profile.

I called the hospital and learned she had survived but was not yet available for visitors. So, I decided to get some help for that night with the girls. I knew I faced some life-changing decisions, and I planned to take no more time than necessary. I drove over to the girls' Montessori school about ten minutes away and talked with one of their teachers who was well-acquainted with the soap opera that had engulfed their lives. Without any judgmental remarks, she agreed to take them to her house that night while I sorted out the final details of life as I had known it. And, as I looked around her school, I quickly reached a crucial decision about my daughters. A sense of relief engulfed me as I could see the place had been an oasis of stability in their lives throughout the turmoil of the past year. And, why not? They had lived here eight hours each day, just like me going to my job. This school *was* their life. Whatever I did, I decided, one thing was clear. My daughters would not lose this place until they grew out of it.

At the same time, I contrasted their school with the room I still rented from Strong. I laughed, trying to imagine the three of us shut in there on weekends, watching television. It was time to get out of there, and, I decided, this weekend would be a perfect time for the three of us to go apartment hunting. I'd have to cash in some of my share from the sale of our house for furniture, but it still sounded like fun.

Thinking about the future reminded me of a need to call my lawyer and see what legal maneuvers we would have to perform after this latest development. I could feel Fred Dailey sitting with his own Wile E. Coyote face on the other end of the line while I told him about Cindy and the formerly-closed divorce case he now would have to reopen.

"OK," he said. "Let's think this through. She's in Ben Taub and probably going to be locked away for a while. She will recover while in therapy and come out of the hospital looking for her kids. My advice is to get an emergency temporary custody order tomorrow, if we can find a judge who will hear it. He'll tell you she's eventually going to blame it all on you, but he'll have to sign it because we probably can't even serve her where she's going. So there'll be no one to object."

"Then what?"

"Then we should file for an immediate jury trial on permanent custody and hope we can pull that off before she's released. Your costs should be minimal. But if you wait for her release, it could get expensive, and there's a better chance you'll lose after she gets sorted out. Courts hate to take girls from their mothers."

"Let's get the temporary order like you said. I don't know about moving so fast on the permanent order. I don't really want to cause her any more harm than I have to…"

He cut me off and asked sarcastically, "Are you going to go ahead and send flowers to Mehaffey, too, since you're feeling like such a nice, generous guy today?"

"I just can't let Cindy feel like I went behind her back and completely destroyed her life. Can't the temporary order be written to last until she gets the court to change it back?"

"Don't bring Mehaffey to court again with you this time. I'll call you when I get something ready. And good luck with this latest situation. I knew I shouldn't have stuck that file in the storeroom."

It had been a hectic day with my body in fight-or-flight mode again since the moment Cindy shocked me with her wake-up call. I was checking off the items on my mental to-do list rapidly but still had a couple of important things left. As evening arrived, I headed for the "Tub" to visit my ex-wife, and I found her in no good mood at all.

"Maybe I'm not pleased with what you did," she said, still sounding too groggy for serious conversation. I ignored her whining and tried to redirect her mind to more uplifting subjects.

"The girls are doing fine. All I'm going to tell them is that you've gotten sick, and they need to live with me. Don't worry about them. You know I can handle it."

"Why did you send me here?"

Her attitude both worried and disappointed me. I had hoped she would revive from her stupor grateful to be alive. Instead, she seemed agitated and abrupt, sounding like she might want to try again.

"C'mon," I said. "You know why you came here. If you get hurt in Houston, you go to Ben Taub. We all go to Ben Taub."

Darkness had fallen by the time I left her there, pouting and still goofy from whatever drugs remained in her system. But I managed to quickly put her out of my mind as I focused on the last item from my list—the one that would be the hardest. I had been working at *The Houston Post* for nearly ten years, and it had become *my* oasis of stability. It had seen me through two marriages and the birth of my children. It had been more than just a place I could work. It had been the anchor for the most important facet of life—my career. It had been in the back of my mind all day.

Earlier, when Cindy's therapist had steered me to the sheriff, I had taken Johnny B aside and asked to take a couple of vacation days to handle this latest abruption. He bit his tongue, but I could tell from the roll of his eyes that he was getting fed up with my soap opera. At first I found his reaction an irritant but didn't have the time for an argument. As I thought about *The Post* and my changing future throughout the day, however, I began to sympathize with him. He had simply given me time off for both of the Mehaffey trials without a word. All this ruckus had not been fair to him, and now it looked like I had only scratched the surface. As a single dad, I would be hobbled for years to come, unable to work the kind of haphazard schedule required to do the newspaper job with the focus it deserved.

More importantly, I could not let that job distract me from the more important work of fatherhood. The girls needed a full-time parent—

something they had not had in at least a year. I would no longer make them compete with anything else. I was sure Johnny B and Logan could have found some kind of place for me at *The Post* with a schedule that could accommodate my new lifestyle, once I had things organized. I knew I would miss the newspaper life more than I had missed anything else that had ever been taken away. And I also knew I would need the income stream that life had provided.

As I drove away from *The Post's* big white stone building, where my resignation sat in Johnny B's mailbox, I snuffed back a nostalgic tear. But I still had a smile on my face. For the first time since the age of twelve I would face the morning unemployed. Most crucial parts of my life suddenly had changed in the span of a single day. But I knew the most important thing remained in place.

I checked my reflection in the rear view and then whispered with confidence: *I'll figure something out.*

SIXTY-NINE

September 15, 1980

I should have known that the eleven-month anniversary of my first date with Catherine could not pass without a reunion of sorts. By then I had reordered my life around my daughters, and things were working well. I used some of my savings to set us up in a little two-bedroom apartment near Houston's Astrodome complex, across the street from a grade school and a church. I also found quickly that my journalism talents were much in demand as a freelance reporter. Until then, I always had considered the word "freelancer" a synonym for "unemployed" and scoffed at the concept of living that way. But Houston at that time had become an international news center, and I was learning that most national news outlets needed freelance help covering the place. Given my local news reporting experience and my newfound availability, I started getting calls for assignments I could handle on my own schedule. With only a little marketing, I began to believe I might be able to succeed at self-employment for a while.

But mostly I focused on making the girls the center of my life. Little E started her advanced kindergarten program that required a bus trip for several miles each morning and afternoon. The bus stopped right outside our small apartment building, and the church across the street offered an after-school program where she could go in case I was out when it came home. Despite the expense, I kept Shannon in the Montessori pre-school on the belief that she needed the most stability I could provide. Lots of things were in flux around her, but I wanted to make sure her oasis of stability remained in place.

I swore off women, at least for a while, or, perhaps, as best I could. When Barbara heard about Cindy's suicide attempt she called one night from a bar and offered to help any way she could. I was flattered. But I told her I thought the time had come for my daughters to be the only girls in my life, at least for a little while.

Cindy spent a month in a Houston mental hospital, then emerged reluctantly accepting the court order I had obtained while she was there. Although that order did not grant her any visitation, I agreed to split each week with her as long as Little E could reach her bus stop in the mornings. Cindy appeared to have successfully eliminated Uncle Al from her life, and she returned to her job as the child welfare worker for Ben Taub, almost as if nothing had happened. But she had experienced an epiphany of some sort in the form of a religious conversion and had become involved in a Roman Catholic group. The religious experience appeared to have a calming effect, and she seemed to be taking life one day at a time while sorting out her personal plans for the future. She certainly showed no signs of challenging my new role as the primary custodian and, in some ways, appeared relieved she no longer had the responsibility.

To accumulate pocket change as well as for therapeutic reasons, I also took a menial job waiting tables weekdays over lunch at one of Houston's mid-range seafood restaurants called Pier 21. Waiting tables gave me something constructive to do for a couple of hours in the middle of each day while adding a nostalgic feel to this new period in my life. I felt as if I were back in college, reviewing my options for the future, and having a little fun. I knew I wouldn't be there very long, either, and it was nice to scrape the tips off the table for a wad of instant money in my pocket every day.

Pier 21 stood walking distance from the offices for the Houston Oilers pro football franchise, and we often saw sports luminaries stop for lunch. I waited on future NFL Hall of Famer Earl Campbell one day and laughed when he sent his fish back to the kitchen. I didn't get a tip from this multi-millionaire running back, but I didn't ask him for an autograph, either. I just treated him like he was any other guy sitting down with his wife and kid for a lunch. Maybe that insulted him. More entertaining, however, were the times when members of the Oilers cheerleading squad, the Derrick Dolls, sat in my section. They laughed a lot, tipped well, and flirted even better. So, I always made sure their fried shrimp and pasta salads received special treatment from the kitchen.

Several of the dolls were there when I looked up to see Catherine stroll into the dining room with the Last Cowboy on one arm and one of the local district criminal court judges on the other. It was obvious someone had tipped her that my waiter skills were on display at Pier 21, and she demanded a table in my section to see for herself. Ever the professional at whatever I'm doing, I took their orders politely and refilled their tea glasses repeatedly. Watching her watching me made me curious about what had happened to her since the trial. I knew she had been released on bond pending appeal, an option for anyone sentenced to a term of fifteen years or less. Of course, I also knew she wasn't able to practice law while appealing a felony conviction like attempted murder. And, I was glad to see that she apparently hadn't taken any shots at Skelton—yet. Maybe the conviction had placed her on best behavior. So, once again, I simply could not resist when she asked if she could return after the lunch rush to have a drink at the end of my shift.

"The terms of your bond require you not to violate any laws, and I am assuming that also means you can't kill me," I said sitting down and ordering a scotch from Sally the barmaid, who had agreed to keep an eye on us while cleaning up from lunch.

Catherine laughed meekly as I removed my black bow tie and pulled my personalized wine opener from my pocket. She sighed.

"What have we done to ourselves?" she asked. I raised my eyebrows and took a sip of scotch. She continued, "Look at you. You're a waiter?"

"Yes," I joked. "But that's only until I can pass the test for driving a cab."

"It's been so bad for me. Skelton has finally given me a job in a machine shop he owns. I do the books and answer phones. I have nothing any more. No money or anything. I heard about Cindy, and it is good you finally have those kids from that bitch."

"We're getting along. You know, I got a call from the state's program to help victims of crime. They said I am eligible for a rehabilitation grant. I told them they should find some real victims and give the money to them."

"Ha! Maybe I should apply. I'm the real victim here," Catherine said and then took a pause before making her pitch. "But it doesn't have to be this way. You can fix it. You can tell them you made a mistake. You didn't mean for any of this to happen."

"And why would I do that?"

"Because you know there is going to be another trial. The appeal will be granted. So much happened in that trial that was wrong. And when they order a new trial, you will have to decide again what is best for everyone. And by then I will have something on you."

"Oh, man," I said, shaking my head. "Listening to you is like having the same bad dream over and over. I wake up, take a piss or get a drink of water.

Then I lay back down, close my eyes, and here you come again. Squawk, squawk, squawk. You make my ears hurt."

"Gary, please listen to me, listen to how desperate I am. I got a job at *The Post.*"

"*The Houston Post*?" I asked, astonished. She nodded and I said, "They circulated your picture after the shooting and told the guards to arrest you on sight. And then you just stroll in over there, and they give you a job doing…what?"

"Just making sales calls at night."

I started laughing at the image of her walking into *The Post* and actually getting a job there while she was atop the security team's list of most wanted potential trespassers.

"Talk about your sleeping watchdogs," I said.

"No," she said, "it wasn't for the job. I wanted to get in there and sneak into the personnel files, find yours, and get something on you."

"Did you?"

"Of course," she beamed with pride. Then she continued, "Well, I got in there and saw your file. But I couldn't find anything in it that was useful."

"Catherine, I truly am sorry your life has crumbled like this. It is such a waste. You don't have to be like this. You could have been a successful attorney. But I can't do anything about it now. If you win an appeal, so be it. I'll be there to testify again. Until then, you just need to suck it up and do the best you can. All you have to worry about is yourself. I've got a couple of kids, and I certainly don't have time for your bullshit any more."

Her patented Medusa stare failed to materialize. All she could muster was a timid scowl that vanished almost as soon as she tried. She looked beaten and shaking, and I realized how far she had fallen just to come here and beg me to do something she knew could never be done. If our attraction indeed had been fatal, I realized, the fatality was her.

"Remember what you always said?" I asked. She squinted as I continued. "You always told me 'Nothing is free' and you were correct. I paid for our relationship with a bullet in the back. And you paid for taking your shots with a conviction. Nothing is free. And, now I think we are done here, correct?"

She stared a moment, then got up and walked out. I walked over to flirt with Sally.

"Is she the one?" Sally asked, revealing that she, too, had heard rumors of my turbulent past. I grinned because I did have plans for Sally, and I hoped it would be sooner, rather than later.

"What do you think?" I asked.

She smiled and whispered, "You can do better."

Just then, Catherine emerged from the back door of the restaurant, and I whirled when I spotted her in the corner of my eye. I expected an attack but it didn't come. Instead, she looked at me with painful eyes.

"My car won't start. Can you come take a look?"

I started laughing.

"Sorry, Catherine. You will have to call Triple A."

With that I walked outside, climbed into my Bronco, and drove toward the parking lot exit. I checked the rear-view mirror and watched as Catherine approached her Mercury Cougar with its hood at a 45-degree angle. She stared in my direction, then reached up and slammed the hood closed. She climbed inside, started the car, and headed for the other exit.

I didn't know what she had had in mind with that stunt. But it reminded me of something important. I knew I would spend the rest of my life looking over my shoulder anyway, waiting for that moment when it came time for her to settle all scores.

And, at the risk of getting too metaphysical, another thought crossed my mind—a new response to Catherine's lingering question about how I had managed to escape her attempt on my life. If I had been destined to square things for Tedesco, maybe also destiny had a larger plan unfolding to make sure I was available to catch my girls when Cindy fell. I might be uncertain about the existence of God. But it certainly did seem like the universe might have some order in it after all.

I might not understand why things happened, but I certainly had learned a rule of thumb for managing life. It seemed pretty clear that when the bell sounds for any fight—no matter how hopeless it seems—you just need to keep swinging because there is no way to predict what might happen in the second round. And it sure seemed clear to me that honest, open love is a power that will usually find a way to survive. Peel away superficial emotions like lust or jealousy, and you find that basic love—like that of a parent for a child—dictates the real milestone events of our lives. Find that raw, basic emotion, and you can never go wrong. It will survive.

Unlike the Apostle Paul, I would never be struck blind on the road to Damascus. But I had seen a light of sorts, and I recalled in particular Paul's admission to the Corinthians—a solid, real world observation even for an agnostic like me. The time had come to put away my childish things. Catherine Mehaffey and the lifestyle she symbolized certainly topped that list.

But I really had little time that day for further rumination on the mysteries of the universe. Like everything else, they would sort themselves out in time. For the moment, I had more serious responsibilities to attend. Little E would need help prepping for a spelling test. And Shannon would be waiting at school for me to take her home.

Epilogue: ...And they all lived happily ever after?

Just as Catherine predicted, Will Gray successfully worked his appellate magic on her attempted murder conviction, persuading the Texas Court of Criminal Appeals to order yet a third trial in 1983. As we prepared for that event, I told Bert I would be satisfied with a compromise to avoid the risk of submitting the case to another jury. I suggested they allow her to plead guilty to a reduced charge of aggravated assault with a term of ten years probation. She agreed, and the case ended with that conviction. Although some have criticized me for what they considered weakness, that outcome satisfied me for several reasons.

First, that conviction forced the State Bar of Texas to suspend her license to practice law until 1988, when she completed the terms with an early discharge. As a result, she could not work as an attorney, and I knew in 1983 that would be a tremendous punishment for her—likely as severe as time in prison. Also, at that time, the overcrowded Texas prison system was granting early release paroles in record numbers, so I expected she would have spent only a couple of years in prison even if another jury decided to send her. In addition, no one believed she would ever be able to comply with the restrictive terms of probation, and most were stunned to learn five years later that she had.

Most importantly for me, however, was the guarantee that Catherine would march into a courtroom and admit what happened that night as part of a guilty plea. She could never take it back. And she could never complain that a rubber stamp jury of prosecutorial puppets had railroaded her. To me, the guilty plea was worth more than the punishment.

But that still wasn't the end of Catherine as a lawyer. She rose from her own ashes as soon as probation ended. Reinstated and remarried, she moved from her temporary home in West Texas to Dallas and started a new career under her married name there. She developed a successful practice for a few years handling a variety of immigration, divorce, and criminal matters. But then a new controversy disrupted her life in 1999, when a former legal associate and the associate's husband were ambushed outside their home in a shotgun attack that took the husband's life. That investigation ultimately led to conviction of Catherine's husband on a murder charge and a sentence of life in prison for him. Although prosecutors tried to implicate Catherine in the attack, they failed to compile enough evidence. She was never charged, and her husband did not accuse her. Seriously wounded, the associate testified that Catherine had been on the scene of the attack, giving the man instructions, and telling him "Don't be a pussy."

That case put Catherine back in the media spotlight as the subject of a three-part series in *The Dallas Morning News* and a segment of the CBS-TV news magazine *48 Hours*. The reporters dogging her tracks in that case found me in her background as the only alleged target who had successfully orchestrated a conviction. Besides the murder of the associate's husband, police up there also found a man hanging nude with a plastic bag around his head in the closet of a rent house she owned. But they had to settle for a ruling of accidental death during erotic asphyxiation, striking out again with her. That discovery prompted a reporter from one TV station to call me and ask if we were having "kinky sex" back in 1979. I just repeated what Catherine always had said: "We were actually like two little mice. Nothing fancy." I told the newspaper: "She was a lot of fun when she wasn't trying to kill me." And, I said it looked like Catherine had more death and violence in her life than most of my friends who had served in Vietnam.

Following the murder case, the State Bar took a new interest in her and tried to cancel her license to practice law based on complaints from some of the immigrants she had represented. But she stood her ground and had not lost her license as recently as 2007.

Also as predicted by my attorney, Fred Dailey, Cindy did finally sort things out and decide she wanted to be reinstated as primary custodian for the girls. As part of her religious epiphany she had decided to move to central Texas and live on a farm with some of her new friends, taking the girls along. She hired a lawyer and sued to overturn my custody order. After a five-day jury trial, however, I won permanent custody of the girls. I am proud to note that I did everything possible to allow them to develop a relationship with their mother, and they managed to do that. She remarried and returned to Houston a few years later, finding a house just a few miles from me. We developed a shared custody arrangement that helped heal the wounds of the past as much as possible. But our relationship never recovered. At one point, for example, Cindy asked me to sign a Vatican agreement annulling our marriage so she could have a fresh start in the Catholic church. I refused. But I always have considered it a mark of distinction to boast that one of my wives hated me so much she wanted the Pope to erase our marriage from the permanent records. I'm happy to report that Cindy did manage to find true love and rebuild her life.

Jim Strong left journalism and became an emergency services director for a neighboring county. I always assumed his experience dealing with my emergencies had prepared him well for that position, but I still have difficulty imagining it sometimes.

Uncle Al's whereabouts are largely unknown, and that is probably for the best. Someone circulated a rumor he had started a skeet shooting range that flings old telephones into the air for targets—but I never took that seriously.

As for me and the girls, I managed to create a successful freelance writing business that lasted until they graduated from high school. During the 1980s and 1990s I wrote for some of the nation's premier publications while working at home to care for them as they grew. Somehow I managed to keep the lights turned on and the refrigerator full. Although I lost touch with a lot of my friends at the newspaper, I often would hear about someone snickering to learn that I was serving as chairman of a Brownie Scout cookie sale or coaching a little girls' fast pitch softball team. But the girls grew up, went to college, found careers, and started families of their own.

My relationship with Catherine developed some national notoriety of its own in 1987 when the movie *Fatal Attraction* captured the public's imagination. I was interviewed as part of a *People Magazine* cover story about true-life fatal attractions, and that article led to my appearance on a number of television talk shows, including Oprah Winfrey, Sally Jesse Raphael and Regis Philbin. For a brief period in the late 1980s, I became the poster boy for true-life fatal attractions. Although often invited to join me on these shows, Catherine never did. I received no financial compensation for my appearances. But I always enjoyed the experiences and found it educational to sit in the interview subject's seat for a change of pace. I always learned something about the interview process on each of these shows. I also found it difficult to deny interview requests from my brethren in the media, even when they tried to get tough with their questions. And I always enjoyed the reaction from audiences who heard the story. I remember one guy in Sally Jesse's audience shouting, "Hey man, that's really cool. You ran a sting on a killer."

Besides stimulating *Fatal Attraction* talk show attention, our story also caught the eye of television docudrama producers who twice optioned parts of it for fictionalized treatments. Two scripts were written and one of them produced. But neither ever aired, to my knowledge.

After Catherine's probation was announced in 1983, George Tedesco's father invited me to lunch. We met at a place called Zimm's Wine Bar, and he came straight to the point, inviting me to join him in a plot to kill her. I guess he thought I would be a natural ally in his vendetta and believed me unhappy with the outcome of my case. I refused his offer and told him abruptly: "This conversation never occurred." Then I returned to my apartment to find it had been burglarized during our lunch, with my .357 Magnum pistol the only thing missing. I reported the burglary to the police and to Bert Graham. I suspected someone wanted to use my pistol on Catherine so they could blame me, but that apparently never happened. And I never replaced the gun.

As I write this on my sixtieth birthday in 2007, I have not seen Catherine since that afternoon at Pier 21 in September 1980. But I think about her often, and I consider that healthy. I'm always looking over my shoulder and try to stay prepared for the day when she returns to complete her list of unfinished business. I believe she would have no logical reason beyond mere vengeance to make another attempt on my life, since all the damage already is done. On the off chance that I have underestimated her, however, I have made arrangements for a backup plan. I retained the Tedesco family's private investigator, Kent Ferguson, to investigate *my* death whenever it occurs. Catherine might take the last action in our turbulent relationship. But I remain determined to have the final word.